HTML 3.2 CD
with JavaScript

For Windows® 95

VIVIAN NEOU

•

MIMI RECKER

To join a Prentice Hall PTR
Internet mailing list, point to
http://www.prenhall.com/register

Prentice Hall PTR
Upper Saddle River, New Jersey 07458
http://www.prenhall.com

Library of Congress Cataloging-in-Publication Data

Neou, Vivian.
    HTML 3.2 with JavaScript for Windows 95 / Vivian Neou, Mimi Recker.
       p.   cm.
    Includes index.
    ISBN 0-13-270125-1
    1. HTML (Document markup language)   2. JavaScript (Computer program language)
    3. Microsoft Windows (Computer file)   I. Recker, Mimi. II. Title.
    QA76.76.H94N434   1997
    005.7'2--dc20   96-36121
                                                CIP

Editorial/Production Supervision: Lisa Iarkowski
Interior Design: Gail Cocker-Bogusz
Acquisitions Editor: Mary Franz
Manufacturing Manager: Alexis R. Heydt
Cover Design Director: Jerry Votta
Cover Design: Anthony Gemmellaro

The publisher offers discounts on this book when ordered in bulk quantities.
For more information, contact:

    Corporate Sales Department
    PTR Prentice Hall
    One Lake Street
    Upper Saddle River, NJ 07458
    Phone: 800-382-3419
    FAX: 201-236-7141
    e-mail: corpsales@prenhall.com

Printed in the United States of America

10 9 8 7 6 5 4 3 2 1

ISBN 0-13-270125-1

Prentice-Hall International (UK) Limited, London
Prentice-Hall of Australia Pty. Limited, Sydney
Prentice-Hall of Canada, Inc., Toronto
Prentice-Hall Hispanoamericana S.A., Mexico
Prentice-Hall of India Private Limited, New Delhi
Prentice-Hall of Japan, Inc., Tokyo
Simon & Schuster Asia Pte. Ltd., Singapore
Editora Prentice-Hall do Brasil, Ltda., Rio de Janeiro

CONTENTS

Paint Shop Pro   181

Creating Interactive and Dynamic Documents 207

Introducing JavaScript 259

JavaScript Examples   **291**

Design Guidelines, Styles and Tips   **315**

Designing Home Pages 347

Publicizing Your Web Pages 371

LIST OF TABLES

ACKNOWLEDGMENTS

The authors both gratefully acknowledge the following people and companies for granting permission to include their software with this book: Leonardo Loureiro for LView Pro, Chris Pearce for Color Manipulation Device, Todd Wilson for MapThis!, Alchemy Mindworks for Graphic Workshop and GIF Construction Set, Chris Lemler at Foghorn Software, Inc. for 8Legs Web Studio, Nick Bradbury for HomeSite, JASC Software for Paint Shop Pro, and Microsoft for PowerPoint Player and Publisher and Internet Assistants for Microsoft Word, Excel and Access.

We would like to thank our more adventurous friends for contributing lively source materials: Jim Herson, Neil Larsen, and Nancy Marx. Ray Curiel helped with the JavaScript chapter, and reviewed many pieces of the book. Tomás and Alejandro Neou-Curiel contributed the artwork for the KidArt Gallery. Our editor, Mary Franz, and our production supervisor, Lisa Iarkowski, guided this book through the production process.

Mimi would like to thank Jim Pitkow for sharing his enthusiasm for and in-depth knowledge of the Web, and Marina Volkov for commenting on early writing. Her thanks go to the warm folks at the UTDC, Victoria University of Wellington (Cedric Hall, Joanna Kidman, Lorna Murray, and Iivi Turner) for maintaining her sanity by dragging her away from her keyboard for those all-important tea breaks. She would also like to thank her parents, Dede and Bruce, for continual support and encouragement.

Vivian is especially grateful to Scott Meyers for providing guidance at crucial times. She also thanks her husband, Ray Curiel, since she would not have been able to write her portion of this book were it not for his support and willingness to take care of the important things in life. And of course thanks to "the important things in life," her kids, Tomás and Alejandro, for occasionally allowing her to write.

INTRODUCTION

When Thomas Jefferson first conceived of public libraries, he could not have imagined a world where people would have instant access to vast, globally distributed repositories of information. Today, the Internet is making this possibility a desktop reality. However, until recently much of the information on the Internet was difficult to locate and use. Fortunately, the World Wide Web and its browsers, such as Netscape and Internet Explorer, are leading the way in providing easy-to-use, seamless methods for navigating, and finding information on, the Internet.

The World Wide Web, commonly known as the Web, has made many gigabytes of digital data available to Internet users with a few mouse clicks. Data on the Web consists of documents. These documents, sometimes called Web pages, may contain text, images, video, audio, even executable programs. The Web is thus called a multimedia system. In addition, Web documents often have embedded cross-references or *links* to other Web documents. This automatic cross-linking of documents to other relevant documents is called hypertext. Because the Web links data presented in many media, it is called a hypermedia system.

For example, a document on the Web about tandem bicycles may include pictures of the author's bicycle, a recording of *A Bicycle Built for Two,* and some information about spoke tension in wheels. The author of the document may know of another document located somewhere on the Internet that has extensive information about bicycle wheels. Rather than quoting the other document or merely listing its location, the author of the tandem document makes a link to the document about wheels. Now, when reading the tandem document, the reader can click (or issue the appropriate command) on the link to view the wheel document.

Documents on the Web such as the one we just described are written in HyperText Markup Language (HTML). If you want to make your own documents available through the Web, you need to learn how to use this language. HTML conforms to the Standard Generalized Markup Language (SGML) standard, which is an international standard (ISO 8879) for defining structured document types and the markup languages used to represent those document types.

The HTML Number Jumble

Like most things in the computer world, HTML has gone through many revisions. Some revisions have been given official blessing by a standards committee, others have been vendor initiated, and still others have expired without gaining any official recognition. Thus, there is HTML 2.0, HTML 3.0, HTML 2.0 with Netscape extensions, HTML with Microsoft Internet Explorer extensions, and so on.

The latest entry in the game is HTML 3.2, which was still being revised at the time this book was written. We cover the incarnation of this version at the time of the writing of this book. However (we will explain why in the next chapter), it is not enough to simply learn about a specific version of HTML, because different browsers support different versions. We will guide you through the morass of HTML versions and vendor-specific extensions so that you can create documents that will be presented in the best possible manner for your audience.

Who Needs HTML?

The most obvious use for HTML documents is to make information available on the Internet. The World Wide Web is the fastest growing Internet resource, and HTML is its "language." This book will provide guidance for your HTML project—whether you are writing an extensive document to advertise your company's products or want to link some personal documents into the Web.

Even if you do not plan to publish documents on the Internet, HTML can still be useful. Documents written in HTML can be viewed on almost all computer platforms thanks to the vast number of WWW browsers available (both free and commercial versions) for almost every type of computer system. Thus, HTML is an excellent choice for authoring on-line manuals or company documents for in-house use.

What About JavaScript?

An additional layer of interactivity has been introduced to the Web through the addition of browser support for a number of scripting and programming languages. These languages allow more information to be processed directly by the browser, making response to user requests quicker and easier.

The most popular and widely supported scripting language for the Web is JavaScript. Incorporating JavaScript in your HTML documents will allow you to add even greater levels of interaction to your documents.

What This Book Can Do for You

By the time you are done reading this book, you should be able to write sophisticated, snazzy-looking documents in HTML. You'll learn about all the basic formatting commands, as well as how to use links and forms. We'll also teach you how to add pictures and sound to your documents. We go beyond the plain mechanics of HTML document creation—we also show you how to organize and lay out your documents so that they look as good as possible.

We'll introduce you to the basics of JavaScript and lead you through several basic scripts—including a simple database and an order form verifier. You'll find all of our examples on the CD, so you can incorporate them into your documents.

But that's not all! We also show you how to convert existing documents into HTML. You will learn how to set up a Web server so that you can publish your HTML documents on the Web. Best of all, you will find the tools to do all of these things on the included CD—you don't need to get anything else to produce and publish HTML documents.

Conventions Used in This Book

When we refer to actions within browsers, we will say to "click" on the item. If you are not using a mouse with your browser (for example, if you are using a line-mode browser), you should use the command that is equivalent to "clicking" on an item with a mouse.

We use a couple of icons throughout the book to point out important information:

We use this *tips* icon to point out useful tips and tricks. You should pay close attention when you see this icon.

We use this *warning* icon to draw your attention to areas where you can get into trouble. Follow our advice to keep from drowning in the rapids!

In chapters where HTML elements are discussed, we close with a section called *The Good, the Bad and the Ugly.* In these sections you will find a summary of the design tips and warnings introduced in the chapter.

Contents of the CD

This book comes with a cornucopia of HTML tools. You will find everything you need to turn a PC into a complete HTML authoring and publishing system—even servers and connectivity tools that will enable you to publish your HTML documents on the Internet. Here's a summary of the CD's contents.

HTML Editors and Converters

- *HomeSite, Version 1.2.* One of the best freeware editors around.
- *8Legs Web Studio.* One of the best shareware Web site creation packages available. Supports Java applets and includes an automatic publishing feature for transferring files to a server. It is well suited for team maintenance of a web site.
- *Microsoft Internet Assistants for Microsoft Word, Excel and Access,* free add-ons for these Microsoft packages that allow you to easily produce HTML documents from existing documents and data
- *Microsoft PowerPoint Player and Publisher*

HTTP Servers and Associated Software

- *fnord,* a great free HTTP server
- *Perl*, a popular scripting language for CGI applications
- *Example Perl CGI applications*

Utilities

- *Color Manipulation Device*, a color picker for setting background, text and link colors
- *MapThis!*, a free image-map maker
- *PaintShop Pro*, an image creation and manipulation tool
- *Gif Construction Set*, a tool to create animated GIFs and much more
- *Graphic Workshop,* an image creation and manipulation tool
- *LView Pro,* an image manipulation tool

HTML Document Treasure Chest

One of the best ways to learn about HTML is to look at HTML documents. We've provided a "treasure chest" of HTML pages, including:

- Templates for personal home pages
- Sample business home page templates
- JavaScript examples
- HTML element demonstration pages so you can see how different HTML elements look in different browsers
- Form templates (order forms and response forms)
- HTML document to download over 10 Windows Web browsers—including Microsoft Internet Explorer, Netscape Navigator, Oracle's PowerBrowser and more
- Free icons and images

and much more!

We have incorporated real links to documents on the Internet in some of the documents. These links all worked at the time the documents were written. However, the Internet is constantly changing, and since documents often move or are deleted, we cannot guarantee that all of the links will work when you try them.

What You Should Know

This book will teach you everything you need to know about HTML. Before starting this book you should already have a basic understanding of the Internet and World Wide Web. Although we will go over some basic Internet and Web applications in this book, you should get and read one of the general reference books on the Internet if you plan to do HTML publishing on the Internet.

However, you may just want to use HTML to develop in-house documentation or information manuals; for that, you should find everything you need in this book.

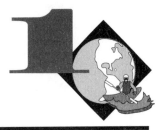

IN THIS CHAPTER YOU WILL LEARN

- HOW HTML ALLOWS YOU TO PUBLISH MULTIMEDIA DOCUMENTS ON THE WORLD WIDE WEB
- HOW HTML AND DOCUMENT DISPLAY VARIES AMONG WEB BROWSERS
- HOW TO DOWNLOAD A VARIETY OF WEB BROWSERS

THE WORLD WIDE WEB AND BROWSERS

What's In This Chapter

In this chapter we will explain more about the World Wide Web and its relation to HTML. We'll explain how HTML is dependent on Web browsers. We will also explain how to download a variety of Web browsers on the Internet using the browser document included on the CD. If you are already familiar with the Web and Web browsers, skip to the section on the HTML templates on the CD at the end of this chapter.

HTML and the Internet

As we mentioned in the introduction, HTML is a hypermedia document description language used to publish documents on the World Wide Web. Since the Web spans the Internet, and the Internet is a global network, HTML documents can be, and frequently are, connected internationally. You might think of HTML documents as looking something like Figure 1–1.

From a practical standpoint this means that if you live in California and a colleague lives in New Zealand, the two of you could publish your work together—even though your portion of the work remains on a computer in California and your colleague's on a computer in New Zealand. How? It's simple—by using *links* to join your pieces of the work together. Thanks to the seamless integration of documents on the Web, your readers would be not be affected by the geographic separation of the physical pieces of actual work (although they may notice differences in transmission times between different pieces of the document).

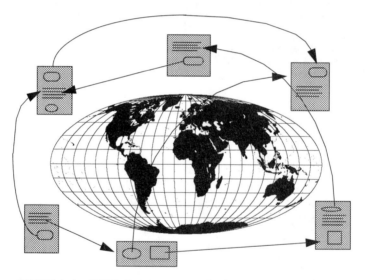

FIGURE 1–1   HTML Documents on the Internet

Let's look at a hypothetical set of documents in HTML to get a better understanding of how all of this fits together. It's time to introduce you to Kelly Kayaker. We will be developing a set of

HTML pages for Kelly in this book to illustrate how HTML works. Kelly's pages can be found on the CD, so you can use them as templates for your own HTML projects.

First, let us give you a little background on Kelly. She writes travel books for a small publishing company named Ozone Books. Kelly lives in Canada, and Ozone is based in New Zealand. Kelly will be breaking new ground for Ozone by developing a document on kayaking that will be published on the Web. Ozone is also planning to begin selling books on the Internet.

One part of Kelly's book will consist of pictures and descriptions of hot kayaking spots. She has friends all over the world who are helping her with these descriptions. Some of these friends would like to provide seasonal updates of their descriptions, so they want to keep their portions of the document on their own computers. Kelly is also planning to let people who read her document add comments to a "guest book." As a result, Kelly's document will be in pieces that are linked in this fashion:

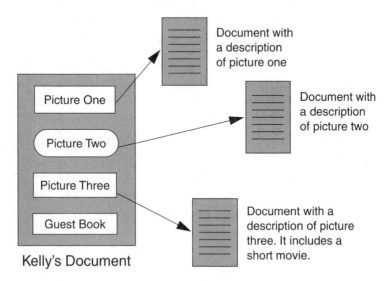

When readers look at Kelly's document with a browser (we'll tell you more about browsers in the next section), they will see a page of pictures. To read the descriptions that correspond to the pictures, the reader clicks on the picture, and the browser then gets the document with the description and displays it. The documents with the descriptions do not have to be on the same computer as Kelly's picture document—they don't even have to be the same type of computer! Even though the actual pieces of the work may be scattered on different computers all around the world, from the reader's standpoint the document is a single, cohesive piece of work.

The guest book will appear as a form, and people reading the document will have the opportunity to sign in and leave comments about it.

Version, Version, What Version Should I Use?

Writing documents that conform to the latest version of HTML can be a stressful activity (not to mention deciding on a version number to include in a book title). Why? Because the HTML standard's version numbers are in a state of flux. This is a result of chaos in the community that sets the standards and different interpretations of the standards by browser manufacturers.

Once upon a time, a single standards committee, the Internet Engineering Task Force (IETF), set the technical standards (including HTML) used on the Internet. However, the IETF process for releasing a new standard can be very lengthy, and the Web's evolution depends on rapid changes in the standard to reflect new technologies. Rather than waiting for the HTML 3 standard to complete the IETF review process, the W3 Consortium has tried to speed up the process by creating HTML 3.2, which is an attempt to describe the most common use of HTML today.

Although HTML 3.2 is still not finalized, we've chosen to make it the primary focus of this book, since it is most likely to be the standard to which browser vendors will try to conform.

We also cover the Netscape and Microsoft Internet Explorer extensions to HTML that did not make it into the HTML 3.2 specification.

Browsers

We've mentioned browsers a number of times. Where do they fit into the picture? Browsers are the applications used to display HTML and other kinds of formatted documents. They understand HTML commands and interpret the commands to format the document for display. Although there are many types of browsers now, the first widely used graphical browser was Mosaic from the National Center for Supercomputing Applications. Currently Netscape Navigator from Netscape Communications—a browser with roots from members of the NCSA team—is acknowledged as the most popular browser. As a result, many people now refer to Web browsers as "Netscape," although Netscape is actually just the name of one type of Web browser. Figure 1–2 shows how the Web browser fits into the Web.

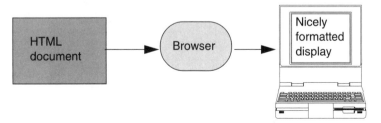

FIGURE 1–2   Web Browser

If you are already familiar with the Web, you may be thinking, "Hey, they left something out!" You are right. Figure 1–2 illustrates the flow of information for a local on-line help system and local review of HTML files (for example, you will probably use a browser to review your document before publishing it on the Internet). There is another piece in this picture, the Web server. If your eyes are starting to glaze over because you thought you were going to learn about HTML in this book, not computer networking, please stick with us. You actually need to know this to effectively use HTML. We'll keep the networking stuff short and simple.

Browsers are applications called *clients*. They get most of their information from *servers*. We say most rather than all because browsers can get their information directly from local files, as illustrated in Figure 1–2. Servers are the applications that allow HTML files to be linked across the network. A Web server is a program that waits for requests to get documents; when it receives a request, it gets the appropriate document and sends it to the browser that made the request. Requests can come from the computer the server is on, or from computers on the other side of the world. The server doesn't care—as long as the request is valid, it will return the requested document. Figure 1–3 shows the flow of information when HTML documents are shared across a network.

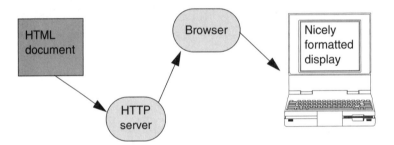

FIGURE 1–3 Web Browser and Server

Web servers talk to browsers by using a network protocol called the Hypertext Transport Protocol (HTTP). Protocols are the languages used by different applications on networks to talk to each other. Although HTTP is the primary protocol used to support the Web, Web browsers can actually get information from other types of servers that use different protocols, such as FTP, mail or gopher. As a result, you can put links in your HTML documents that will allow your readers to download documents and applications or to make a telnet connection to another computer. We'll explain how to do this in the section on Uniform Resource Locators (URLs) in "URLs and Links" on page 67.

Whew. That was a lot of jargon and acronyms. But now we're done with the network for a little while. Let's take a closer look at browsers.

HTML and Browsers

HTML is used to define the *structure* of a document. However, the browser used to display the document dictates how each structural element should be rendered. *Although general element display guidelines are provided in the HTML specification, in practice there is wide variation in display between browsers.*

Browsers also vary widely in their recognition of HTML elements. Most browsers try to support Version 2 of HTML; some browsers do not recognize anything above Version 1, while others (most notably Netscape Navigator) use vendor-specific extensions to HTML. To muddy things even further, most browsers are also willing to accept documents that violate all of the specifications for HTML. When a browser encounters a noncompliant document, it will typically ignore noncompliant portions of the document and do its best to interpret the rest.

In other words, there is nothing to force you to write HTML documents that fully adhere to any of the HTML specifications. In fact, if you are writing for an audience that will be using a specific browser (for example, you may be writing in-house documentation for a company Intranet), you should become familiar with the way that browser handles HTML so you can tailor your documents in an appropriate fashion. However, if you are writing documents that will be published on the Internet, you will need to make sure that your documents look okay on a broad range of browsers.

To complicate things even more, the same browser may have different features or slightly different ways of doing things from one platform to another. There are also differences between the way that the same browser may do things from one version of the browser to the next. Let's take a quick look at the way different browsers display a simple HTML document. The HTML source we will display is this:

```
<P>The logical tags in HTML are:
<DL>
<DT><STRONG>Citation:&lt;CITE&gt;</STRONG>
<DD><CITE>This paragraph is in a citation tag, and is
typically rendered in an italic font.</CITE>
<DT><STRONG>Code: &lt;CODE&gt;</STRONG>
<DD><CODE>CODE is intended for code examples, and is
typically displayed in a fixed-width font.</CODE>
<DT><STRONG>Emphasis: &lt;EM&gt;</STRONG>
<DD><EM>This paragraph is in an emphasis tag. It is usually
displayed in italics.</EM>
<DT><STRONG>Keyboard: &lt;KBD&gt; </STRONG>
<DD><KBD>This paragraph is in a keyboard tag. It is typically
displayed in a fixed-width font.</KBD>
<DT><STRONG>Sample: &lt;SAMP&gt;</STRONG>
<DD><SAMPLE>This paragraph is in a sample tag. The sample tag
is intended for sequences of literal characters and is
typically displayed in a fixed-width font.</SAMPLE>
<DT><STRONG>Emphasis: &lt;STRONG&gt;</STRONG>
<DD><STRONG>Strong Emphasis. It is usually displayed in a
boldface font.</STRONG>
<DT><STRONG>Variable Name: &lt;VAR&gt;</STRONG>
<DD><VAR>Variable Name. This is intended for variable names,
and is typically displayed in an italic font.</VAR>
</DL>
```

Now let's see how it looks in different browsers.

Netscape

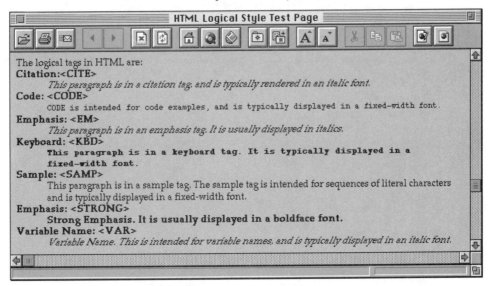

Microsoft Internet Explorer

Lynx (A line-mode browser)

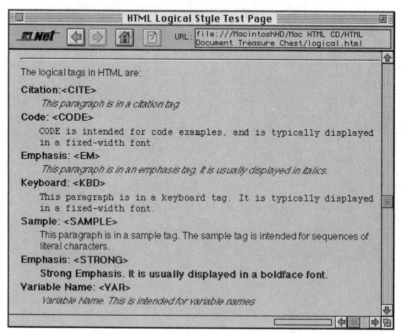

MacWeb (EiNET)

NCSA Mosaic

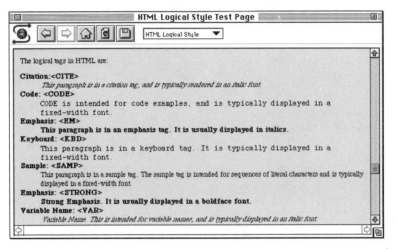

As you can see, these browsers display the same simple document in a variety of ways. From the background to line spacing to the fonts, you cannot count on anything to be consistent between browsers.

Compare the Lynx display with the graphical browsers'. If you've only used a graphical browser, the way that a document looks in a line-mode browser may seem like going back to the dark ages. However, as a designer of Web pages, it is important for you to keep line-mode browsers in mind. There are still many people using these types of browsers—for example, in some libraries, there is public Web access—but only through line-mode browsers.

Many browsers also allow users to customize the way that various HTML elements are displayed, causing even greater discrepancies between the way a document may be displayed from one browser to another. For example, compare the following display of our document in Netscape with the way that Netscape displayed it on page 9.

Netscape: HTML Logical Style Test Page

Back | Forward | Home | Reload | Images | Open | Print | Find | Stop

The logical tags in HTML are:

Citation:<CITE>
   This paragraph is in a citation tag, and is typically rendered in an italic font.
Code: <CODE>
   CODE is intended for code examples, and is typically displayed in a fixed-width font.
Emphasis: <EM>
   This paragraph is in an emphasis tag. It is usually displayed in italics.
Keyboard: <KBD>
   This paragraph is in a keyboard tag. It is typically displayed in a fixed-width font.
Sample: <SAMP>
   This paragraph is in a sample tag. The sample tag is intended for sequences of literal characters and is typically displayed in a fixed-width font.
Emphasis: <STRONG>
   Strong Emphasis. It is usually displayed in a boldface font.
Variable Name: <VAR>
   Variable Name. This is intended for variable names, and is typically displayed in an italic font.

Document: Done.

In more complex documents, especially ones that incorporate multimedia elements, the differences between browsers become even more pronounced. Unfortunately, there is no simple solution to this problem. As we introduce new HTML elements, we make design recommendations that will help you to author documents that will look good regardless of the browser used to display them.

You can preview your document in most browsers by specifying the Open Local *or* Open File *command, which can usually be found in the* File *menu.* This allows you to see your document as it is being developed and to correct potential errors. If you find a problem, correct it within the editing environment. Then use the *Reload* command to see if your changes have fixed the problem.

Getting Browsers

If you do not have any browsers, or only one, you are probably anxious to get some more now. On the CD we've included a browser document that will help you to locate a number of Windows 95 browsers including:

- Microsoft Internet Explorer
- NCSA Mosaic
- Netmanage's WebSurfer
- Netscape Navigator
- Winweb from Trade Wave (formerly EINet)
- Oracle's PowerBrowser
- SPRYNET Mosaic
- SlipKnot

A line-mode browser for DOS, Unix or VMS:

- Lynx

Our browser document will also help you to locate a number of browsers for other platforms.

To download most of these packages, all you need to do is load browsers.html into your favorite browser. You will see the list of browsers along with some information about each one. When you choose the link in a browser's description, either the browser will be downloaded to your system, or you will be placed at a home page for the browser that will provide you with information about the browser and an opportunity to download it.

We urge you to install at least two or three browsers to review your documents. If your intended audience is the general Internet population, we recommend (at a minimum) checking your documents in Netscape Navigator, Microsoft Internet Explorer and Lynx.

Screenshots in this Book

While there is still much debate about which browser is used by which percentage of the Internet population, at the time this book was written the most popular browser was widely recognized as being Netscape Navigator, and the most popular platform was Windows. Unless otherwise indicated, Netscape Navigator, Atlas Preview Release 2 on Windows 95, is used for screenshots in this book.

However, Microsoft seems determined to overtake Navigator with its Internet Explorer browser, and there are many other entries in the browser dominance war due to arrive soon. We will periodically show you how documents look in some of these other browsers to help you understand the importance of designing pages that can be viewed and used in any browser.

IN THIS CHAPTER YOU WILL LEARN

- How to author a basic HTML document
- How to use basic HTML commands
- How to use Netscape extensions to these commands
- How basic HTML elements look in a browser

THE BASICS

What's In This Chapter

This chapter shows you how to create a basic HTML document. It discusses setting up your document and introduces the basic formatting commands.

Creating an HTML Document

HTML documents are written in plain text (ASCII). There are a number of ways to create an HTML document:

1. You can use your favorite editor and add in the HTML commands yourself.
2. You can use an HTML editor that inserts the commands in the appropriate locations for you.
3. You can also use a conversion utility that takes a document from some other format and converts it to HTML.

We discuss all of these methods in this book. We start with the text editor method, since it is important to understand how HTML works, even if you decide to use a system that inserts HTML commands for you.

The first step is to create a file to hold your HTML document. The file should have the *.html* or *.htm* file extension. On most systems that can handle extensions with more than three letters, the .html extension is most commonly used. However, since DOS and Windows 3.1 could handle only three-character extensions, many of the HTML documents authored in Windows 95 environments stick with the three-character extension as well. Both extensions are acceptable. In this book we will use the .html extension for our documents.

Browsers and servers make some decisions on the way they deal with documents based on the file extension, so it is important to choose the correct extension for your document.

In this chapter we will author a document on the sport of kayaking as an example. Hence, we call this file, kayak.html. We have included a copy of this document on the CD.

Document Tags: <HTML>, <HEAD>, and <BODY>

Several tags do not affect the presentation of documents but convey important information to browsers and users. As you will find, most browsers do not complain if you forget to put these tags in your document, but it is safer to include them.

First, HTML documents should contain an <HTML> tag. Note that the document should have a corresponding <HTML> at the end. HTML is *not* case sensitive. <HTML> is treated the same as <html> or <HtMl>.

The document should be organized into <HEAD> and <BODY> sections. Like an electronic mail message, the <HEAD> tags surround the introductory section, while the <BODY> tags surround the main part of the document.

Although these tags do not affect the presentation of a document, they are important. The HTTP protocol includes a "HEAD" command, which returns the information included in the head of a document. Although most browsers do not currently use this feature, many Web-searching robots use it to build their databases. If you want your documents to be catalogued in an understandable fashion, make sure that you include a HEAD section.

The TITLE element in a document must occur within the <HEAD> tags of the document, and it is the only element that goes in the head section. Within the <BODY>, the document can be structured in paragraphs, lists and so on, using HTML tags. The basic framework for our kayak document is shown in Figure 2–1.

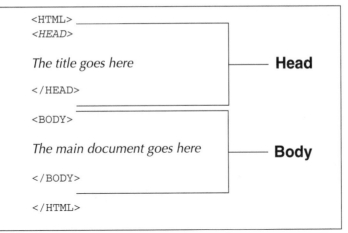

FIGURE 2–1   Basic Document Framework

Document Type: <!DOCTYPE>

In theory, every HTML document should begin with a document type identifier. This statement should be placed before the <HTML> tag and contain information about the version of

HTML used in the document. For example, the official document type declaration for HTML 2 is:

```
<!DOCTYPE HTML PUBLIC "-//IETF//DTD HTML 2.0//EN">
```

and for HTML 3.2:

```
<!DOCTYPE HTML PUBLIC "-//W3C//DTD HTML 3.2//EN">
```

This tag is intended to help browsers make useful inferences about the type of tags it will find in the document. It is also used by HTML validators (programs that check HTML documents for errors).

Unfortunately, in practice using DOCTYPE can be difficult. As a result of the intensive development work going on with the HTML language, there are many variations of HTML—including vendor-specific extensions and evolving official standards. Some of these extensions do not have official DOC-TYPEs. Additionally, some documents include a mix of extensions from different sources. In these cases, it is almost impossible to decide which DOCTYPE to use.

The DOCTYPE tag is a place where theory and reality come into conflict. With the current state of browsers, it is unlikely that the lack of a DOCTYPE tag will affect the presentation of your document. We mention DOCTYPE here primarily so that you will know what it is when you encounter it.

A list of valid DOCTYPES is available at:

http://ugweb.cs.ualberta.ca/~gerald/validate/lib/catalog

Markup Tags

If you've used a WYSIWYG (What You See Is What You Get) word processing program such as Microsoft Word, you have probably formatted your documents so that some words are displayed in italics or boldface. You have also probably designated portions of your text as titles, headings or lists.

HTML provides some of this functionality for documents that are published on the Internet. However, there is a significant difference between HTML and a WYSIWYG word processing system. Like many word processing systems, HTML allows you to define the *structure* of a document—you can specify such things as lists, titles, headings and so forth. However, the way these things will be displayed to the reader is determined by the browser used to display the document.

If you like to have complete control over the look of your document (for example, adjusting font sizes, or placing text on the page in a specific location), you will probably find working with HTML frustrating. HTML was designed so that authors could mark up the text in documents to indicate *types* of text. However, since HTML was designed to allow the same document to be meaningfully displayed on a wide variety of platforms with vastly different capabilities, it is generally left up to the browser (which understands the limitations and abilities of the platform on which it is running) to decide how each type of text will be displayed.

Thus, you cannot specify that text should be displayed in a 9-point Courier font, or that an item designated as a heading will be centered and displayed in a bold 20-point font[1]. These decisions are left up to the browser—and, as you will see, even on the same platform there is wide variation in how different browsers display the same document. We will provide guidelines to make your documents look as good as possible in the wide variety of browsers that may be used to display them. But first, let's look at how different types of text are defined in HTML.

HTML commands use *markup tags* to specify structural elements in a document. These tags tell the browser about the type of text being displayed, such as headers, titles, lists or plain text.

HTML markup tags consist of a left angle bracket (<), followed by the name of the tag, and then a right angle bracket (>). Tags usually come in pairs in order to act as *containers* of

---

1. Microsoft Internet Explorer 3 and above supports extensions to HTML that allow authors to request that specific font sizes and styles be used. However, these extensions are not widely supported by other browsers and also depend on whether the requested fonts are installed on the user's system.

the affected text. The second tag in a pair looks just like the first, except that a slash precedes the name. This second tag tells the browser that the command is done. Thus, an HTML statement looks something like this:

```
<TagName>Some Text</TagName>
```

Many tags also may be used with *attributes*, which are additional commands that specify additional information about the way that the tag should be used. For example, the ALIGN attribute allows you to specify alignment information:

```
<P ALIGN=CENTER>Some centered text</P>
```

As we introduce each markup tag, we will also let you know about any attributes that are defined for that tag.

Title: <TITLE>

The first essential item you should include in an HTML document is a title. We start our document with this title line:

```
<TITLE>The Sport of Kayaking</TITLE>
```

As you can see in this example, the markup tags for the title are <TITLE> and </TITLE>. Of course, since HTML is not case sensitive, we could have written our tags in lower-case:

```
<title>The Sport of Kayaking</title>
```

We will use upper-case letters in the rest of our examples, but it is fine to use lowercase tags if you prefer. In the above example, the title of the document is "The Sport of Kayaking." In Netscape Navigator it would look like this:

As you can see, Netscape, like most browsers, displays the title of a document in a special area of the window.

A DOCUMENT MAY HAVE ONLY ONE TITLE.

You should include only one title in your document. Including multiple TITLE tags in the same document not only violates the official HTML standard but also forces browsers to choose which tag to display since most do not have a place to display multiple titles.

You may have seen documents that violate this rule. Most such documents that we have encountered were due to an attempt by their authors to take advantage of an unfortunate feature in Version 1 of Netscape. This version allowed multiple title tags in a document to be displayed in succession in the title bar. Some writers took advantage of this feature by including titles such as:

```
<title>K</title>
<title>Ka</title>
<title>Kay</title>
<title>Kaya</title>
<title>Kayak</title>
<title>Kayaki</title>
<title>Kayakin</title>
<title>Kayaking</title>
```

in their documents. This would result in the title appearing to scroll into the title bar. Netscape corrected this problem in Version 2 and above of Navigator, which displays only the first title tag in the document. Thus, authors trying to use this scrolling feature will find that their documents appear with a single-letter title in newer versions of Netscape.

This illustrates one of the pitfalls of creating documents that do not adhere to the HTML standard—although documents with multiple title tags looked good in one version of one type of browser, they looked bad in later versions of the browser as well as other types of browsers.

USE DESCRIPTIVE YET SUCCINCT TITLES.

An HTML document should have a title that succinctly describes its contents. This title, like the title of a book, can be used by readers to decide if they wish to view the entire document. If the title is too generic, the reader will be unable to determine whether the document is of any interest. For example, a bad title would be:

```
<TITLE>Introduction</TITLE>
```

This title does not provide any significant information about the contents of the document. Since links (we'll explain more about links in the next chapter) may be made to any document from any other document, this title makes it difficult for readers to decide whether the document contains information they want. A better title would be:

```
<TITLE>Introduction to Kayaking</TITLE>
```

The following two titles are also poor choices. Although they tell something about the content of the document, they are too general to be useful:

```
<TITLE>Security</TITLE>
<TITLE>Paddles</TITLE>
```

Better alternatives would be:

```
<TITLE>Computer Security Hints</TITLE>
<TITLE>Guidelines for Choosing a Kayaking Paddle</TITLE>
```

KEEP TITLES SHORT!
TITLES WITH NO MORE THAN FIVE OR SIX WORDS
HAVE THE GREATEST IMPACT.

Although the HTML standard does not set a limit on the number of characters that may be included in a title, most browsers display only as much as will fit into the section of the window reserved for the title. This area is typically no longer than one line. If you keep your title under 64 characters, you can be reasonably well assured that it will fit into the allocated space.

DO NOT PLACE ANY MARKUP TAGS IN A TITLE!

A title may not contain anchors, highlighting or paragraph tags (these types of tags are described later). If you try to include these tags, the behavior from browser to browser is unpredictable (and, in most cases, undesirable). Some browsers may show the tags as part of the title, while others may actually pull the text out of the title area and display it as part of the document.

We've provided a document on the CD that deliberately violates the guidelines for good title composition. You can find the file in longtitle.html. Here's the beginning of the document:

```
<HTML>
<HEAD>
<TITLE>Will This Title Show Up</TITLE>
<TITLE>This Is A Very Very <H1>Long Title</H1> That Tells You
Nothing About The Document And May Not Fit In The Area That
Browsers Set Up For Titles.</TITLE>
</HEAD>
```

And here's what happens when we load this document into Netscape Navigator:

Notice that the heading titles are displayed as part of the text. Now let's see how this looks in Microsoft Internet Explorer:

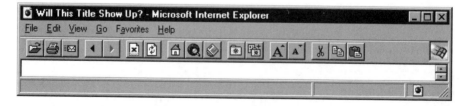

As you can see, these browsers make different choices about the title that will be displayed. Netscape chose the last title in the document while Internet Explorer used the first title. Of course, every browser will get confused in different ways when you violate the rules. Try loading this document into several different browsers and see for yourself.

Meta Information: <META>

The META tag allows you to include "meta-information" in your document. Clear as mud? We could give you the official line, but for now let's leave it as being the place where additional indexing information and extra document control information (such as expiration dates) can be placed. We mention this tag now because it goes in the HEAD portion of the document. However, its use will be described more fully in later chapters where we describe advanced HTML concepts.

Headings: <H1> through <H6>

Now we move on to tags that belong in the BODY portion of your document. The first tag you will probably want to use in the body of your document is one of the header tags. For example, the first header in our document is "White Water Kayaking." Thus, the next tag we use is H1:

```
<H1>White Water Kayaking</H1>
```

As you can see, H1 is a container and is denoted by <H1>...</H1>. HTML allows you to specify up to six levels of headers, <H1> through <H6>. The first header, H1, is the largest, most prominent header. It is typically displayed in a large and bold font, while each subsequent header is displayed in an increasingly smaller size. Here is a sample document that illustrates the six levels of headers:

```
<H1>Level 1 Heading, H1</H1>
<H2>Level 2 Heading, H2</H2>
<H3>Level 3 Heading, H3</H3>
<H4>Level 4 Heading, H4</H4>
<H5>Level 5 Heading, H5</H5>
<H6>Level 6 Heading, H6</H6>
```

Here it is in Netscape:

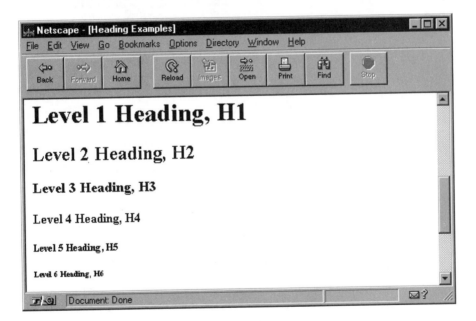

and in Lynx:

```
                                                          Heading Examples
                          LEVEL 1 HEADING, H1
Level 2 Heading, H2

  Level 3 Heading, H3

    Level 4 Heading, H4

      Level 5 Heading, H5

        Level 6 Heading, H6




Commands: Use arrow keys to move, '?' for help, 'q' to quit, '<-' to go back.
  Arrow keys: Up and Down to move. Right to follow a link; Left to go back.
  H)elp O)ptions P)rint G)o M)ain screen Q)uit /=search [delete]=history list
```

ALIGN Attribute

You can control the way that the header is aligned by the browser by using the ALIGN attribute. You can choose from values of LEFT, CENTER and RIGHT. Since this attribute was introduced after HTML 2.0, many older browsers do not support it.

Here is a sample document using these attributes with H2:

```
<H2 ALIGN=LEFT>ALIGN=LEFT</H2>
<H2 ALIGN=CENTER>ALIGN=CENTER</H2>
<H2 ALIGN=RIGHT>ALIGN=RIGHT</H2>
```

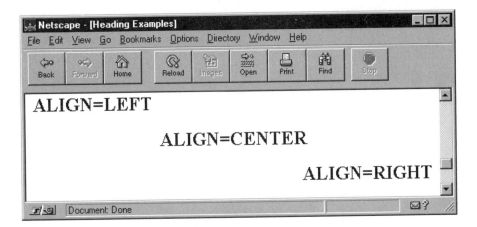

The header test document is in heading.html on the CD. Load it in several browsers to see the different ways browsers choose to display headings.

Paragraphs: <P>

Now we want to include some general text:

```
<P>Kayaking is an outdoor sport, practiced by adrenaline
junkies, in which enthusiasts paddle wild rivers and creeks
in small, enclosed boats. Most people are a bit nervous the
first time they kayak.</P>
```

The <P> specifies a paragraph break. Unlike most tags, it is an example of an *empty container* since it does not require an end tag, although it is preferable to include it. HTML performs automatic word wrap in documents and ignores carriage returns. Therefore, you must explicitly signal paragraph breaks in text with the <P> tag. *If you do not include any paragraph breaks in your HTML text, it will appear as one long paragraph.* Some exceptions do exist, as we will explain later. Let's digress from our kayaking document for a moment to illustrate this point.

Let's look at a short and simple HTML document. The document source looks as if there should be three paragraphs. However, notice that there are no P tags in this document.

```
<HTML>
<HEAD>
<TITLE>Paragraph Break Test Document</TITLE>
<HEAD>
<BODY>
<H1>Paragraph Break Test Document</H1>
Paragraph tags delineate paragraphs. Browsers typically render
a blank line between paragraphs. This section of this document
illustrates the need to include paragrpaph tags in your HTML
sources. If you do not include &lt;P&gt; tags in your
documents, your document will appear as one long paragraph
(perhaps with some breaks if you use other elements such as
lists or headers).

Although there is a blank line before this sentence in the HTML
source, there is no P tag, so the browser will not recognize
the start of a new paragraph. It should appear as one long
paragraph in your browser.

In HTML 2, there is no requirement to close a P tag. However,
it is good practice to do so since later versions of HTML
include extra attributes for the P tag (such as ALIGN) that
will work more cleanly if P tags are closed.
</BODY>
</HTML>
```

Now let's see how it looks:

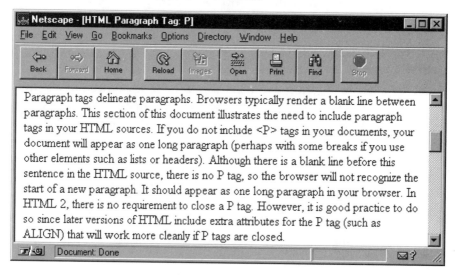

The browser did not pay attention to the blank lines in our HTML source and placed the whole document in one long paragraph. As you can see, it is important to include paragraph tags in your documents.

In HTML 3.2 an ALIGN attribute was added to the paragraph tag to allow authors to control the alignment of individual paragraphs. ALIGN may be set to one of three values: CENTER, LEFT and JUSTIFY.

```
<P ALIGN=CENTER>This is a paragraph with ALIGN=CENTER.</P>
<P ALIGN=RIGHT>This is a paragraph with ALIGN=RIGHT.</P>
<P ALIGN=LEFT>This is a paragraph with ALIGN=LEFT, which is
the default.</P>
```

Note that although we include closing tags for our paragraphs, they are not required. Some browsers will add a blank line whenever they encounter a </P> tag, so be sure to check your documents in a variety of browsers to make sure that you do not have too much empty space

```
Netscape - [HTML Paragraph Tag: P]
File  Edit  View  Go  Bookmarks  Options  Directory  Window  Help

 Back   Forward   Home     Reload  Images   Open    Print    Find    Stop

              This is a paragraph with ALIGN=CENTER.

                                    This is a paragraph with ALIGN=RIGHT.

This is a paragraph with ALIGN=LEFT, which is the default.

Document: Done
```

As soon as a tag for a new structural element is seen, the alignment will revert to the default (left). If you want to align sections of your document rather than a single paragraph, you should use DIV or CENTER. These tags are described later in this chapter.

Logical and Physical Styles

HTML provides two methods for influencing the way that text is displayed: logical and physical styles. Logical style tags describe the type of text being displayed. The <CITE> tag is an example of a logical tag. It is intended to demark a bibliographic citation, and it is left to the browser to determine how to display such a field. Physical styles, on the other hand, specify the desired physical appearance of the affected text, such as the <I> tag for italics. There is a list of logical style tags in Table 2–1, and a list of physical style tags in Table 2–2.

TABLE 2–1 Logical Style Tags

Style Marker	Description
<CITE>	Used for bibliographic citations. Browsers usually display citations in italics.
<CODE>	Used to display snippets of computer code. Browsers usually display in a fixed-width font.
<EM>	Used to denote emphasis of the affected text. Browsers usually display emphasis in italics.
<KBD>	Used to denote user keyboard entry. Browsers often display in a bold fixed-width font.
<SAMP>	Used to denote a sequence of literal characters.
<STRONG>	Used to denote strong or important text. Browsers usually display in bold font.
<VAR>	Used to indicate a variable name.

TABLE 2–2 *Physical Style Tags*

Command	Description
<B>	Bold style.
<I>	Italic style.
<TT>	Use typewriter text or fixed-width font.
<STRIKE>	Strikeout the text.

Each logical style tag is commonly associated with a specific type of text format. For example, most browsers choose to display citations in italics. However for logical styles the HTML standard only recommends a display style rather than requiring one. This allows the browser to choose the most appropriate display style for its platform. Since some browsers (such as the linemode browser, Lynx) cannot display some types of text (such as italics or strikeout), the browser can use the logical description of the type of information being displayed to choose the appropriate display style.

On the other hand, physical styles are associated with specific display formats. Since some formats cannot be displayed on all platforms, the browser must either ignore markup it cannot display or choose some other method to display that text. In either case, the text will not appear in the format specified by the tag. For this reason, it is preferable to use logical over physical styles—the browser has a better chance of understanding what is being displayed and choosing an appropriate format for the display.

Let's see how we can use these tags to dress up our documents. Let's use a description list and add some physical and logical style commands:

```
<P>Essential items to have while kayaking:</P>
<DL>
<DT><STRONG>Life jacket</STRONG>
<DD>A life jacket is essential while kayaking as it provides
flotation.
<DT><B>Helmet</B>
```

```
<DD>A helmet protects the head against blows against rocks.
</DL>
<P>Other things you need include:</P>
<DL>
<DT><EM>Spray skirt</EM>
<DD>The spray skirt fits between the torso of the kayaker and
the boat, and prevents water from swamping the kayak.
<DT><I>Paddle</I>
<DD>A paddle allows the kayaker to navigate in the water.
</DL>
```

Now let's see how this looks:

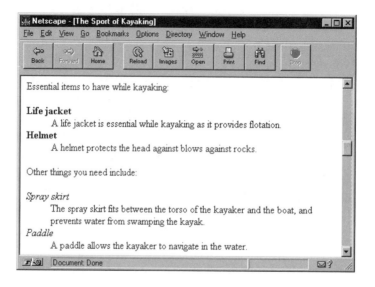

Notice that we used a different style command for each term in our list. As you can see, in this version of Netscape Navigator STRONG and B are treated in the same fashion, and EM and I are displayed in the same font. Now let's see how it looks in Lynx:

```
                                        The Sport of Kayaking (p1 of 4)
 Essential items to have while kayaking:

 Life jacket
         A life jacket is essential while kayaking as it provides
         flotation.

 Helmet
         A helmet protects the head against blows against rocks.



 Other things you need include:

 Spray skirt
         The spray skirt fits between the torso of the kayaker and the
         boat, and prevents water from swamping the kayak.

 Paddle
         A paddle allows the kayaker to navigate in the water.
 -- press space for more, use arrow keys to move. '?' for help, 'q' to quit
  Arrow keys: Up and Down to move. Right to follow a link; Left to go back.
 H)elp O)ptions P)rint G)o M)ain screen Q)uit /=search [delete]=history list
```

Not surprisingly, all four tags are displayed in the same way in Lynx.

There are times when it might be necessary to use physical tags. For example, if you are providing instructions, you may want to put optional portions of commands in italics and include a statement in your document explaining this convention. In this case you would need to be sure that certain portions of text really are in italics. Since browsers have more leeway on the rendering of <EM>, it would be safer to use <I> in a case like this—although, as you can see in our Lynx illustration, you cannot count on I to be displayed in italics.

We have included two documents—physical.html and logical.html—on the CD that you can use to check how different elements look in different browsers.

HTML 3.2 Formatting Extensions

The formatting extensions described in this section were originally introduced by Netscape and have been incorporated in the HTML 3.2 specification. As a result, they are not as widely supported as the other tags that have been described. For example, they are only supported in Version 2 and above of Netscape Navigator, so you will not see any change in the display of your document if you add them and then view your document with Version 1.x of Navigator.

Big and Small Print: <BIG>, <SMALL>

The <BIG> and <SMALL> elements specify that the enclosed text should be displayed, if practical, using big or small fonts relative to the current font size. You can get a similar effect through the use of the FONT tag with a SIZE attribute, which is described later in this section.

Subscript and Superscript: <SUB>, <SUP>

The <SUB> element specifies that the enclosed text should be displayed as a subscript, while the <SUP> element specifies that the enclosed text should be displayed as a superscript. Both will be displayed in a smaller font relative to the regular font size.

Let's look at an example:

```
<DL>
<DT><STRONG>Large Font: &lt;BIG&gt;</STRONG>
<DD>Use a <BIG>larger font</BIG> than surrounding text.
<DT><STRONG>Small Font: &lt;SMALL&gt;</STRONG>
<DD>Use a <SMALL>smaller font</SMALL> than surrounding text.
<DT><STRONG>Subscript: &lt;SUB&gt;</STRONG>
<DD>Text should be in <SUB>Subscript</SUB>.
<DT><STRONG>Superscript: &lt;SUP&gt;</STRONG>
<DD>Text should be in <SUP>Superscript</SUP>
</DL>.
```

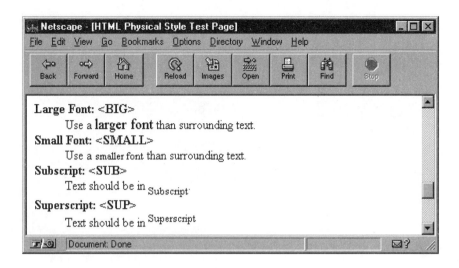

Font Size and Color: <FONT>

The FONT tag allows you to control the size and color of the font used for a section of text. Remember that this tag will be ignored by browsers on platforms that do not support colors and variable font sizes. Also, since it is a fairly new tag, many older browsers do not support it.

The SIZE attribute allows you to change font size. Valid values range from one to seven, with the default being three. The value given to size can optionally have a '+' or '-' character in front of it to specify that it is relative to the current base font size. Here's our test document:

```
<FONT SIZE=1>1</FONT>
<FONT SIZE=2>2</FONT>
<FONT SIZE=3>3</FONT>
<FONT SIZE=4>4</FONT>
<FONT SIZE=5>5</FONT>
<FONT SIZE=6>6</FONT>
<FONT SIZE=7>7</FONT>
<FONT SIZE=+3>6</FONT>
<FONT SIZE=+2>5</FONT>
<FONT SIZE=+1>4</FONT>
<FONT SIZE=+0>3</FONT>
<FONT SIZE=-1>2</FONT>
<FONT SIZE=-2>1</FONT>
```

In the first half of the document we use absolute values for the font size, and in the second half we use relative values to produce the same result. The relative values are based on the default base font size of 3. Now let's see how this looks:

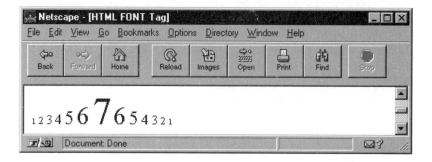

You can use the COLOR attribute to set a color for your font. The value for this attribute may be one of the 16 widely recognized color names: aqua, black, blue, fuschia, gray, green, lime, maroon, navy, olive, purple, red, silver, teal, white, or yellow, or it may be set to a hexadecimal RGB value. The format is:

```
<FONT COLOR=LIME>Lime-colored text</FONT>
<FONT COLOR="#rggbb">Colored text</FONT>
```

The *#rrggbb* in this example represents a color code. For a detailed explanation of the codes please refer to the multimedia chapter. To find the code for a specific color, you can use the Color Manipulation Device, a shareware color application that is included on the CD. You can find more information on this application in the multimedia chapter. You should also be familiar with the discussion of the use of color in HTML documents in the multimedia chapter.

Here is a sample snippet of code using the color attribute:

```
<P><FONT COLOR=RED>NEW</FONT> Ozone Books now carries the
latest book by Kelly Kayaker.
```

If you set a font color, be sure you choose a color that will appear clearly against your background. A yellow font over a white background is very difficult to read. You should also be careful to choose colors that are not used to highlight links. For example, many browsers use blue text to indicate the presence of a link. If you use blue text, and do not set the link text color value to something other than blue, your readers will be confused. You can find more about setting background, link and text colors in the multimedia chapter.

Special Characters

HTML reserves four special ASCII characters for its own use. These are the left angle bracket (<), right angle bracket (>), ampersand (&) and double quote ("). The alert reader will have noticed that the angle brackets are used to mark tags. The ampersand is used to signal the start of an escape sequence, while the quote is used around filenames and URLs. These characters are frequently used in HTML documents, and browsers rely on these characters to interpret the documents. If you wish to display these characters in your documents, you must use special escape sequences.

In addition to the escape sequences defined for these characters, the HTML specification also includes special sequences for the copyright (©) and registered (®) symbols as well as a nonbreaking space. A list of these sequences can be found in Table 2–3.

TABLE 2–3 Special Characters

Escape sequence	Description	Symbol
&copy;	Copyright symbol,	©
&reg	Registered symbol,	®
	Nonbreaking space	
&lt;	Less than symbol	<
&gt;	Greater than symbol	>
&amp;	Ampersand	&
&quot;	Double quote	"

Unlike other HTML markers, escape sequences *are* case sensitive. Escape sequences are also used in HTML for accented characters that occur in other languages. You can find a table of these in Appendix A.

Horizontal Lines: <HR>

Sections between documents are often separated by a horizontal line that runs the length of the browser window. The <HR> tag produces a horizontal line in HTML. For example, in our kayak document we placed a line between the introductory paragraph and the rest of the document.

HR Attributes

Netscape introduced four attributes, which have been incorporated into the HTML 3.2 specification. Table 2–4 describes these attributes.

TABLE 2–4 HR Attributes

Attribute	Description
SIZE	A number giving an indication (in pixels) of how thick the rule should be.
WIDTH	A number or percentage. The number is the number of pixels, the percentage is the width relative to the page size. To indicate a percentage, follow the number with a "%", otherwise it will be treated as a pixel width.
ALIGN	This may take one of three values: left, right or center (the default).
NOSHADE	Use a plain line—no shading.

It is easier to see an illustration than to go into detail on what each of these attributes does. Here are some samples:

```
A plain &lt;HR&gt;<HR>
&lt;HR SIZE=5&gt;<HR SIZE=5>
```

```
&lt;HR SIZE=50&gt;<HR SIZE=50>
&lt;HR WIDTH=200&gt;<HR WIDTH=200>
&lt;HR WIDTH=70%&gt;<HR WIDTH=70%>
&lt;HR WIDTH=70% ALIGN=LEFT&gt;<HR WIDTH=70% ALIGN=LEFT>
&lt;HR WIDTH=70% ALIGN=RIGHT&gt;<HR WIDTH=70% ALIGN=RIGHT>
&lt;HR NOSHADE&gt;<HR NOSHADE>
```

Notice that we have used symbol names for "<" and ">" so that each line in our example will be labeled with the tag used to make it. Let's see how this looks:

If you use these attributes, remember that many older browsers do not support them.

Lists

HTML provides several ways to display information in lists. These include:

- Unnumbered lists
- Numbered lists
- Menu lists
- Directory lists
- Definition lists

Table 2–5 describes the various tags used to create lists.

TABLE 2–5 *List Tags*

Command	Description
<OL></OL>	Numbered or ordered list.
<UL></UL>	Unnumbered or unordered list.
<DIR></DIR>	Directory list. Looks like an unordered list in most browsers. List entries should be no longer than 20 characters.
<MENU></MENU>	Menu list. This list also looks similar to an unordered list in most browsers. The display is supposed to be more compact.
<LI>	Item in a list.
<DL></DL>	Definition list.
<DT>	Defined item in a definition list.
<DD>	Definition of an item in a definition list.

Specifying Items in Lists: <LI>

Lists share a common format. Like most HTML objects, they should start and end with the appropriate markup tags. However, the tags used to mark items within a list are empty container tags (like paragraph tags, they need only a start tag). For example:

```
<OL>
<LI>Paddles
<LI>Kayaks
</OL>
```

As you can see in this example, another markup tag is used to label each item in the list. With the exception of definition lists (which need two types of item tags, since they have two types of items), items in lists are specified with the <LI> tag. You indicate that something is an item by starting it with the <LI> tag. Since this is an empty container tag, there is no need to close the item (although you can add a closing </LI> if you prefer).

With the exception of items in a directory list (which should be kept under 20 characters), items in a list can be longer than a single sentence. If you wish to have multiple paragraphs within a list item, don't forget to separate them with the <P> paragraph separator.

Creating a List

The process of creating a list is simple. Here are the basic steps:

1. *Begin with the opening list tag for the type of list you wish to create.*
2. *Enter the <LI> tag, followed by a list item.*
3. *Continue entering list items, with an <LI> tag preceding each item. No closing tag is needed for items.*
4. *End the list by typing the appropriate closing container tag for your list.*

Unnumbered Lists: <UL>

Unnumbered lists, which are also known as unordered lists, are typically displayed by browsers with a bullet in front of each item. The markup tags for unnumbered lists are <UL> and </UL>. For example, in our kayak.htm document, we would specify an unordered list as follows:

```
<P>There are many types of kayak paddles:</P>
<UL>
<LI>Feathered
<LI>Dihedral
<LI>Break-down
</UL>
```

When viewed with a browser, the above snippet would look like this:

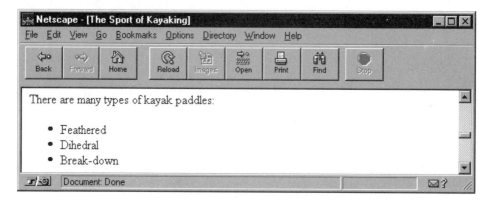

TYPE Attribute

In the HTML 3.2 standard, a type attribute is available with the UL tag. This attribute allows you to specify the type of bullet to use with your list. Possible values are DISC (the default), CIRCLE and SQUARE.

Here is an example:

```
<UL TYPE=CIRCLE>
<LI>Circle: &lt;TYPE=CIRCLE&gt;
</UL>
<UL TYPE=SQUARE>
<LI>Square: &lt;TYPE=SQUARE&gt;
```

```
</UL>
<UL TYPE=DISC>
<LI>Disc: &lt;TYPE=DISC&gt;
</UL>
```

Here is how it looks in Netscape:

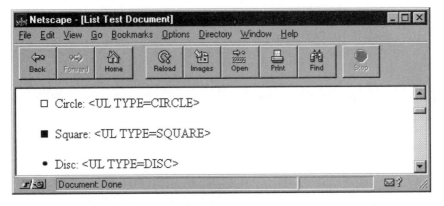

This particular version of Netscape Navigator uses a square rather than a circle for the CIRCLE type. However, other non-beta versions display a circle.

As with most 3.2 extensions to HTML, keep in mind that this attribute will be ignored by many browsers, so when viewed in such a browser, your lists will be displayed with whatever bullet that browser uses by default. For example, Version 2 of Microsoft Internet Explorer did not change the bullet style:

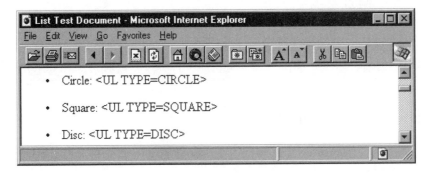

Numbered Lists: <OL>

Numbered, or ordered, lists have numbered items. The markup tags for ordered lists are <OL> and </OL>.

In our kayak.html document, we specify an ordered list as follows:

```
<P>Kayaking and other river sports are very popular
recreational activities in New Zealand. Popular rivers for
these sports are</P>
<OL>
<LI>The Shotover River, South Island
<LI>The Buller River, South Island
<LI>The Karamea River, South Island
<LI>The Rangitikei River, North Island
<LI>The Mohaka River, North Island
</OL>
```

Our ordered list looks like this:

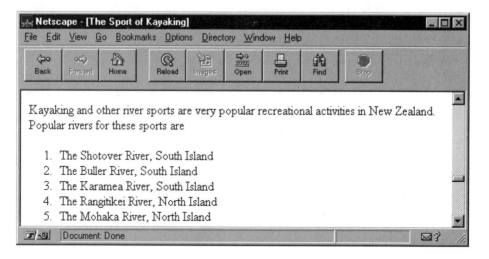

OL Attributes: TYPE and START

A couple of attributes for ordered lists were introduced in HTML 3.2. The TYPE attribute is used to set the number type, with possible values being:

A   Upper-case letters (A, B, C,...)

a   Lower-case letters (a, b, c,...)

I   Large Roman numerals (I, II, III,...)

i   Small Roman numerals (i, ii, iii,...)

1   Numbers—the default (1, 2, 3...)

The START attribute is used to designate a starting place other than one. The start should always be specified as a number—the browser will automatically translate it into whatever type is specified for the list.

Here is our sample list:

```
<OL TYPE=1 START=9>
<LI><STRONG>TYPE=1 START=9</STRONG>
<LI>Plain arabic numbers (the default), start at 9
</OL>
<OL TYPE=A START=27>
<LI><STRONG>TYPE=A START=27</STRONG>
<LI>Capital letters, start at 27.
</OL>
<OL TYPE=a START=3>
<LI><STRONG>TYPE=a START=3</STRONG>
<LI>Lower-case letters, start at 3
</OL>
<OL TYPE=I START=30>
<LI><STRONG>TYPE=I START=30</STRONG>
<LI>Upper-case Roman numerals, start at 30
</OL>
<OL TYPE=i START=100>
<LI><STRONG>TYPE=i START=100</STRONG>
<LI>Lower-case Roman numerals, start at 100
</OL>
```

And here is how it looks:

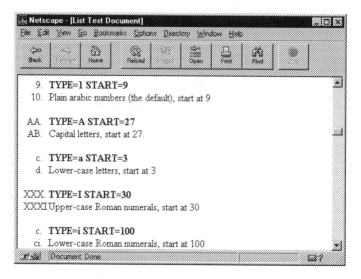

As with other extensions that were added in 3.2, these attributes will be used only if your documents are viewed with a browser that supports the 3.2 standard. When your document is displayed in other browsers, your lists will be shown without the bells and whistles provided by these attributes. This is especially important if you use the START attribute, since numbering in older browsers will start at 1 even if you use START to specify something else. For example, let's look at our document in NCSA Mosaic:

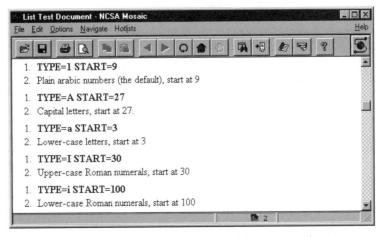

As you can see, both our START and TYPE attributes are ignored in this browser.

LI Attributes

With HTML 3.2, the TYPE attribute may be used with the LI tag. It can take the same values as TYPE for UL or OL (depending on the type of list it is in), and it changes the list item type for that item and all subsequent items in the list.

```
<UL>
<LI TYPE=CIRCLE>Circle: &lt;LI TYPE=CIRCLE&gt;
<LI TYPE=SQUARE>Square: &lt;LI TYPE=SQUARE&gt;
<LI TYPE=DISC>Disc: &lt;LI TYPE=DISC&gt;
</UL>
```

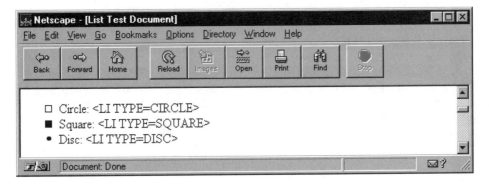

As with the TYPE attribute for UL, use caution when you use this attribute. Many browsers do not yet support it.

In addition to the TYPE attribute, a VALUE attribute was also added for ordered lists so that the count may be modified at any point in the list. Here's our test document:

```
<OL>
<LI TYPE=A>Use capital letters: &lt;LI TYPE=A&gt;
<LI TYPE=a>Use lower-case letters &lt;LI TYPE=a&gt;
<LI TYPE=I>Use upper-case Roman numerals &lt;LI TYPE=I&gt;
<LI TYPE=i>Use lower-case Roman numerals: &lt;LI TYPE=i&gt;
<LI TYPE=1>Use regular numbers (default): &lt;LI TYPE=1&gt;
<LI VALUE=10>Start numbers (or letters) at a specific number.
In this case, 10: &lt;LI VALUE=10&gt;
</OL>
```

And here is how it looks:

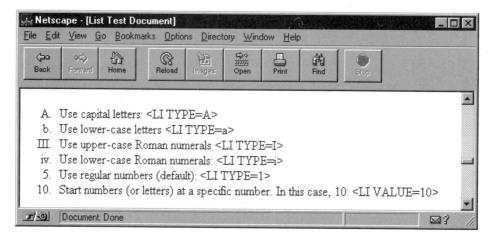

Directory List: <DIR>

Directory lists are intended for short lists. They should be enclosed in <DIR> and </DIR> tags. Each item should be no more than 20 characters. If space is available, the HTML specifications recommend that browsers try to display directory lists in multiple columns. However, in our tests with various browsers we have yet to find one that does this.

```
<P>Following is a list of kayaking resources you will find in
this document:</P>
<DIR>
<LI>Books
<LI>Magazines
<LI>Outfitters
<LI>River descriptions
<LI>Travel agencies
</DIR>
```

Now let's see how this looks:

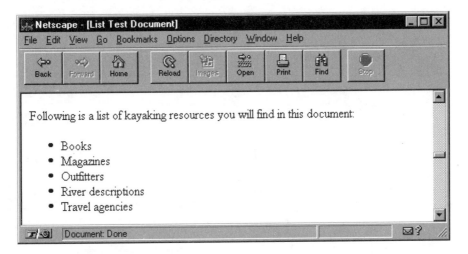

Menu List: <MENU>

A menu list functions much like an unordered list, except it is supposed to be displayed in a more compact style by browsers. We've found that menu lists look exactly like unordered lists in many browsers. However, as development on browsers continues, this may change.

A menu list is enclosed in <MENU> and </MENU> tags, and each item in the list is preceded by the <LI> tag.

```
<P>Kayaking is especially rewarding on those rivers in the
United States that have been designated by Congress as part
of the Wild and Scenic River system. These rivers include:</P>
<MENU>
<LI>The Tuolumne River, California
```

```
<LI>The Chattooga River, Georgia
<LI>The Rogue River, Oregon
<LI>The Illinois River, Oregon
<LI>The Middle Fork of the Salmon, Idaho
<LI>The Selway River, Idaho
</MENU>
```

Now let's see how this section looks:

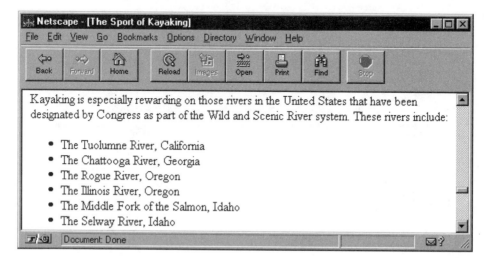

As you can see, unordered, menu and directory lists look fairly similar in Netscape Navigator. However, keep in mind that some browsers allow readers to specify different formats for different types of lists, and that browser writers may decide to use different default formats for different types of lists. Therefore it is not advisable to use these types of lists interchangeably.

Definition Lists: <DL>

Definition lists should be used when specifying a set of terms followed by their definitions. Most browsers format the definition text on a new line. Definition lists are specified as follows:

1. *Begin with an opening definition list <DL> tag.*
2. *Enter the <DT> tag, followed by the text for the defined term.*
3. *Enter the <DD> tag, followed by the text for the definition.*
4. *Continue entering definition terms with the <DT> tag, followed by their definitions, with the <DD> tag. No closing tags are needed.*
5. *Type the closing container tag, </DL>.*

For example, in our kayak.html document, we would specify a definition list as follows:

```
<DL>
<DT><EM>Life jacket</EM>
<DD>A life jacket is essential while kayaking as it provides
flotation.
<DT><EM>Helmet</EM>
<DD>A helmet protects the head against blows against rocks.
<DT><EM>Spray skirt</EM>
<DD>The spray skirt fits between the torso of the kayaker and
the boat, and prevents water from swamping the kayak.
<DT><EM>Paddle</EM>
<DD>A paddle allows the kayaker to navigate in the water.
</DL>
```

The previous snippet would looks like this:

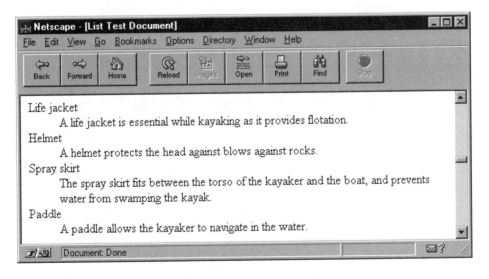

COMPACT Attribute

The COMPACT attribute may be used with DL, OL, UL, DIR or MENU lists. It indicates that interitem spacing should be reduced if possible. In our browser test we were unable to find any browsers that made significant changes to the appearance of the list based on this attribute.

Multiple-Paragraph List Items

Any list item (whether specified via LI, DT or DD), may need to be multiple paragraphs. Although the HTML standard encourages the use of the P tag to delineate paragraphs, the tendency for browsers to insert a blank line between paragraphs may result in confusing or ugly displays of list elements. Let's look at the way that the Lynx and Navigator browsers display an unordered list and a definition list with multiple paragraphs. The segment of HTML we use is this:

```
<UL>
<LI>First, an unordered list. We will separate this item into
two paragraphs using the P tag.
<P>Here is the second paragraph in our first item.
<LI>Now our second item.
<LI>This item is divided into two sections using BR.<BR>
Here is the portion of the item that appears after the BR tag.
</UL>
```

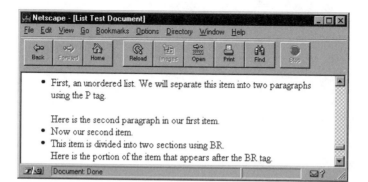

```
<DL>
<DT>This is a definition list.
<DD>We separate this definition item into two paragraphs
using the P tag.
<P>Here is the second paragraph in our first item.
<DT>Now our second item.
<DD>This definition item is divided into two sections using
BR.<BR>
Here is the portion of the item that appears after the BR tag.
</DL>
```

As you can see, the blank line that appears as a result of the P tag breaks the list's continuity. In cases like this, it makes sense to use a BR tag rather than P.

Nested Lists

The lists you use can be nested to an arbitrary level. When you nest lists, keep your poor readers in mind. Nest too deeply, and not only will you have an ugly document, you'll be guaranteed a confused audience!

We might use a nested list in our kayak document as follows:

```
<OL>
<LI>Kayaks
<UL>
<LI>White water kayaks
<LI>Sea kayaks
<LI>Squirt kayaks
</UL>
<LI>There are many types of kayak paddles:
<UL>
```

```
<LI>Feathered
<LI>Dihedral
<LI>Break-down
</UL>
</OL>
```

And here it is:

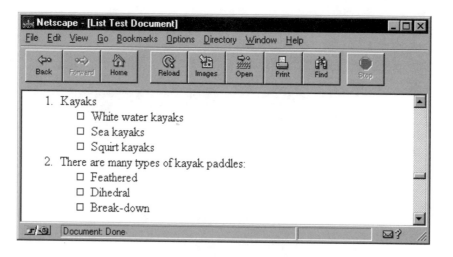

WHEN NESTING LISTS, DON'T FORGET TO CLOSE EACH LIST AND SUBLIST WITH THE APPROPRIATE TAG.

Some browsers choose a different type of bullet for each level of nesting. We made a little test list to illustrate this:

```
<P>You can also nest unordered lists within each other.
Notice how some browsers change the bullets each level:</P>
<UL><LI>Level One
<UL><LI>Level Two
<UL><LI>Level Three
<UL><LI>Level Four
<UL><LI>Level Five
</UL></UL></UL></UL></UL>
```

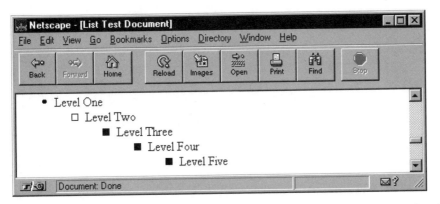

As you can see, Netscape automatically changes the bullet type for the first three levels of nesting. If you use more than three levels of nesting in Netscape, you may wish to explicitly set the bullet type beyond the third level.

Preformatted Text: <PRE>

Sometimes you don't want the Web browser to change the formatting of plain text. You may wish line breaks and spaces to be significant in a piece of text, not ignored by the browser. For example, you may need to display columns of data or show some computer program code. Another example would be a map drawn with ASCII characters. In all of these cases, you want the layout, spacing and line breaks to be exactly reproduced by the browser.

The <PRE> tag tells the browser to display the text in a fixed-width font and to faithfully reproduce spaces, line breaks and tabs. The closing tag is, not surprisingly, </PRE>.

You should not nest other kinds of tags within preformatted text because browsers may interpret such tags strangely. The only exception is the anchor tag, <A>, which is explained in the next chapter.

For example, in our kayaking document, we might want to have a silly ASCII drawing of a kayak paddle. In this example, spaces and line breaks are crucial:

```
<P>Kayaks are navigated using a long paddle, which looks
something like this:</P>
<PRE>
```

```
</PRE>
```

This would be displayed in the browser as:

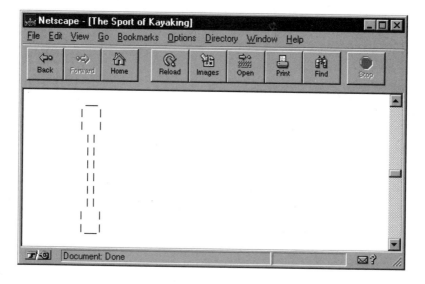

Long Quotations: <BLOCKQUOTE>

The <BLOCKQUOTE> tag is used to mark long quotations in documents. Browsers typically display quotations as indented text. For example, to include a quotation in our kayak document:

```
A first-time kayaker describes his experiences:
<BLOCKQUOTE>
<P>Sir William Francis Butler (1872) explains the thrill of
kayaking:</P>
<BLOCKQUOTE>
It is difficult to find in life any event which so
effectually condenses intense nervous sensation into the
shortest possible space of time as does the work of shooting,
or running an immense rapid.
</BLOCKQUOTE>
```

The resulting text is displayed as:

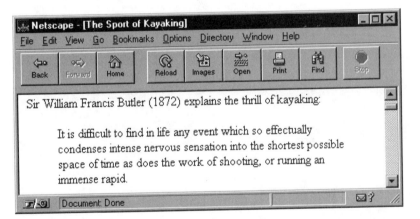

Line Breaks:

A line break is indicated by the <BR> tag. Unlike the <P> tag, the <BR> tag does not insert an extra blank line. The <BR> tag simply forces a line break in the text.

Clear Attribute

HTML 3.2 includes a CLEAR attribute, which provides control for text that is next to an image or table (we'll explain how to add these elements to your documents in the following chapters). It breaks the line and moves down vertically until there is a clear margin. Values that CLEAR may take include ALL, LEFT or RIGHT. You should use the option that matches the side on which you placed your image. So if you have an image with ALIGN=RIGHT, use a BR tag with CLEAR=RIGHT to break the line and move down vertically until there is a clear right margin. If you have images on both sides of your paragraph, use CLEAR=ALL. Let's look at an example now.

```
<P> <IMG SRC="../Images/htmllogo.gif" ALIGN=left BORDER=2>
Here is an example using the CLEAR attribute with the BR tag.
We'll float some text to the right of our CD logo image by
using the ALIGN=LEFT attribute with our image. Since our
image is on the left, let's use the LEFT value to break this
line.<BR CLEAR=LEFT>
```

Here is how this snippet looks in Netscape Navigator:

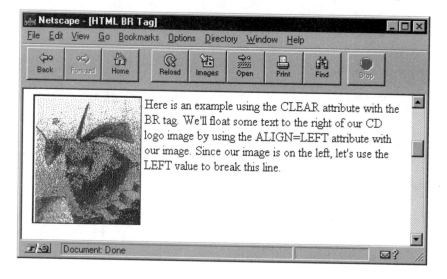

For comparison, let us look at a similar paragraph when we omit the CLEAR attribute:

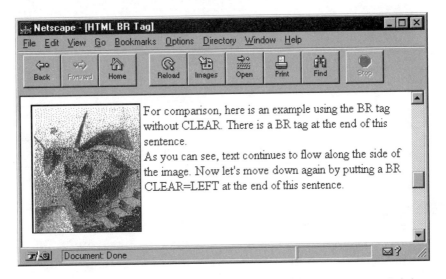

As you can see, the CLEAR attribute can be useful for putting comments about an image next to the image.

Addresses: <ADDRESS>

The <ADDRESS> tag is used to mark—surprise—addresses. Typically, it occurs at the end of documents and is used to enclose the author's name and electronic mail address. Browsers usually display addresses in italic style. For example, the author of the kayak document might include the address as follows:

```
<P>For more information, contact:</P>
<ADDRESS>
Kelly Kayaker<BR>
kayaker@kayak.com
</ADDRESS>
```

This would be displayed as:

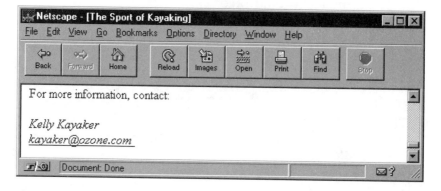

Center: <CENTER>

This tag was originally created by Netscape to allow text to be centered. It is now part of the HTML 3.2 standard, primarily in recognition of its wide use. To use this tag, the text to be centered should be placed in <CENTER></CENTER> tags.

```
<P>To use it, simply place the opening CENTER tag before the
element(s) that are to be centered, and then close it after
you are done. For example, here is a single line:
<CENTER>Here is some centered text!</CENTER>
```

And here it is:

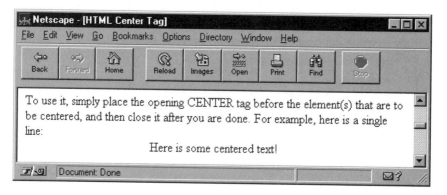

Note that CENTER may also be used to center other objects such as images and tables.

```
<P>Now we use CENTER to center a table, heading and image:
<HR>
<CENTER>
<TABLE BORDER>
<H2>The Thrill of Kayaking</H2>
<CAPTION>New Zealand Kayaking Locations</CAPTION>
<TR><TH>South Island Rivers<TH>North Island Rivers
<TR><TD>Shotover <TD>Rangitikei
<TR><TD>Buller <TD>Mohaka
<TR><TD>Karamea<TD>
</TABLE>
<P><IMG SRC="../Images/kayak.gif" ALT="[Kayak Logo]">
</CENTER>
```

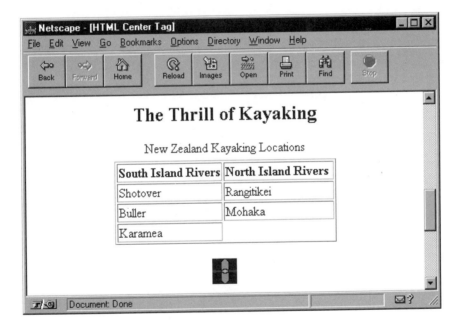

DIV

The DIV tag allows you to specify how a section of text and objects should be aligned. Unlike CENTER, it can be used for different types of alignment. DIV has one attribute: ALIGN, which may take the values LEFT, RIGHT or CENTER. Unfortunately, since DIV is a relatively new tag, at the time this book was written CENTER was still more widely supported than DIV. Here is an example using DIV:

```
<DIV ALIGN=RIGHT>
Right aligned section of text.
<UL>
<LI>The Tuolumne River, California
<LI>The Chattooga River, Georgia
</UL>
</DIV>
<DIV ALIGN=CENTER>
Center aligned section of text.
<UL>
<LI>The Rogue River, Oregon
<LI>The Illinois River, Oregon
</UL>
</DIV>
<DIV ALIGN=LEFT>
Left aligned section of text.
<UL>
<LI>The Middle Fork of the Salmon, Idaho
<LI>The Selway River, Idaho
</UL>
</DIV>
```

And here is how it looks:

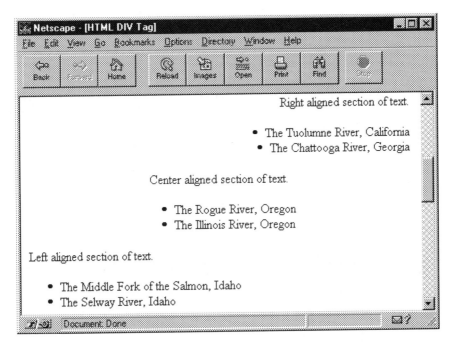

Comments: <! -->

Comments may be included in HTML documents by using the comment tags, <!-- and -->. Text appearing within comment tags will be ignored by browsers. You can use comments to make notes about your documents that you do not want to be displayed to your readers.

Comments cannot be nested within one another. Comments are useful for embedding information for authors, such as document creation date. For example:

```
<!-- The file was created on Jan 1, 1996, by Kelly Kayaker-->
```

Many browsers do not treat embedded HTML tags in a comment correctly. Let's write some lines of HTML that have a nested comment line and a comment line containing several HTML tags.

```
<P>The following line is &lt;!-- Comment --&gt; It should not
be displayed</P>
<!-- Comment -->
<P>Now we try a comment that contains a tag: &lt;!-- Testing
&lt;H1&gt;test&lt;/H2&gt; --&gt; If your browser handles tags in
comments, nothing should appear between the end of this
sentence and the word "Now" in the next paragraph.</P>
<!-- Testing <h1>test</h1> -->
<P>Now we try nesting some comments: &lt;!--&lt;!-- Testing
&lt;H1&gt;test&lt;/H2&gt; --&gt; Note that we only nest the
starting tag for the comment. Since "--&gt;" is defined to be
the end of a comment, the comment should end as soon as the
browser sees one -- there is no provision for nesting end tags
in the HTML standard. Nothing should appear between this
sentence and the horizontal rule if your browser can handle
nested comments.</P>
<!-- <!-- Testing <h1>test</h1> -->
```

Here it is:

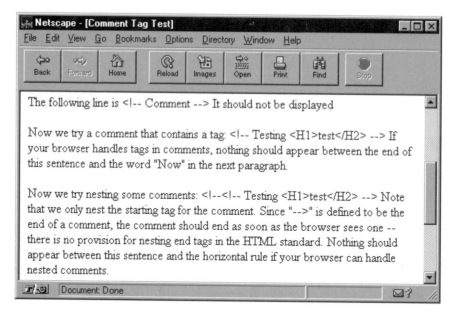

 Although the HTML specification does not restrict you from including HTML tags in a comment, it is better to be safe and avoid placing any tags in a comment. This means that you should not try to use a comment to prevent sections of a document from being displayed!

The Good, the Bad and the Ugly

Let's sum up some of the lessons we've learned in this chapter:

- Divide your documents into head and body parts.
- Don't forget closing tags.
- Never use more than one title in a document.
- Never use other tags in a title.
- Keep your titles fairly short—no more than 64 characters.
- Make your titles meaningful. For example, "Games" is a poor choice for a title; "Games on the Internet: MUDs" is better.
- When nesting lists, don't forget to close each list with the appropriate tag.
- Avoid HTML tags in comment fields—it is not a good idea to place portions of your document in a comment field to try to prevent it from being displayed. Browsers do not always handle tags within comment fields correctly.
- Look at your documents in more than one browser. Different browsers may display the same elements in dissimilar ways.

URLS AND LINKS

What's In This Chapter

This chapter introduces links—the "hyper" part of HTML. We also explain URLs and how to use them in links. As a hypertext system, HTML allows you to link portions of a document to other locations that can be in either the same document or other documents. The links may be made from regions of text, icons, or graphics. They may point to a specific location within another document, or even to another section in the original document.

When a Web browser sees a link, it signals its availability to the user by underlining or coloring the link region. The link destination is communicated to the browser via a uniform resource locator (URL).

Uniform Resource Locators

In the previous chapters we have mentioned URLs a number of times. You can think of URLs as addresses for documents on the Internet. In order to make links you will need to understand what the different parts of a URL are. There are usually three parts in a URL: *protocol, hostname* and *filename*. These three parts are put together to make a URL as follows:

```
protocol://hostname/filename
```

A typical URL looks something like this:

```
http://www.ozone.com/kayak/top.html
```

In this example, "http:" indicates the name of the protocol that should be used for transfer, "www.ozone.com" is the name of the host, and "/kayak/top.html" is the name of the document.

Markup Tag: <A>

The link markup tag in HTML is <A> (denoting "anchor"). This is followed by the URL of the destination document. Then the content or name of the hypertext link (that is, the pointing link) is entered. The closing anchor tag is, of course, </A>.

Specifically, you specify a hypertext anchor in a document with the following somewhat cumbersome set of commands:

- Begin your anchor with "<A ". Don't forget the space after the A.
- Enter the URL of the destination document by typing HREF="*URL*".
- Enter ">".
- Enter the text that serves as the name or pointer to the destination document.
- Enter the closing container tag, </A>.

For example, we might wish to add to our kayak document a pointer to an FAQ on sea kayaking. The FAQ document is stored on another Web server, named ozone.com, and the document is called /kayaking/seakayaker. This link would be entered as follows:

```
Sea kayaking is also exciting. You can find out more about sea
kayaking in the <A
HREF="http://ozone.com/kayaking/seakayaker.html"> sea kayaking
FAQ</A>.
```

Let's see how this looks in Netscape:

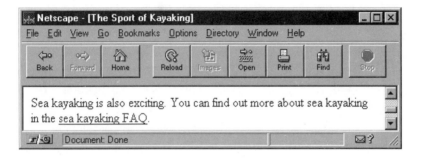

As you can see, the link shows up with an underline. It is also displayed in a different color.

The anchor tag is not supposed to be case sensitive, but many systems (mostly UNIX) will not be able to find the file unless the pathname portion of the URL is treated in a case-sensitive fashion. This is not supposed to be the case according to the HTML specification, but in practice it is. Thus, http://ozone.com/myfile.html is not necessarily the same as http://ozone.com/MyFile.html. Make sure that you check your capitalization as well as spelling for URLs!

Partial Links

You can also make a link that points to a file that is stored on the same machine and is in the same directory or subdirectory as the original document. In this case, you use a partial, or relative, URL as follows:

```
A number of <A HREF="magazine.html">kayaking magazines</A>
are also available to help you learn more about the sport.
```

In this case, the browser assumes that the pointed-to document, magazine.html, is located in the same directory as the original document, kayak.html. It also assumes that the http protocol is used to retrieve the document.

In general, you should use partial links when pointing to related sets of documents. This way, it is easy to move entire sets of documents to a new location on the server if it becomes necessary. Be careful about trying to use relative URLs when your files are not on the same partition as your original file. These URLs may work correctly while checking your files with a browser locally, but will almost always fail when you try to access them through a server. For example, using an anchor that looks like this:

```
<A HREF="/HardDisk1/html/magazine.htm">kayaking magazines</A>
```

may work correctly when you test your document with a browser locally; but when you move it to a server, you will probably find that the link no longer works. You should also use caution when trying to traverse a directory tree in an upward direction with "..". For example, you might be tempted to try something like the following:

```
<A HREF="../html/magazine.htm">kayaking magazines</A>
```

Like our previous example, this anchor works when the file is checked locally, but may not work correctly when moved to a server (depending on the server used). If you know that you will be using a server that can handle ".." as a means for traversing the directory tree, then it is an easy convention for accessing files in different subdirectories. Be sure to check whether you can do this with your server before including it in many documents—otherwise you may have to make extensive changes later.

Rather than trying to use relative URLs when pointing to documents that are in neither the same directory nor one of its subdirectories, you could use complete URLs. Note that some servers (primarily on UNIX systems) allow links to be made between unrelated directories. If you wish to make links between documents in unrelated directories, check with your site's webmaster to see whether this capability is supported by the local server.

YOU SHOULD USE COMPLETE URLs WHEN POINTING TO UNRELATED DOCUMENTS, OR DOCUMENTS ON OTHER MACHINES.

Specific Locations in Other Documents

In addition to pointing to other documents, links can be used to jump to specific locations within other documents, or even to another location within the same document.

For example, let's add a link within our kayak.htm document that specifically points to information about our favorite kayaking magazine in magazine.htm. To do this, we need to insert a named anchor to mark the location within magazine.htm. We name the destination location as follows:

```
<A NAME="wave">Wave~Length</A>
```

Then, when we create our link in the original document, kayak.htm, we include the URL pointing to the destination document, magazine.htm, as well as the name of the pointer to the desired destination anchor within the document. This is done using the hash mark (#), as follows:

```
<A HREF="magazine.html#wave">Wave~Length</A>
```

Now the reader who clicks on the link "Wave~Length" will be taken not only to the new file, magazine.html, but directly to the specific location within that document. This is an especially useful feature when the destination document is long, and you don't want your reader to have to wade through a long document in order to find the section of interest.

Specific Locations within the Current Document

This notion of marking specific locations within documents using named anchors also applies within one document. Thus, we may choose to name several locations in one document, then have pointers to these locations within the same document. This is a quite useful feature if we wish to have a table of contents at the top of a long document. Readers may select an item in the table of contents and be taken directly to that section of the document.

Naming anchors within one document works exactly the same way, except that the name of the destination document is omitted. Only the name of the anchor is included. For example, we may wish to put a pointer to the kayaking resource section at the top of the kayak document. First, we add a label to the beginning of the resource section, as follows:

```
<H2>Kayaking <A NAME="resources">Resources</A></H2>
```

Then, at the beginning of the document we add a link to this label:

```
<A HREF="#resources">kayaking resources</A></P>
```

Be careful when you reference links in the same document. Unlike links to other sites or files, which will usually cause browsers to leave your reader in the same location if something is wrong at the other end (for example, the other host is down or the browser is unable to find the file), browsers will not treat your readers kindly if something is wrong with the other end of a same-document link. Some browsers will dump your reader at the end of the document, while others may not do anything. Unlike links that go to other sites or files where you may have no control over the other end, you *do* have control over both ends of links within the same document. Make sure that you get it right!

Special Characters in URLs

URLs may include any alphanumeric character and the symbols: hyphen (-), dollar sign ($), period (.), plus (+), exclamation point (!), star (*), left parenthesis "(", right parenthesis ")", single quote (') and underscore (_), typed in directly.

However, you may occasionally want to make a link to a file on some other operating system that allows authors to be more creative with filenames. It is common for Macintosh filenames to include spaces, and it is not uncommon to find files with even more unusual characters in their names. When you run into this problem, you will need to encode the character. You encode characters by preceding the ASCII code for the character with a percent sign (%). For example, the ASCII code for the space character is 20. Thus, the URL for a file named "My Kayak" would be:

```
http://ozone.com/My%20Kayak
```

You can find an ASCII table in Appendix B, and on the CD in characters.html.

Other Ways to Use Links

Although at the beginning of this chapter we said that you can think of URLs as addresses for documents on the Web, they are actually much more than that. The key is the protocol portion of the URL. So far, all of our examples have used the Hypertext Transfer Protocol (http). However, you can specify protocols other than http, such as ftp, gopher, telnet, news or mail. By specifying the appropriate protocol in the URL, you can use links to ask the browser to send mail, transfer files or even make a telnet connection. Keep in mind that some browsers do not support all of these actions, so readers using them will not be able to use these links.

One significant difference between the specification of the protocol and markup tags is that some browsers treat the protocol specification in a case-sensitive fashion. Therefore, it is not safe to assume that FTP is the same as ftp.

ALWAYS SPECIFY PROTOCOLS IN LOWER CASE.

A note of caution about the use of protocols other than http: as with markup tags, it is up to the browser to take the appropriate action for each protocol. Some browsers may not support all of the protocols. In these cases the browser will probably just ignore the reference.

We'll explain now how to use some of the most popular protocols in URLs.

FTP

When you specify FTP as the protocol in a URL, the browser will automatically make an anonymous FTP connection to the specified location and transfer the requested file or provide a directory listing (depending on what you specify). Here is the format for an anonymous FTP URL:

```
ftp://hostname/directoryname/filename
```

Let's look at a few examples to see how this works. The following link will transfer a file called "kayak.zip" from the host ozone.com:

```
<A HREF="ftp://ozone.com/kayak.zip">Kayak Trip Planning
Program</A>
```

If a reader chooses this link, the browser will try to open an FTP connection to the host ozone.com and download the file kayak.zip. If you do not specify a filename, a directory listing will be provided:

```
Here are the files in our <A HREF="ftp://ozone.com/">
kayak repository </A>.
```

Although ftp uses anonymous FTP as a default, you can also have the URL specify a particular user. We'll explain how to do this, but first a word of caution. After opening an FTP connection, browsers do not offer you the option of entering a password for the account if one is not provided. This means that you must include the password and account name as part of the URL if you want to use a specific account. This is a huge security hole, since the password is not encrypted—anyone reading your document will be able to see it. Unless you have some special application that requires the use of a specific account, we strongly recommend that you avoid using this feature. The format for a URL that includes an account and password is:

```
ftp://username:password@hostname/path
```

For example, if we want to see a directory listing of Kelly Kayaker's account we could include the following in our kayaking document:

```
<p>Here is a <A HREF="ftp://kayaker:badidea@ozone.com/">
directory listing</A> of Kelly's account.
```

We have made extensive use of the ftp protocol in our browser.html document (this is the document that you can use to get a variety of browsers) on the CD. You should look at this document for more examples of this protocol.

File

The file protocol is for accessing files on a local disk. It is related to ftp because it will try to use FTP if you have specified a host other than the one on which the browser is being used. Here is the format for a file URL:

```
file://localhost/pathname
```

Mail

Using a link to send e-mail is an easy way to allow your readers to provide feedback about your document. The name for this protocol is *mailto*. Thus, the format for e-mail URLs is:

```
mailto:username@hostname
```

Two of the best places to put this option are in a short request for feedback at the beginning of the document, or as part of the address at the end of the document. Let's modify our kayak document to allow readers to send Kelly a message:

```
For more information contact:
<ADDRESS>Kelly Kayaker<BR>
<A HREF="mailto:kayaker@ozone.com"> kayaker@ozone.com </A>
</ADDRESS>
```

If the reader is using a browser that can send e-mail, kayaker@ozone.com will be highlighted in some fashion. If the reader clicks on it, it will provide a mail window that looks something like this:

As you can see, the browser inserts the address specified in the URL in the "To" field.

Telnet

You can also use URLs to provide a telnet connection to the site of your choice. Telnet URLs appear in this format:

```
telnet://hostname:portnumber
```

You do not need to specify a port number if you want a connection made to the default telnet port. However, if you are making a link to a special service at a certain port, you will need to make the connection directly to that port. For example, the University of Michigan offers weather information on port 3000 on the host downwind.sprl.umich.edu. Let's incorporate this information in our kayak document:

```
It is important to know what the weather will be like before
going on a kayak trip. You can get National Weather Service
forecasts for any location from the  <A
HREF="telnet://downwind.sprl.umich.edu:3000"> University of
Michigan WEATHER UNDERGROUND</A>. <P>
```

When the reader chooses this link, the browser will call a helper application to make a telnet connection to port 3000 on the host downwind.sprl.umich.edu. You can try this yourself by loading the kayak document into a browser and choosing this link.

Gopher

Gopher is an information service developed at the University of Minnesota. It provides easy transfer of files because it encodes information about many types of files. However, since the Web includes similar file transfer facilities, it is usually easier to access files through http if a site offers both types of services. However, some sites still offer only gopher service. In this case, you will need to make a link through gopher. A gopher URL looks like this:

```
gopher://hostname:port/gophertype[item]
```

Gophertype is a single character indicating the type of thing to expect (see Table 3–1).

TABLE 3–1 Gophertypes

Type	Description
0	A text file.
1	A directory.
2	A CSO phone-book server.
3	Error.
4	A BinHexed Macintosh file.
5	A DOS binary archive of some sort.
6	A UNIX uuencoded file.
7	An Index-Search server.
8	The item points to a text-based telnet session.
9	The item is a binary file.
g	The item is a GIF format graphics file.
T	The item points to a text-based tn3270 session.
I	The item is some kind of image file.

The two most commonly used types are 0 (text) and 1 (directory). Let's add a link to a gopher site with kayaking information to our kayak document:

```
You can get more kayaking information from this <A
HREF="gopher://ftp.std.com/11/nonprofits/canoe.kayak">gopher
server</A>.
```

News

Newsgroups are an extensive set of electronic bulletin boards. There are newsgroups covering almost every conceivable topic. The news protocol allows you to make a link to a specific newsgroup. The format for URLs using this protocol is:

```
news :newsgroup
```

For example, we might want to make a link to the news-group rec.boats.paddle in our kayak document:

```
You can find more information about kayaks in the newsgroup
<A HREF="news:rec.boats.paddle"> rec.boats.paddle</A>.
```

You can also specify specific articles by replacing the name of the newsgroup with an article ID in the URL. However, since news turns over so rapidly, this link would remain valid only a short time.

In order to use a newsgroup link, the reader's browser must support some news-reading mechanism and must be configured to use a news (NNTP) server. While it is not your responsibility to make sure that your reader's browsers are set up correctly, if you make heavy use of news URLs, it might be helpful to your readers to include a warning about configuring their browsers to use an NNTP server before trying those links.

Link Trivia

There are a few things about links that we have not yet mentioned. We've left them for last, not because they are the best, but because right now they are not terribly important. Feel free to skip this section. We've told you about the attributes HREF and NAME in the anchor tag. We expect these tags to be the only ones you'll ever need to use. However, there are actually a number of other attributes that can be used with anchor tags, and so for completeness they are listed in Table 3–2. Browser support for these attributes is fairly spotty, and there is still debate about these attributes in the Web development community. For now, use them at your own risk.

TABLE 3–2 Additional Anchor Tag Attributes

Attribute	Description
REL	This is currently only proposed. It is supposed to give the relationship described by the link.
REV	Another proposed attribute. It is supposed to give the relationship described by the link in the opposite direction to REL.
URN	This stands for Uniform Resource Number and is supposed to help the browser avoid reloading a document it has already acquired.
TITLE	This is only for information. It should provide the title of the document whose address is in the HREF attribute.

JavaScript Extension: onMouseOver

Although we won't be getting to our formal description of JavaScript for several more chapters, we're going to introduce a handy JavaScript function (formally known as an Event Handler) that you can use with your links. As you probably know, most browsers display the destination of a link in the status bar when the mouse is over the link.

The onMouseOver JavaScript function allows you to display a message rather than the URL in the status bar when the mouse is over the link. Since this function may be used in a similar fashion to most markup tag attributes, even if you don't want to learn JavaScript, you can still take advantage of this function. The syntax for this function is:

```
onMouseOver="window.status='your message';return true"
```

JavaScript is case sensitive, so you must put the function name in exactly as it appears here. To incorporate it in a link, simply add it to the link as you would any other attribute. Let's add a message to the magazine link example we used earlier in this chapter:

```
My favorite kayaking magazine is <A
HREF="magazine.html#wave" onMouseOver="window.status='My
Favorite Magazine!';return true">Wave~Length</A>.
```

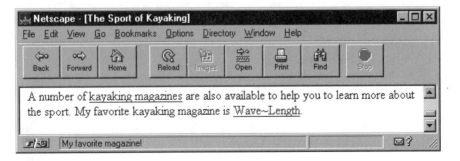

As you can see, the status bar shows our phrase rather than the URL now. Remember that the phrase will be displayed only in browsers that support JavaScript (and that have JavaScript enabled). The URL will show up as usual in other browsers.

The Good, the Bad and the Ugly

Now that you know how to make links, it is time to go over some guidelines on when and where you should use them.

Don't fall into the *click here* trap. Many people have chosen to make links that look like this:

```
If you want to see my document on kayaking click <A
HREF="kayak.htm">here</A>.
```

While one "click here" in a document isn't necessarily a bad thing, it does not make good use of the browser's display features. Since most browsers highlight links, the links in a document are more conspicuous than the rest of the text. If most of your links are made to the same word, there is no way for the reader to quickly distinguish between the links. For example:

```
<UL>
<LI>Click <A HREF="bird.htm">here</A> for a document on birds.
<LI>Click <A HREF="cat.htm">here</A> for a document on cats.
<LI>Click <A HREF="dog.htm">here</A> for a document on dogs.
<LI>Click <A HREF="fish.htm">here</A> for a document on fish.
</UL>
```

When we see this in a browser, the word "here" leaps out. It is difficult to see what the links are actually for.

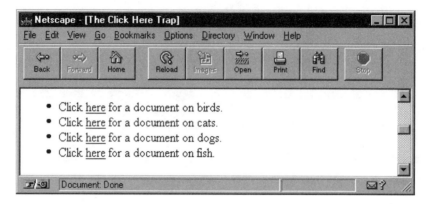

However, simply shifting the link over to the subject of each document and slightly rewriting each line clears up the problem.

```
<UL>
<LI>A document about <A HREF="bird.htm">birds</A>.
<LI>A document about <A HREF="cat.htm">cats</A>.
<LI>A document about <A HREF="dog.htm">dogs</A>.
<LI>A document about <A HREF="fish.htm">fish</A>.
</UL>
```

Now we have:

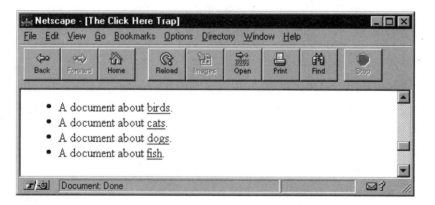

In our new and improved version, the topic of the document behind each link is easy to see.

It is easy to make links in inappropriate places. There are so many resources on the Internet, you may be tempted to make a link every time you mention something for which you have an Internet resource. Place links only where they really contribute something to the content of your document.

Finally, don't make your anchor text too long. While there is nothing to stop you from making a whole sentence into a link, doing this is unsightly and does not make it any easier for your reader to follow the link. Rather than using a long phrase as a link, choose the words in the phrase that most clearly describe the link and place your anchor tags around them.

TABLES, FRAMES AND MORE

What's In This Chapter

This chapter introduces tables and frames. It also includes descriptions of the nonstandard HTML elements available in the Netscape and Internet Explorer browsers. We urge you to use these nonstandard HTML elements with caution, since it is difficult to make documents that use nonstandard elements look good when viewed by different types of browsers. Additionally, unlike official HTML elements, these elements have bypassed the rigorous screening process that official HTML elements must pass. Instead they rely on a single company for advocacy and support.

Tables: <TABLE>

So far, the only way that we could line up text in columns was to use the PRE tag and lots of space. The table tag allows you to easily set up text in columns and much more. A table should be enclosed in the <TABLE></TABLE> tags. Within the table, the <TR> tag is used to designate rows. Individual cells are designated by <TH> for a header cell or <TD> for a data cell. A caption may also be included by using the <CAP-TION></CAPTION> tags. You can find the tables presented in this section on the CD in the documents table.html and toc.html. Let's look at a table that simply places text in two rows.

```
<TABLE>
<TR><TH>South Island Rivers<TH>North Island Rivers
<TR><TD>Shotover <TD>Rangitikei
<TR><TD>Buller <TD>Mohaka
<TR><TD>Karamea<TD> 
<CAPTION>New Zealand Kayaking Locations</CAPTION>
</TABLE>
```

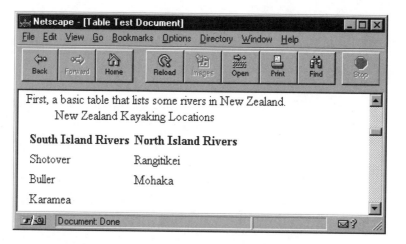

While this is a simple way to align text in columns, a rich set of attributes provides a wide variety of ways to use tables.

Attributes that are available with TABLE in the HTML 3.2 standard include:

ALIGN

This specifies horizontal alignment for the table itself. It may be set to: CENTER (center table between text margins, the default value), RIGHT (flush with right margin), LEFT (flush with left text margin)

BORDER=N

Render borders around the table and between cells. N is the width of the border and is optional. This attribute is supposed to be superseded by the FRAME attribute.

CELLSPACING=n

Cell spacing—spacing between cells. N should be a value in pixels.

CELLPADDING=n

Cell padding—spacing within cells. N should be a value in pixels.

WIDTH=n or n%

Allows you to specify the width for the table. The width may be entered as a total number of pixels or as a percentage of the page width. A WIDTH attribute is also available for TD and TH. The width may be expressed in pixels or as a percentage of the table width.

Let's see how the addition of some of these attributes changes our table. We replace our opening TABLE tag with:

```
<TABLE BORDER CELLSPACING=5 WIDTH=400 ALIGN=CENTER>
```

```
┌──────────────────────────────────────────────────────────────────┐
│ ≋ Netscape - [Table Test Document]                    _ □ ✕ │
├──────────────────────────────────────────────────────────────────┤
│ File  Edit  View  Go  Bookmarks  Options  Directory  Window  Help │
├──────────────────────────────────────────────────────────────────┤
│  ⇦      ⇨      🏠       ⟳       📷       ⇨        🖨      🔍     ⬤   │
│ Back  Forward  Home   Reload  Images   Open    Print   Find   Stop │
├──────────────────────────────────────────────────────────────────┤
│              New Zealand Kayaking Locations                    ▲   │
│                                                                    │
│  ┌──────────────────────────┬──────────────────────────┐        │
│  │   South Island Rivers    │   North Island Rivers    │         │
│  ├──────────────────────────┼──────────────────────────┤         │
│  │ Shotover                 │ Rangitikei               │         │
│  ├──────────────────────────┼──────────────────────────┤         │
│  │ Buller                   │ Mohaka                   │         │
│  ├──────────────────────────┼──────────────────────────┤         │
│  │ Karamea                  │                          │         │
│  └──────────────────────────┴──────────────────────────┘        ▼  │
├──────────────────────────────────────────────────────────────────┤
│ 🖭  Document: Done                                      ✉?       │
└──────────────────────────────────────────────────────────────────┘
```

As you may notice, this table is not centered, even though we included an ALIGN=CENTER attribute. We have found that most browsers do not yet support this attribute. However, you can still center tables in some browsers by placing the table in a CENTER or DIV tag.

The table could still use some work. Rather than having each river in a separate cell, it would be nice to have each set of lists in an unordered list. Since you can place almost any HTML element in a table cell, this is a simple change. We modify our table as follows:

```
<TABLE BORDER CELLSPACING=5 WIDTH=400 ALIGN=CENTER>
<TR><TH>South Island Rivers<TH>North Island Rivers
<TR><TD><UL><LI>Shotover
<LI>Karamea
<LI>Buller
</UL>
<TD><UL>
<LI>Rangitikei
<LI>Mohaka
</UL>
<CAPTION>New Zealand Kayaking Locations</CAPTION>
</TABLE>
```

```
┌────────────────────────────────────────────────────────────────┐
│ ⋈ Netscape - [Table Test Document]                    _ □ X     │
│ File  Edit  View  Go  Bookmarks  Options  Directory  Window  Help│
│ ┌─────┬─────┬─────┬─────┬─────┬─────┬─────┬─────┬─────┐         │
│ │ ⇦   │ ⇨   │ 🏠  │ ⟳   │ 📷  │ 📂  │ 🖶   │ 🔍  │ ●   │         │
│ │Back │Forward│Home │Reload│Images│Open │Print│Find │Stop │       │
│ └─────┴─────┴─────┴─────┴─────┴─────┴─────┴─────┴─────┘         │
│ ┌──────────────────────────────────────────────────────┐ ▲     │
│ │        New Zealand Kayaking Locations                 │       │
│ │                                                       │       │
│ │ ┌──────────────────┬──────────────────┐              │       │
│ │ │ South Island Rivers │ North Island Rivers │         │       │
│ │ ├──────────────────┼──────────────────┤              │       │
│ │ │  • Shotover      │                   │              │       │
│ │ │  • Karamea       │   • Rangitikei    │              │       │
│ │ │  • Buller        │   • Mohaka        │              │       │
│ │ └──────────────────┴──────────────────┘              │ ▼     │
│ ┌──────┬──────────────────────────────────┐ ✉?         │
│ │ 🔲🔳 │ Document: Done                   │            │
│ └──────┴──────────────────────────────────┘            │
└────────────────────────────────────────────────────────────────┘
```

Cell Attributes

The following attributes may be specified for table cells (TD) and table headings (TR).

ALIGN

The ALIGN attribute allows you to specify the horizontal alignment of paragraphs within a table row. In the absence of this attribute, the default may be overridden by the presence of an ALIGN attribute on the parent TR element. Allowed values include:

LEFT   Flush left, default for data cells (TD)

CENTER   Center contents, default for header cells (TH)

RIGHT   Flush right

VALIGN

This attribute is used to explicitly specify the vertical alignment of material within a table row. Using it with an individual cell will override the setting for a row. It can take one of the following four values:

TOP   Align contents with the top of the cell, default

MIDDLE   Center contents vertically

BOTTOM   Place contents at the bottom of the cell

BASELINE   Ensure that all cells in a row share a baseline—applies only to the first text line for each cell

COLSPAN

The number of columns spanned by the cell. It allows you to merge cells across columns. It defaults to one.

ROWSPAN

The number of rows spanned by the cell. Allows you to merge cells across rows. It defaults to one.

Let's look at a table example that uses some of these attributes. Here is a rather silly table:

```
<P>Here is a table with funny alignment and spanning columns
and rows:</P>
<TABLE BORDER>
<CAPTION><H3>A Very Silly Table</H3></CAPTION>
<TR><TH>Column One<TH>Column Two<TH>Column Three<TH>Column
Four
<TR ALIGN=CENTER><TD>La<TD>De<TD>Da<TD>Ta Dum!
<TR><TD COLSPAN=2>Next cell is right justified<TD
ALIGN=RIGHT>Da<TD>Ta Dum!
<TR><TD ROWSPAN=2>La De<TD>Da<TD>Ta Dum!<TD>Ta Dum!
<TR ALIGN=RIGHT><TD>Da<TD>Ta Dum!<TD>Ta Dum!
</TABLE>
```

And here is how our silly table looks:

```
┌─────────────────────────────────────────────────────────────────┐
│ ▒▒ Netscape - [Table Test Document]                    _ □ ✕      │
├─────────────────────────────────────────────────────────────────┤
│ File  Edit  View  Go  Bookmarks  Options  Directory  Window  Help │
├─────────────────────────────────────────────────────────────────┤
│  Back  Forward  Home   Reload  Images  Open  Print  Find   Stop   │
├─────────────────────────────────────────────────────────────────┤
│              A Very Silly Table                                    │
│                                                                   │
│  Column One  Column Two  Column Three  Column Four                 │
│      La          De           Da          Ta Dum!                 │
│  Next cell is right justified         Da  Ta Dum!                 │
│  La De       Da           Ta Dum!         Ta Dum!                 │
│                      Da        Ta Dum!       Ta Dum!              │
│                                                                   │
├─────────────────────────────────────────────────────────────────┤
│  ▒▒  Document: Done                                     ✉?        │
└─────────────────────────────────────────────────────────────────┘
```

Nonstandard Cell Attributes

Microsoft Internet Explorer and Netscape Navigator both support additional attributes that are not part of the 3.2 standard. Some of the following attributes are supported only by Explorer.

BACKGROUND

Used to set a background image, which is tiled behind the table. Internet Explorer only, and support varies between platforms and versions.

BGCOLOR

Used to set a background color for the table. Value may be an RGB in the form #RRGGBB or one of the predefined color names (see the multimedia chapter for more information on color). Navigator and Internet Explorer.

BORDERCOLOR

Set a color for the border. Must be used in conjunction with the BORDER attribute. The value may be any color in the standard formats. Internet Explorer.

BORDERCOLORLIGHT

Set the lighter border color used to draw 3-D borders. Must be used in conjunction with the BORDER attribute and preferably with the BORDERCOLORDARK attribute. Internet Explorer.

BORDERCOLORDARK

Set the darker border color in 3-D borders. Must be used in conjunction with the BORDER attribute and preferably with the BORDERCOLORLIGHT attribute. Internet Explorer.

With the exception of BGCOLOR, we found that support for these attributes in Internet Explorer varied between platforms and versions. However, since these attributes merely provide additional control over the color of various table elements, tables that include these attributes should still be useable even if the document is viewed in a table-aware browser that does not support these attributes.

Here is a sample table using some of these attributes:

```
<P>Here is a table with some color attributes set on the
table itself.
This table includes BGCOLOR=fuschia BORDERCOLORLIGHT=lime
BORDERCOLORDARK=green
BORDERCOLOR=RED
<CENTER><DIV ALIGN=CENTER>
<TABLE BORDER ALIGN=CENTER
BGCOLOR=fuschia
BORDERCOLORLIGHT=lime
BORDERCOLORDARK=green
BORDERCOLOR=RED>
<CAPTION><H3>Internet Growth</H3></CAPTION>
<TR><TH>Date <TH>Number of Hosts
<TR><TD>8/81 <TD ALIGN=CENTER> 213.0
<TR><TD>5/82 <TD ALIGN=CENTER> 235.0
<TR><TD>8/83 <TD ALIGN=CENTER> 562.0
```

```
<TR><TD>10/84<TD ALIGN=CENTER> 1,024.0
</TABLE>
</DIV></CENTER>
```

Here it is in Internet Explorer:

Table Test Document - Microsoft Internet Explorer

File Edit View Go Favorites Help

Here is a table with some color attributes set on the table itself. This table includes BGCOLOR=fuschia BORDERCOLORLIGHT=lime BORDERCOLORDARK=green BORDERCOLOR=RED

Internet Growth	
Date	Number of Hosts
8/81	213.0
5/82	235.0
8/83	562.0
10/84	1,024.0

and in Netscape Navigator:

Netscape - [Table Test Document]

File Edit View Go Bookmarks Options Directory Window Help

Back Forward Home Reload Images Open Print Find Stop

Here is a table with some color attributes set on the table itself. This table includes BGCOLOR=fuschia BORDERCOLORLIGHT=lime BORDERCOLORDARK=green BORDERCOLOR=RED

Internet Growth

Date	Number of Hosts
8/81	213.0
5/82	235.0
8/83	562.0
10/84	1,024.0

Document: Done

This is another example of the way that one vendor's browser may present the same document quite differently than another vendor's browser. Although you can't see the colors in this picture, you can see how the addition of a background color has shaded the background of the table and caption area in the Internet Explorer display, while Navigator shades only the table itself.

Also notice that we have centered the table. The tag that Internet Explorer used in this case is the CENTER tag. However, if you look at the document, you will see that we have included three centering commands: CENTER, DIV ALIGN=CENTER, and an ALIGN=CENTER attribute on the table itself. Although it may seem to be redundant, some browsers support one tag but not the others. By including as many supported tags as possible, we increase the likelihood that our table will be displayed in a centered fashion.

Bar Graph Example

Tables can be used for much more than simple text layout. For example, they provide an easy way to position images on a page. We provide examples of this use for tables in the multimedia chapter. Here we demonstrate how a table can be used to create a bar chart. Our table is a production chart for apples, oranges and grapes:

```
<TABLE CELLPADDING=0 CELLSPACING=0 COLS=4 WIDTH=50%>
<CAPTION>Fruit Production</CAPTION><TR><TD WIDTH=10>50<TD
WIDTH=30><TD BGCOLOR=GREEN WIDTH=30><TD WIDTH=30>
<TR><TD>40<TD BGCOLOR=RED><TD BGCOLOR=GREEN><TD>
<TR><TD>30<TD BGCOLOR=RED><TD BGCOLOR=GREEN><TD
BGCOLOR=FUSCHIA>
<TR><TD>20<TD BGCOLOR=RED><TD BGCOLOR=GREEN><TD
BGCOLOR=FUSCHIA>
<TR><TD>10<TD BGCOLOR=RED><TD BGCOLOR=GREEN><TD
BGCOLOR=FUSCHIA>
<TR><TD><TH>Apples<TH>Oranges<TH>Grapes
</TABLE>
```

We know of two browsers that support the BGCOLOR attribute, Internet Explorer and Netscape Navigator. Here is our table in Internet Explorer:

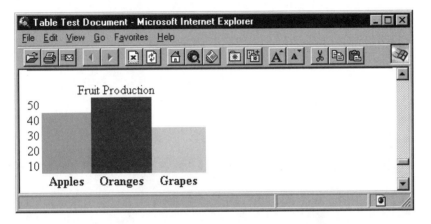

Here it is in Navigator:

Where's the graph? It turns out that the version of Netscape Navigator we used does not put anything in empty cells (including the background color). Fortunately, this problem is easily remedied by putting a nonbreaking space in our "empty" cells:

```
<TABLE CELLPADDING=0 CELLSPACING=0 COLS=4 WIDTH=50%>
<CAPTION>Fruit Production</CAPTION>
<TR><TD WIDTH=10>50<TD WIDTH=30> <TD BGCOLOR=GREEN
```

```
WIDTH=30> <TD WIDTH=30> 
<TR><TD>40<TD BGCOLOR=RED> <TD
BGCOLOR=GREEN> <TD> 
<TR><TD>30<TD BGCOLOR=RED> <TD BGCOLOR=GREEN> <TD
BGCOLOR=FUSCHIA> 
<TR><TD>20<TD BGCOLOR=RED> <TD BGCOLOR=GREEN> <TD
BGCOLOR=FUSCHIA> 
<TR><TD>10<TD BGCOLOR=RED> <TD BGCOLOR=GREEN> <TD
BGCOLOR=FUSCHIA> 
<TR><TD><TH> Apples <TH> Oranges <TH> 
;Grapes
</TABLE>
```

Here it is in Navigator with the spaces:

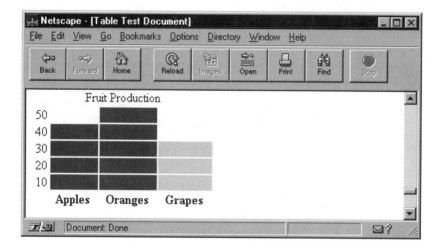

Tables in Browsers without Table Support

As we've mentioned before, knowing which browsers your audience uses can be a helpful aid in developing your documents. The example given in the section made use of the background color attributes for table cells. Since this is not a widely supported feature, it is important to test it in the browsers that you expect your audience to use. And what about people that view your documents in browsers that do not have any table support?

Browsers that do not support tables typically display the entire table as a running section of text. You can preserve your lines by inserting a BR tag at the end of each row. Be careful to place the BR tag inside the TR or TD at the end of your row:

```
<TR><TH>Date <TH>Number of Hosts<BR></TR>
<TR><TD>8/81 <TD ALIGN=CENTER> 213.0<BR></TR>
```

not:

```
<TR><TH>Date <TH>Number of Hosts</TR><BR>
<TR><TD>8/81 <TD ALIGN=CENTER> 213.0<BR></TR><BR>
```

In the second case, most browsers will see the BR as being outside any table element and will display it outside the table.

While the BR strategy will preserve the line breaks in your table, it will not help with column alignment. For those of you who would like to do this as well, you can line up your columns with spaces, and place the table in a PRE tag:

```
<PRE>
<TABLE>
<TR><TH>Date <TH>Number of Hosts<BR></TR>
<TR><TD>8/81 <TD ALIGN=CENTER> 213.0<BR></TR>
</TABLE>
</PRE>
```

We will discuss methods for diverting readers to specific versions of documents based on their browser type later in the book.

Frames: <FRAMESET>, <FRAME>, <NOFRAME>

Frames provide a way for you to divide a window into separate sections or "frames" and load a different document into each window. Documents in one frame may update other frames, allowing you to create an index in one frame that will display the requested topic in another frame. If this seems like it can't work without departing from standard HTML, you're right. At the time this book was written the only browsers that supported frames were Netscape Navigator Version 2 and above and Microsoft Internet Explorer Version 3 and above.

Documents that use frames have a structure that looks like this:

```
<HTML>
<HEAD>
</HEAD>
<FRAMESET>
</FRAMESET>
</HTML>
```

As you can see, BODY has been replaced by FRAMESET. Framesets allow you to set up the layout for a window. It takes two attributes: COLS and ROWS. Both attributes take a list of values. The values may be in:

- number of pixels
- percentage
- *number** where * indicates that the frame corresponding to this value gets whatever space is not used by the other frames. *Number* is optional and indicates the percentage of remaining space to be allocated to that frame (if there is more than one such frame).

For example, to make a simple window divided into equally sized quarters, you could use:

```
<FRAMESET ROWS="50%,50%" COLS="50%,50%">
```

The result would be:

![Netscape - [Quartered Window] showing a browser window divided into four equal quadrants with menu bar (File Edit View Go Bookmarks Options Directory Window Help) and toolbar (Back, Forward, Home, Reload, Images, Open, Print, Find, Stop). Status bar reads "Document: Done".]

Actually we cheated a bit. This snippet would not display anything, because there are no frames in it. Before anything is displayed, you need to specify what will go in the frames you laid out. You do this with the FRAME tag.

You can nest FRAMESET tags to create just about any layout you want. For example, if you wanted to have a narrow frame across the top of your window for a banner or introductory material, and another narrow banner at the right of your window to hold an index, you could use the following:

```
<FRAMESET ROWS="20%,80%">
<FRAME>
<FRAMESET COLS="80%,20%">
<FRAME>
<FRAME>
</FRAMESET>
</FRAMESET>
```

Here is how this looks:

Frames: <FRAME>

Once you have finished the layout for your window, you will need to place content in each frame. You do this with the FRAME tag. The two most important FRAME attributes are:

SRC=_URL_

> This attribute allows you to specify the URL of the document that is to be displayed in the frame. If you do not specify an SRC, the frame will be left empty (as in our examples above).

NAME=_window-name_

> NAME is used to give the frame a name so that it may be updated by links in other documents. Names must begin with a number or letter.

You use these attributes to load information into the frame and to set up a reference name for each frame. For example:

```
<FRAME SRC=kidwelcome.html NAME=artwindow>
```

Several other attributes are available that give you greater control over the look of each frame:

FRAMEBORDER=_value_

> Used to set the width of the frame borders and takes a value in pixels. Setting the value to 0 will create borderless frames if the document is viewed in a browser that supports borderless frames[1].

MARGINWIDTH=_value_

> Used to control the width of the left and right margins, _value_ should be expressed in pixels and may not be less than one (so the frame's contents do not touch the edge of the frame).

MARGINHEIGHT=_value_

> Same as marginwidth, except that it controls the width of the top and bottom margins.

---

1. At the time this book was written borderless frames were only supported by Microsoft Internet Explorer.

SCROLLING=*yes | no | auto*

This attribute controls whether a scroll bar will be available for that frame. AUTO is the default; it will cause a scroll bar to be placed only if it is needed. YES causes scroll bars to be displayed even if the frame is not full, and NO prevents scroll bars from being displayed even if some of the information cannot be displayed. NO is a dangerous choice, since it can create situations in which readers may be unable to see the entire document.

NORESIZE

This prevents readers from resizing a frame. (Readers are normally permitted to resize frames by dragging frame edges using their mouse.)

For example, let's fill in our frames from the previous section:

```
<FRAMESET ROWS="20%,80%">
<FRAME SRC=menubar.html NAME=topframe FRAMEBORDER=3>
<FRAMESET COLS="80%,20%">
<FRAME SRC=sidebar.html NAME=sideframe MARGINWIDTH=1>
<FRAME SRC=greeting.html NAME=mainframe SCROLLING=NO>
</FRAMESET>
</FRAMESET>
```

Frame Navigation: TARGET and <BASE>

Navigating around a document that uses frames can be confusing for readers. This is because documents that do not include appropriate navigational control may leave readers stuck with a window divided into multiple frames even though they are no longer viewing a frame document. This happens when links in a frame document do not include directives for the placement of the new document. Without a target directive, new documents are loaded in the current frame, leaving the other frames in the window intact. Making matters even worse, if the reader wants to return from the link, the familiar "Back" button in the browser may not be of any help, since some browsers consider the top-level frame document the one that is loaded in the window. As a result, a click on "Back" would return the reader to the document that was loaded before the top-level frame document rather than returning the frame to the previous document loaded in it.

There are a number of methods for specifying where a link should be displayed. These methods allow you to create links in any frame that can update another frame (or window), which is known as the target. When a reader clicks on a link for which a target has been specified, the requested document will appear in the target frame or window.

The default target frame is the current frame, so if you do not specify a target, the document will be displayed in the current frame. If you specify a target frame that does not currently exist, a new frame (in a new window) will be opened and given that name.

Target names must begin with a number or a letter. They are also case sensitive, so be careful when you enter the name. For example, the target names Frame, fRame, frAme, and fraMe are not the same.

You can set a default target for all of the links in a document by using the BASE tag with the TARGET attribute. This tag sets a named target window for every link in a document that does not have an explicit TARGET attribute. The format for this tag is:

```
<BASE TARGET="default_target">
```

You can set a target for a specific link by using the TARGET attribute with the A tag. The syntax for this attribute is:

```
<A HREF="url.html" TARGET="window_name">Click here and open a
New Window</A>
```

Predefined Targets

As we said in the previous section, the names that you choose for targets must start with a number or letter. This is in part because other characters are reserved for predefined target names. At the time this book was written, the predefined targets shown in Table 4–1 were available:

TABLE 4–1 *Predefined Targets*

Target	Description
_blank	Load this link into a new unnamed window
_self	Load link into current window (default)
_parent	Load link over parent (self if no parent exists)
_top	Load link at the top level (self if you are currently at the top)

Notice that all of these target names begin with an underscore. They are also composed of lower-case letters. As we stated before, target names are case sensitive, so be sure that you enter the names exactly as they appear in Table 4–1.

Frame Navigation Guidelines

If you do not want to trap your readers in a single frame, you should set your base target to _top:

```
<BASE TARGET="_top">
```

This will cause references in your document that do not have an explicit target to be loaded in the full window rather than into the current frame. If you have links that you want to be loaded into the current frame, you can then target them to the frame by including a target attribute with the link. For example, if the current frame is named "MyFrame", you would include a target attribute with the link like:

```
<A HREF=kayak.html TARGET="MyFrame">kayaking</A>
```

Alternatively you may wish to have all of your links target another frame in the window. This is useful if you are using frames to create a table of contents. In this case you may wish to make the default target be another frame in the window. For example, we have a document with two frames, one named "toc" that contains the table of contents, and one named "content" that contains the documents referenced by the table of contents:

```
<FRAME SRC=toc.html NAME=toc>
<FRAME SRC=intro.html NAME=content>
```

In our toc.html document, we include:

```
<BASE TARGET="content">
```

Thus any document linked in the table of contents will be loaded into the "content" frame, unless an alternate target has been set for that link.

If you choose to use the predefined target "_blank" or an undefined target name, be careful to use them sparingly. Both of these targets will force the browser to open a new window. Extra windows use system memory, and gratuitously forcing the browser to open new windows may cause problems for your reader's system. Additionally, many readers are annoyed by the creation of extra windows that they have not explicitly requested.

It is almost always desirable to load external links that are not under your control into the "_top" target. If you don't, they may appear to be part of your document, or they may not be designed for a frame. Either way, you will detract from the document's presentation.

Updating Multiple Frames: onClick

It is possible to simultaneously update multiple frames through the JavaScript function onClick. We will provide a complete introduction to JavaScript later in this book. However, you do not need to know how to use JavaScript in its entirety to make use of this function. This section is for those of you that would like to incorporate this functionality in your documents without having to learn all about JavaScript.

JavaScript uses names for windows in a similar fashion to the frame predefined targets. The top-level window's name is "parent", and each frame in the parent window can be referenced by the name set for that frame when the frame is created. The names are separated by periods, so a frame that is named "frame2" would be referenced as "parent.frame2".

Each frame has a "location.href" object that holds the reference for the current document. To update a frame, simply set this object to the location of the new document. For example, if we wanted to update our "frame2" frame to point to a document named "newdoc.html", we would set the new location with the command:

```
parent.frame2.location.href=newdoc.html
```

Of course simply placing this command in your document won't do anything. You will need to call it with the onClick function. To use onClick, simply treat it as another attribute for the A tag. String together your update commands separated by semicolons. The set of update commands should be placed in double quotes. We could simultaneously update four frames with the following snippet:

```
Use onClick to <STRONG><A HREF="makenewframe4.html"
onClick="parent.frame2.location.href='makenewframe1.html';
parent.frame3.location.href='makenewframe2.html';
parent.frame1.location.href='makenewframe4.html';
return true">rotate the frames</A>
```

JavaScript is case sensitive, so onClick must be capitalized exactly. At the time this book was written, all the browsers that supported frames also supported JavaScript. However, this may change as other browsers are released. Additionally, readers have the option of turning off JavaScript capability in some browsers. If they do this, the multiple update will not work.

Content for Browsers without Frame Support:
<NOFRAMES>

Since the content of frames is completely contained within FRAME tags, browsers that do not have frame support will not see anything to display. Since many browsers do not have frame support (including early Netscape browsers), you can lose a substantial number of readers unless you provide some content that does not require frame support. You do this with the <NOFRAMES> tag.

Officially you should place your content in a <NOFRAMES> tag after the last FRAME, but before the closing FRAMESET tag. For example:

```
<FRAMESET ROWS="10%,90%">
<FRAME SRC=row1.html>
<FRAME SRC=row2.html>
<NOFRAMES>
<P>This should be visible if your browser does not support
frames, while an alternative set of documents will be
displayed if your browser does support them.
</NOFRAMES>
</FRAMESET>
```

When this is viewed by a frame-aware browser, the frames will be displayed, and the NOFRAME section will be ignored. Other browsers will not recognize the <NOFRAMES> tag and simply display the content as any other HTML document.

However, we prefer to place our NOFRAMES tag outside the FRAMESET tag and include a BODY tag within the NOFRAMES section:

```
<FRAMESET ROWS="10%,90%">
<FRAME SRC=row1.html>
<FRAME SRC=row2.html>
</FRAMESET>
<NOFRAMES>
<BODY BGCOLOR=#FFFFFF>
<P>This should be visible if your browser does not support
frames, while an alternative set of documents will be
displayed if your browser does support them.
</NOFRAMES>
```

This allows us to set BODY attributes such as a background color. If you want to include a BODY tag, the NOFRAME section must be placed outside the FRAMESET—if it isn't, frame-aware browsers will see the BODY tag and ignore the frames. Note that although this usage varies from the Netscape specification for frame documents (since they are not supposed to include a BODY tag), we have not found any browsers that have a problem with it.

Frame Document Example

Let's look at an example. We've created a set of documents for a Kids Art Gallery. You can find the document in netscape-frames.html. We divide our window into three frames. The top frame contains the logo for the Gallery, and clicking on the logo will refresh the welcome message in the main frame. The rest of the window is divided into two parts—one for the welcome message and display of full-size images, the other for an index to the art. Clicking on thumbnail images in the index will cause a full-size version of the image to be displayed in the main window.

Our top-level frame document looks like this:

```
<HTML>
<HEAD>
<TITLE>Netscape Frames Test Document</TITLE>
</HEAD>
<FRAMESET rows="90,*">
<FRAME SRC=kidbanner.html SCROLLING=NO MARGINHEIGHT=0
MARGINWIDTH=0 NORESIZE>
<FRAMESET cols="75%,25%">
<FRAME SRC=kidwelcome.html NAME=artwindow>
<FRAME SRC=kidindex.html>
</FRAMESET>
<NOFRAMES>
```

NOFRAMES portion of the document removed for brevity

```
</HTML>
```

Our first frameset divides the window into two rows. The first row will hold the Gallery banner, which is 81 pixels tall. We set the height for this row to 90 pixels so that there will be some space around the banner.

We want our second row to use the rest of the space in the window, so we set its value to "*". Next, we specify the frame that will be loaded into the first row, using a FRAME tag. Our second row will be divided into two frames, which we set up with another FRAMESET tag. This time we do not need a fixed width for either row, so we use percentages to split it up.

Notice that we have set a name for only one of our three frames, since this is the only frame that we plan to refresh. The other two frames contain documents with links that target this frame.

Now let's look at two of the documents loaded by our top-level frame document. Our top frame contains only a logo for our gallery. We use the NORESIZE attribute with this frame, since there is no reason for readers to resize it. Since it will not be resized, and since we know that it is tall enough to hold the banner, we also set the SCROLLING=NO attribute as well.First, our banner document, kidbanner.html:

```
<TITLE>Kid Gallery Banner</TITLE>
<BODY BGCOLOR=#0000FF VLINK=#0000FF>
<CENTER>
<A HREF=kidwelcome.html TARGET=artwindow><IMG
SRC=kidbanner.GIF ALT="Kid Gallery Logo"></A>
</CENTER>
```

We only have one link in this document, so we do not bother including a BASE tag. Instead, we include a TARGET attribute in our link tag to specify that the linked document should be displayed in the frame named artwindow.

The second document is our gallery index, kidindex.html:

```
<HTML>
<HEAD>
<TITLE>KidGallery Index</TITLE>
</HEAD>
<BODY BGCOLOR=#000000 TEXT=#FFFF00>
<H1>Kids Art Gallery</H1>
<BASE TARGET=artwindow>
<P><A HREF="kidpictures/kidpict10.gif"><IMG
SRC="kidpictures/kidpict10-thumb.gif" ALT="[Picture
1]"></A><br>187Kb image
<P><A HREF="kidpictures/kidpict2.gif"><IMG
SRC="kidpictures/kidpict2-thumb.gif" ALT="[Picture
2]"></A><br>44Kb image
<P><A HREF="kidpictures/kidpict3.gif"><IMG
SRC="kidpictures/kidpict3-thumb.gif" ALT="[Picture
3]"></A><br>33Kb image
```

Additional image links removed for brevity

```
<HR>
<P><A HREF="index.html" Target="_top"><IMG
SRC=pictures/CDTHUMB.GIF ALT="[HTML CD Home Page]"></A></P>
<ADDRESS>Vivian Neou, <A
HREF="mailto:vivian@catalog.com">vivian@catalog.com</A><BR>
Copyright &#169; 1995 Vivian Neou</ADDRESS>
</HTML>
```

Notice that each thumbnail image is linked to a large image, and that the link is targeted to be displayed in the artwindow frame. Our final link goes to the index for the HTML CD. Since this document has nothing to do with the Kids Gallery, we target this link to the predefined target "_top", which will cause the document to be loaded in the whole window rather than in one of the Kids Gallery frames.

Now let's see how our document looks:

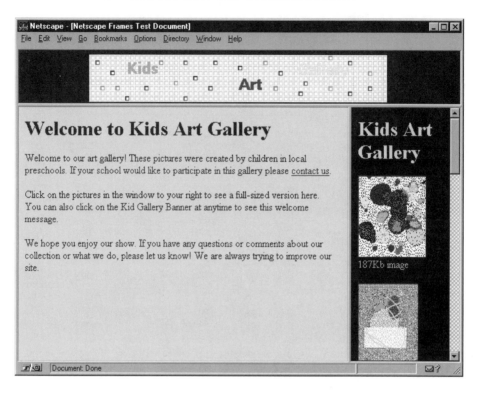

Clicking on any of the images in the index will cause a full-size version of the image to appear in place of the "Welcome to Kids Art Gallery" message. Readers may click on the banner at the top of the window at any time to have the welcome message reloaded in the large frame. Finally, readers can return to the HTML CD index by scrolling to the end of the gallery index and clicking on the link to the CD index. Since the link to the CD index is targeted for loading to "top," it will the be loaded using the entire window, rather than in an individual frame.

The NOFRAMES portion of the document duplicates the information in the documents referenced by the FRAMES. Although we do not show this part of the document here, you can see it on the CD.

Common Errors

If you create a Frame document that isn't displayed correctly in a Frame-aware browser, you should first check your document and make sure that you have not included any BODY tags before the FRAMESET in your document. Also be sure no other tags that would normally appear in the body of your document are included before your FRAMESET.

Netscape Extensions

This section describes some additional elements that are supported (at least at the time of this writing) in the Netscape browser. Netscape also supports many custom attributes to standard HTML tags. These attributes are described along with their related tags elsewhere in this book.

Note that the tags described in this section were introduced by Netscape, and Navigator is the only browser that definitely supports these tags. However, Microsoft announced that it would be supporting all of the Netscape extensions to HTML, and with a few limited exceptions (which are described below) we found this to be true. If you know that your documents will be viewed in one of these two browsers, it is likely that the effects you try to achieve with these tags will appear as expected.

If your goal is to produce documents that look good in a wide variety of browsers, use these extensions to HTML at your own risk.

Blink: <BLINK>

The BLINK tag does exactly that—makes your text blink on and off. In earlier versions of Netscape this tag would cause the text to disappear momentarily and then reappear. On some versions and on some platforms, Navigator just flashes a shaded box around the text. Here's a sample from our Netscape document:

```
<P><BLINK>Now you see me.<BLINK></P>
<P>Now you don't</P>
```

And here is how it looks:

None of the versions of Microsoft Internet Explorer that we tested supported this tag.

No Break: <NOBR>

The NOBR element stands for no break. This means all the text between the start and end of the NOBR elements will not have line breaks inserted. As with PRE, long text strings inside of NOBR elements probably will force readers to scroll the window horizontally to see the entire line. For example the following snippet:

```
<NOBR>
Here is a very, very, very, very, very, very, very, very,
very, very, very, very, very, very, long sentence.
</NOBR>
```

results in:

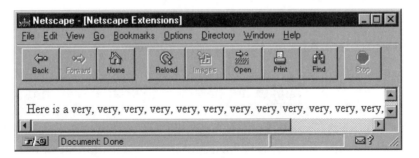

Word Break: <WBR>

The WBR element stands for word break. This is for the rare case when you have a NOBR section and you know exactly where you want it to break. It is also useful any time you want to give the Netscape Navigator help by telling it where a word is allowed to be broken. The WBR element does not force a line break (BR does that); it simply lets the Netscape Navigator know where a line break is allowed to be inserted if needed. If we were to add a WBR to our example from the previous section:

```
<NOBR>
Here is a very, very, very, very, very, very, very, very,
very,<WBR> very, very, very, very, very, long sentence.
</NOBR>
```

we would get:

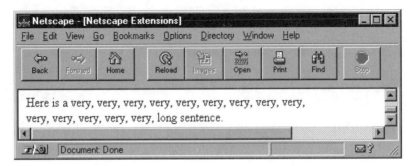

We found that the versions of Internet Explorer that we tested supported the NOBR tag, but not the WBR tag.

Base Font Size: <BASEFONT SIZE=value>

BASEFONT SIZE changes the base size of the font. Relative font size changes are based on this value, which defaults to 3 and has a valid range of 1-7. Here is an example that shows how the same font size can be set using either the FONT SIZE tag, the BASEFONT SIZE tag, or a combination of the two:

```
<BASEFONT SIZE=1>1
<FONT SIZE=+2>3
<BASEFONT SIZE=3>3
<FONT SIZE=+2>5
<BASEFONT SIZE=5>5
<FONT SIZE=+2>7
<BASEFONT SIZE=7>7
<FONT SIZE=-2>5
<BASEFONT SIZE=5>5
<FONT SIZE=-2>3
<BASEFONT SIZE=3>3
<FONT SIZE=-2>1
<BASEFONT SIZE=1>1
```

And here it is:

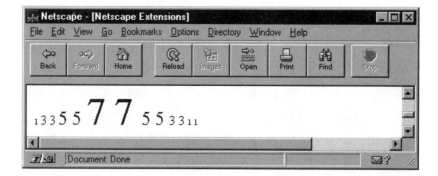

If the base font size is already set to the maximum, trying to set a greater relative font size has no effect.

Internet Explorer Extensions

Internet Explorer supports some tags that are not part of the HTML 3.2 specification. Although Microsoft has announced that it will add support for all of the Netscape tags in future versions of Explorer, Netscape has not made a similar pledge of support for the Explorer tags. Since Explorer still has a relatively small portion of the browser market, you may not want to invest much time in these tags. However, Microsoft is working hard to make Explorer the browser of choice and may very well eventually capture a majority of the market. These tags do provide functionality that is not easy (or possible) to produce with other HTML tags. They are worth using if you want a specific effect and don't care if some of your audience misses it.

FONT Attribute: FACE

This attribute allows you to specify a specific font type. Values may be the name of any font. Multiple fonts separated by commas may be specified. If multiple fonts are specified, the browser will try each font in order until it finds one. If it is unable to match any of the fonts in the list, the default font will be used. Example:

```
<FONT FACE="Helvetica, Times Roman, Palatino">Test of the
FONT FACE attribute</FONT>
```

Scrolling Banner: <MARQUEE>

This tag creates a scrolling banner. While this effect can be achieved with Java or JavaScript, the MARQUEE tag provides a much simpler and cleaner method for creating this effect. To create a section of scrolling text, simply place your text in a Marquee tag:

```
<MARQUEE>Look at me scroll!!</MARQUEE>
```

The default will create a left-scrolling line of text across the window. However, there are many attributes available to tailor your banner:

ALIGN

Controls the alignment of the text around the marquee. Value may be set to TOP, MIDDLE or BOTTOM.

BEHAVIOR

Controls the text movement. The default is SCROLL for scrolling text. Other valid values are: SLIDE (scroll text into the marquee and stop) and ALTERNATE (bounce text back and forth in the marquee area)

BGCOLOR

Set a background color for the marquee. Value may be set to an RGB triplet in the form #RRGGBB or one of the pre-defined color names. See the color section in the multimedia chapter for more information.

DIRECTION

Sets the direction for the text scroll. Value may be set to LEFT (default) or RIGHT.

HEIGHT

Specifies a height for the marquee. Value may be a number of pixels (e.g.: HEIGHT=80) or a percentage of screen height (HEIGHT=10%). Use WIDTH to set the width of the marquee.

HSPACE

Sets left and right margins outside the marquee. Value is a number in pixels. See VSPACE to set top and bottom margins.

LOOP

Sets the number of times that the text should loop. Value may be a number or INFINITE (equivalent to -1)

SCROLLAMOUNT

Sets the number of pixels between each draw of the marquee text. The higher the number, the faster your marquee will scroll.

SCROLLDELAY

Sets the number of milliseconds between successive draws of the marquee text.

VSPACE

Set top and bottom margins for the marquee. Value is the number of pixels. See HSPACE to set the left and right margins.

WIDTH

Set the width of the marquee. Value may be the number of pixels (WIDTH=120) or a percentage of window width (WIDTH=80%). Use HEIGHT to set the marquee height.

You can also make even fancier marquees by combining them with other HTML elements such as tables. Here is an example of a multiple-line marquee inside a table:

```
<TABLE ALIGN=CENTER>
<TR><TD WIDTH=23><img SRC=../Images/ladybug.gif
ALT="[Ladybug]"><img SRC=../Images/ladybug.gif
ALT="[Ladybug]">
<TD WIDTH=400><FONT COLOR=WHITE>
<MARQUEE ALIGN=MIDDLE DIRECTION=RIGHT BEHAVIOR=SCROLL
WIDTH=400 HEIGHT=29 BGCOLOR=RED BEHAVIOR=ALTERNATE
SCROLLAMOUNT=3>
Bouncing Text using
</MARQUEE>
<MARQUEE DIRECTION=RIGHT BEHAVIOR=SCROLL WIDTH=400 HEIGHT=29
BGCOLOR=RED BEHAVIOR=ALTERNATE SCROLLAMOUNT=3>
the BEHAVIOR=ALTERNATE tag
</MARQUEE></FONT>
<TD WIDTH=23><img SRC=../Images/ladybug.gif
ALT="[Ladybug]"><img SRC=../Images/ladybug.gif
ALT="[Ladybug]">
</TABLE>
```

You can also set the typeface and color of your text with the FONT tag or one of the other style tags. For example:

```
<FONT COLOR=WHITE><MARQUEE BGCOLOR=BLUE>Some white text on a
blue background!</MARQUEE></FONT>
```

Notice that the MARQUEE is inside the FONT tag in this example. In our tests we found that the inclusion of style commands inside a MARQUEE were ignored. For example in this section of code:

```
<MARQUEE><STRONG>Hello!</STRONG></MARQUEE>
```

the STRONG tag was ignored. However, if the style command was placed around the MARQUEE, it was used:

```
<STRONG><MARQUEE>Hello!</MARQUEE></STRONG>
```

Obviously we can't show you screenshots of our examples here, but you can display them yourself by loading the msie.html document on the CD.

The Good, The Bad and The Ugly

This chapter covers new and evolving areas in HTML. While many people using the Internet upgrade their browsers frequently so that they can access the latest and greatest enhancements, a significant number of people still are not using browsers that support the features described in this chapter. If you create documents that make heavy use of the features described here, you should try to offer alternative documents for people who do not have browsers that support these elements. This is especially true for FRAME documents, since even pre-Version 2 Netscape browsers do not support this element.

It is very important to include a NOFRAMES section in your frame documents; otherwise, readers viewing the document in a browser that does not support frames will not see anything (other than the title).

IN THIS CHAPTER YOU WILL LEARN

- HOW TO INCLUDE IMAGES IN YOUR HTML DOCUMENTS
- HOW TO PICK THE CORRECT GRAPHICS FORMAT FOR THE IMAGES IN YOUR WEB PAGES
- HOW TO MAKE IMAGES WITH "CLICKABLE" HOT SPOTS
- HOW TO MAKE ANIMATED GIF IMAGES
- HOW TO INTEGRATE VIDEO AND SOUND INTO YOUR HTML DOCUMENTS

MULTIMEDIA: IMAGES, VIDEO AND SOUND

What's In This Chapter

So far, we've covered methods for laying out text in your HTML document. Now it's time to see how to turn your HTML documents into multimedia presentations.

We begin the chapter with a discussion of color—adding it and using it with plain text documents. Next, we discuss image formats and explain why some are better than others for use within HTML documents. We will show you how to manipulate images to improve their appearance in Web documents, and show you how to use Paint Shop Pro. We explain how to include images in your HTML documents and use them as

119

backgrounds. We also show you how to make images with clickable "hot spots." We'll also discuss video and sound and explain how to best incorporate them into your documents.

Color Values

A growing number of HTML tags include attributes that allow you to specify a color to be associated with the tag's text. These attributes typically may be set to one of 16 predefined colors:

aqua	*black*	*blue*	*fuschia*
gray	*green*	*lime*	*maroon*
navy	*olive*	*purple*	*red*
silver	*teal*	*white*	*yellow*

These colors correspond to the fixed windows colors.

Another method for specifying colors is as a red-blue-green (RGB) color triplet: *#rrggbb*. Computers store color information as a set of three numbers, representing the amounts of the primary colors—red, green and blue—used to compose that color. This is known as the RGB representation for a color. The size of the color palette is determined by the range of values that the each number in the RGB set may take. Each pair of letters is a hexadecimal number between 00 and FF that represents one of the shades of a color. The higher the number, the more intense the color will be. For example, a pure red would be FF0000. In other words, we set the red value to the highest setting and set the green and blue to the lowest setting. Table 5–1 shows some more RGB color codes.

On the CD we've included Color Manipulation Device, an application that you can use to translate the color on your screen into the corresponding RGB value. Instructions on the use of this program can be found later in this chapter.

TABLE 5–1 RGB Color Codes

Code	Color
#000000	Black
#FFFFFF	White
#0000FF	Blue
#FF0000	Red
#00FF00	Green
#FFFF00	Yellow
#FF00FF	Purple

While there are millions of possible RGB values, it is best to limit your choices to a fairly narrow range. We explain why in the next section

Netscape Navigator's Window Color Palette

There is a little quirk in the way that Netscape supports graphics on Windows systems (3.1, 95 and NT) running in 8-bit mode that can make your images look awful when viewed on one of these systems.

The quirk? Netscape uses a 216-color palette on these systems. This means that colors that are in the palette will appear as expected, while other colors are "dithered" to approximate the actual color. Dithering means nonpalette colors are represented by using pixels in colors from the palette and intermingling them. Sometimes dithered colors look fairly close to the color they are supposed to represent, but often they are not. Additionally, dithered colors often look slightly textured since they are composed of pixels in different colors. Before we explain how to get around this problem, let's take a closer look at the Netscape palette.

The Netscape Windows color palette is composed of RGB values where the values are always 0, 51, 102, 153, 204, 255 (decimal) or 00, 33, 66, 99, CC, FF (hexadecimal). RGB values are typically represented in hexadecimal. For example, an RGB value of 003399 would be in the Netscape color palette, but 003298 would not. To prevent dithering, you should try to restrict the color tables for your images to values in this palette whenever possible.

Of course this does not work well with photographs. Photographs that are mapped onto the Netscape palette will usually appear blotchy and posterized. Photographs are best left in a JPEG format, which does not use a palette.

Background Color: BGCOLOR

In this section we describe the HTML 3.2 attributes for the BODY tag that allow you to change the background and text color used to display your document. The next section explains how to change the default text colors.

The BODY tag attribute used to set a background color is BGCOLOR. It may be set to one of the predefined colors or an RGB triplet. For example, the following two lines are equivalent:

```
<BODY BGCOLOR=WHITE>
<BODY BGCOLOR=#FFFFFF>
```

Default Text Colors

In Chapter 2, we introduced the FONT tag, which can be used to set a color for sections of text. What if you want to specify a default color for the text in the entire document? This is done through the use of the following BODY attributes. Note that the color value associated with these attributes should be one of the predefined colors or an RGB triplet.

TEXT

Set the default text color.

LINK

Set the color for links that have not been visited.

VLINK

Set the color for links that have been visited.

ALINK

Set the color for links that are active (in the process of being loaded—this state is typically "on" for only a few seconds).

Color Guidelines

Choose colors from the Netscape palette so that they will not be dithered. This also helps to increase the likelihood that your document will look acceptable on multiple platforms.

 If you choose to set a background color, be sure that your text is visible on top of it. Be sure to set text colors for all types of text—TEXT, LINK, VLINK and LINK, and avoid setting the same color for different types of text. Otherwise you lose the visual aid provided by having different colors for visited links vs. unvisited links. You can use the Color Manipulation Device application to quickly and easily experiment with different color scheme looks.

Finally, use a consistent color scheme across your documents. It can be confusing to users if the color use between your documents is not consistent.

Color Manipulation Device

If you wish to set a background or text color, finding the correct code for the colors you wish to use can be a painful process. Fortunately for you, the CD includes Color Manipulation Device, a handy shareware utility by Chris Pearce. This application not only translates colors into their corresponding numerical codes but can create your document framework with the appropriate information. If you prefer to use an image rather than a background color, it offers that option as well. Install it by dragging its folder from the CD to your hard disk. To start Color Manipulation Device, click on its icon:

cmd.exe

It will present you with a dialog window:

Color Manipulation Device 2.0

File   Edit   Tools   Schemes   Help

Color Picker

- Background Color
- Text Color
- New Link Color
- Visited Link Color
- Active Link Color

Red   153
Green   0
Blue   0

Body Tag

<BODY BGCOLOR="#FFFFFF" TEXT="#000000" LINK="#009900" VLINK="#000099" ALINK="#990000" >

Sample Homepage

Color Manipulation Device

Normal text is going to be this color.
New links are going to be this color.
Links that you've already been to are this color.
Links briefly turn to this color when clicked.

For each item's color that you wish to set, click on the color box next to the item and drag the slider until you are satisfied with the color. The program allows you to set almost any color. Remember, though, that if the color is not in the Netscape color palette, it may not be displayed as it appears in Color Manipulation Device. For this reason, it is advisable to watch the hexadecimal value for the color (while the decimal value appears above the slider, the hexadecimal value is displayed in the Body Tag section of the window) and make sure that it is in the Netscape palette.

If you wish to use a background image, go to the Tools menu and choose "Show Backgrounds?":

Go to the tool menu again and choose "Load Background". Note that there should be a check next to the "Show Backgrounds?" menu item. If there isn't, the "Load Background choice will be grayed out.

After you choose "Load Background", another dialog window will appear:

```
Open                                               ? X
Look in:  📁 Images               ▼  🔼 📝 📊 📊

📁 backgrounds    📄 Bear.jpg        📄 Lava.jpg
📁 icons          📄 bear1.jpg
📁 Map Files      📄 bear2.jpg
📁 Pictures       📄 bear3.jpg
📁 Separators     📄 kelly.JPG
📁 spinning-globe 📄 kellythumb.JPG


File name:    [                        ]     [ Open ]
Files of type: [All Supported Images    ▼]   [ Cancel ]
```

Color Manipulation Device does not support GIF format files owing to the licensing issues with the GIF compression algorithm. It does however support JPEG, so if you want to use a GIF file for a background, simply convert it to JPEG (we'll show you how to do this in the chapter on Paint Shop Pro) and use the JPEG version with Color Manipulation Device. You can later switch the tag to point to the GIF version of your image.

To load the tag into a document, copy it to the clipboard by choosing "Copy Tag" from the Edit menu (or using the <CTRL>-T shortcut). Open your document in an editor and paste the tag at the appropriate point. That's it!

You can also save a color scheme by choosing "Save a Scheme" from the Schemes menu. You will be prompted for a filename in which to store the scheme. To load an existing scheme into Color Manipulation Device, simply chose "Load a Scheme" from the Schemes menu.

Images in HTML Documents

Colorful documents are nice, but the addition of images can greatly increase their visual appeal. Let's turn our attention to the ways that HTML supports multimedia authoring on the Web. The first element of multimedia support we examine is the addition of images to documents.

Before we can add an image to a document, we must have an image, and to find images for our documents we need to know which image formats can be used in HTML documents.

Graphics Formats

Images may be stored in many formats. Table 5–2 displays many of the common image file formats used on the Web and their recognized filename extensions. Browsers use the file-name extension to determine which viewer is needed for a par-ticular image, so images *must* be given a filename extension that matches the image type.

TABLE 5–2 Common Image File Extensions

Description	Extension
GIF image	.gif
JPEG image	.jpg or .jpeg
Computer Graphics Metafile	.cgm
Windows Bitmap image	.bmp
PICT image	.pict
Progressive JPEG image	.pjpg
Portable network graphic	.png
Adobe Acrobat file	.pdf
Encapsulated PostScript	.eps
PostScript file	.ps
TIFF image	.tiff
XBM bitmap image	.xbm

Choosing an Image Format

As shown in Table 5–2, there are many formats are available for the storage of images. However, most browsers have built-in or "inline" support for only one or two formats. While most browsers may be configured to support additional formats, it is up to the user to do so. There are two methods that browsers may use to support image formats that do not have built-in inline support. The older method uses an external program to display the image. With this method the image does not appear in the browser window; instead, the browser runs the viewer program, and the image is displayed in the viewer program's window rather than in the browser window with the rest of the document. The newer method employs the use of "plug-ins". A plug-in is a module that the browser uses to add extra functionality to its native capabilities. Since the plug-in is not a part of the browser, readers must still download and install plug-ins before they can use them. Once they are installed, the browser can display images that are stored in the formats that they support within the browser window.

Since you cannot count on your readers to configure their browsers to support additional image formats, it is advisable to choose one of the widely supported formats for your images. Many tools exist to convert images from one format to another (including one of our favorite image tools, Paint Shop Pro), so even if you have images in a less common format, it is a fairly straightfoward task to convert them to one of the popular formats.

At this time this book was written the two most widely supported Web image formats were GIF and JPEG.

Graphics Interchange Format (GIF)

The most common format for images on the Web is Graphics Interchange Format (GIF), which was developed by CompuServe. You can be fairly sure that if you provide images in GIF format, as long as the browser supports any image display, it will be able to display your image. If you already have a collection of images in some other format, consider converting them to GIF. You will find an application called Paint Shop Pro on the CD that can be used to convert many formats to GIF.

Interlaced GIFs

Interlaced GIF images are images in which the scan lines have been rearranged so that a low-resolution version of the image can quickly be displayed. The rest of the image is then filled in over several passes. Although storing images in this format does not speed up their transmission time (in fact, it typically takes slightly more space to store the interlaced version of an image than the noninterlaced version), it does provide readers with a quick preview of the final image and helps to provide the impression that your document has loaded quickly. Paint Shop Pro can be used to convert noninterlaced images into interlaced images.

Keep in mind that some browsers do not take advantage of this feature, waiting until the entire image has been downloaded before displaying it. However, for browsers such as Netscape Navigator that do support this feature, it substantially improves the time in which readers can begin to see your images (although it does not improve the total amount of time that it takes to download the image).

JPEG

JPEG stands for Joint Photographic Experts Group, which is the group that originally developed this standard. A related standard called MPEG is used for video. We will discuss MPEG in the section on video.

JPEG stores information about the image by keeping track of the color changes in the image, rather than storing information about each pixel in the image. It is what is known as a *lossy* format because the final image is not exactly the same as the original. However, the human eye does not usually perceive the tiny differences introduced by the JPEG format.

The big advantage offered by the JPEG storage format is that for certain types of images JPEG images require much less storage space (and hence require less transmission time) than do equivalent GIF images. For example, the picture of Kelly Kayaker on the CD in JPEG format requires 26 kb of storage space, while the same picture in GIF format requires 122 kb of space. This dramatic difference in the storage requirement illustrates JPEG's strength in storing photographs and other images with a wide variety of shadings. This advantage does not hold for line drawings. For those types of images, GIF images may require less storage space.

GIF vs. JPEG

Originally, GIF formatted images had the widest support. However, almost all browsers (with the exception of some older browsers that have not recently been updated), also support JPEG images. The choice between these formats now comes down to the image content. For graphics such as logos or line drawings, GIF will almost always produce sharper results, and may even require less storage space. Photographs and other complex images should be stored in JPEG format—they will be much smaller, and the color issues we discussed in the section on color are not as much of a problem.

The Future of Image Formats

Both the GIF and JPEG formats have limitations that prevent them from being ideal for images on the Web. A number of other image storage formats hold promise for the future.

Progressive JPEG

There is a good chance that progressive JPEGs may become the most popular way to store plain images for the Web. Why? Because this format offers the advantages of interlaced GIF images accompanied by the low storage requirements of the JPEG format. Additionally, progressive JPEG files are frequently smaller than a regular (baseline) JPEG file containing the same image.

The downside? Progressive JPEG files are not readable by regular JPEG decoders. This means that special support has to be added before a browser can display a progressive JPEG image. At the time this book was written browser support for this format was fairly limited—Version 2 of Netscape Navigator was the first popular browser to support it. However, other browsers such as Microsoft's Internet Explorer were also planning to add support, and we expect even more browsers to support it as the format gains in popularity.

You will find references in the utilities.html document to a number of tools that you can download over the Internet to convert your images into this format.

PNG

The Portable Network Graphics (PNG) format was developed in response to legal difficulties with the GIF compression algorithm. It is optimized for the quick delivery of high quality images over the Internet. Some browser vendors such as Netscape plan to support this format in future versions of their browsers.

Image Tips and Tricks

Choosing the basic format for your image is only the first step in making the images in your documents look as good as possible. There are also many other things you can do to make your images more appealing in HTML documents.

We've included a number of GIF and JPEG images in the Images folder on the CD that you can use to experiment with. You are welcome to use these images as you wish.

Transparent Backgrounds

Some images look better if their own backgrounds do not appear, giving them the appearance of floating on the browser's background. For example, if you have made a red button for your links, it would detract from the look of the button to have a white square background appear in back of it. If your image is in GIF89a format (or is in a format that can be converted to GIF89a), you can modify it so that the background is "transparent." What this means is that one color in the image is designated as the transparency color. When the image is displayed, this color is replaced with whatever background color is used by the display window. Let's see what a difference this can make. In the following figure, the image does not have a transparent background:

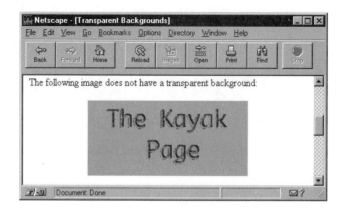

As you can see, there is an unsightly background square behind the text in the image. It would be preferable to display the image without having to see the background, as you can see here:

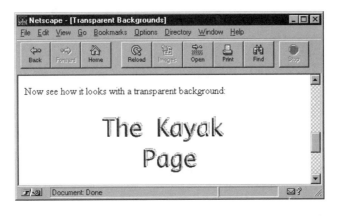

The key to transparency is in the version of GIF. Many GIF images are in GIF87 format, an old version of GIF that does not support transparency. Fortunately it is a fairly simple process to convert your GIF87 images to GIF89a using GraphicConverter. We'll explain how to do this in the section about GraphicConverter that's coming up.

Since there is no way to indicate that only the background is to be made transparent, your image's background should be a solid color, and the color should not be in use elsewhere in the image. For this reason transparent backgrounds are not suited for many types of images. In particular, photographs do not work well with transparent backgrounds, since their backgrounds are rarely solid colors and it is difficult to make sure that the background color is not used elsewhere in the image. However, as mentioned, this technique is an excellent one to use with buttons and other icons.

A note of warning about design decisions for transparent backgrounds: not all browsers currently provide support for them. If a browser does not support transparency, it will display the image's own background. One way to partially get around this problem is by choosing the background to be either gray or white—the colors that many browsers use for their own backgrounds. This way, the image's background will still blend in with the browser's background even if the browser does not support transparent images. However, not all browsers use gray as a background color, so this is not an infallible technique.

Reducing Image Size

Keeping image storage size as small as possible is an important element of creating graphics for the Web. One way to reduce image size is to reduce the number of bits allowed for the storage of color information. When you reduce the number of bits you also reduce the number of colors that can be used in the image. Table 5–3 shows a list of the number of colors that may be stored for a given bit depth. If you are working with a simple image that only uses a few colors, you can reduce to a bit depth of 3. Even with more complex images it is often possible to reduce the depth with only a small reduction in picture quality. It is worth spending some time comparing your images at different bit depths to see if the trade-off between picture quality and storage space (which, of course, translates into transmission time) is worthwhile for a particular image.

TABLE 5–3 Bit Depth vs. Number of Colors

Bit Depth	Number of Colors
3	8
4	16
5	32
6	64
7	128
8	256

You can create 1-, 2-, 3-, 8-, and 16-bit files with Paint Shop Pro. Some other image manipulation programs such as Adobe Photoshop allow you to choose almost any bit depth you want.

Thumbnails

It has been said that a picture is worth a thousand words. In the case of HTML and pictures, a picture can cost much more than a thousand words—at least in transfer time. Pictures can make a document look great, but if it takes your reader a couple of hours or even several minutes to transfer the document, odds are pretty high that he or she won't be willing to wait, no matter how great your pictures are. Image files are usually fairly large, and many people are still reading documents over slow phone lines. The answer? Thumbnail copies of your  images. A thumbnail copy of an image is a small version (typically around one inch wide) that your readers can use to decide whether they want to get the full-size version.

As an example, we have a GIF picture of Kelly in her kayak. The full-size picture is approximately 122 kb, but our thumbnail version is only 5 kb. By putting the thumbnail picture in our document with a link to the full-size picture, we have saved our readers over 100 kb (unless they decide to get the full-size picture). If your reader is using a 14,400-bps modem, this translates to approximately one minute. While one minute is not a lot of time, you can see how this adds up if you have any number of images at all. In the Paint Shop Pro chapter we will explain how you can use it to create thumbnail images.

Image Tag: <IMG>

HTML supports the ability to display embedded images within textual documents. The syntax for an embedded image is similar to the one used for links. The image itself is pointed to with a URL, as follows:

```
<IMG SRC=URL_of_image>
```

Let's use this element to add some pictures to our kayak document. It would be nice to have some pictures next to the choices in the table of contents at the beginning of the document. As you may recall, we had a table of contents that looked like this:

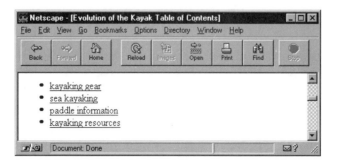

Those bullets are pretty boring, and we just happen to have some small GIF pictures that would work well in their place. We will put the image in the file kayak.gif next to "kayaking gear," and the image in sea.gif next to "sea kayaking." Here are the commands we use to add these images:

```
<PRE>
<A HREF="kayak.htm#gear"><IMG SRC="gif/kayak.gif"> kayaking
gear</A>
<A HREF="kayak.htm#seakayak"><IMG SRC="gif/sea.gif"> sea
kayaking</A>
```

If you look carefully at this example, you will see that we have placed both the images and the descriptive text inside an anchor tag. Although the images did not have to be inside the anchor, placing them includes them in the link. Now the reader can click on either the picture or the text to make the jump. As you will see, Netscape also frames images that are links to let the reader know that the link is there. Most other browsers use a frame to indicate the presence of a link, although some browsers may use other methods to display the link.

Now let's see how our changes affected the document:

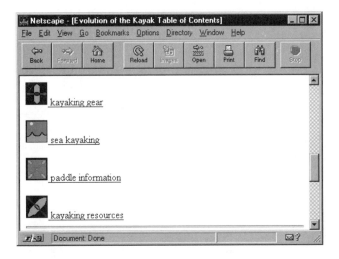

While this is fancier than our original list there is a lot of wasted space. As long as we leave our table of contents in a PRE block we could create columns by manually lining up the images and text. If you try to do something like this, remember that line breaks are significant in areas that are tagged with <PRE>, so be careful not to accidently insert extra lines. This is a fairly cumbersome method to create columns. Fortunately tables provide a better way to do this:

```
<TABLE BORDER=5>
<TR><TD><A HREF="kayak.htm#gear"><IMG SRC="gif/kayak.gif">
kayaking gear</A>
<TD><A HREF="kayak.htm#seakayak"><IMG SRC="gif/sea.gif"> sea
kayaking</A>
</TABLE>
```

We are going to make one more adjustment to the image before we show you how it looks.

Aligning Images: ALIGN Attribute

Browsers generally display an embedded image with the bottom of the image aligned with the text in the document. For those of you who wish to align your images in some other manner, the IMG tag offers the ALIGN option. This attribute may be set to the values: listed in Table 5–4.

TABLE 5–4 ALIGN Attribute Values

Value	Description
TOP	Align text with the top of the image
MIDDLE	Align text with the center of the image
BOTTOM	Align text with the base of the image (default)
LEFT	Align image to the left of the window. Text may appear to the right of the image. Use with <BR CLEAR=LEFT> to move text beneath the image.
RIGHT	Align image to the right of the window. Text may appear to the left of the image. Use with <BR CLEAR=RIGHT> to move text beneath the image.

For example, if we want our kayak images to be aligned with the middle of the text baseline, we would change the image tags to include ALIGN=MIDDLE:

```
<IMG SRC="kayak.gif" ALIGN=MIDDLE>
```

Now let's take a look and see how ALIGN and TABLE changed our document:

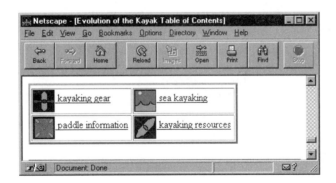

Additional Extensions to ALIGN

For those of you who wish to tailor your documents for readers using the Netscape Navigator browser, there are many additional values available for the ALIGN attribute. In addition to the original options, Netscape has added support for texttop, absmiddle, baseline and absbottom:

TEXTTOP

Align the image with the top of the tallest text in the line (this is usually, but not always, the same as ALIGN=top).

ABSMIDDLE

Align the middle of the current line with the middle of the image. The difference between this option and the standard HTML middle option is that middle aligns the baseline of the current line with the middle of the image.

BASELINE

Align the bottom of the image with the baseline of the current line (identical to ALIGN=bottom). Since ALIGN=bottom is standard HTML, it is better to use it than this Netscape-only option.

ABSBOTTOM

Align the bottom of the image with the bottom of the current line.

Here is an example to illustrate the way these options place images:

```
<PP>These images are aligned
<IMG SRC=gif/sailb2.gif ALIGN=texttop>
<IMG SRC=gif/sailb2.gif ALIGN=baseline>
<IMG SRC=gif/sailb2.gif ALIGN=absbottom>
<IMG SRC=gif/sailb2.gif ALIGN=absmiddle>
in this order: texttop, baseline, absbottom, absmiddle.</P>
<P>These images are aligned
<IMG SRC=gif/sailb2.gif ALIGN=baseline>
<IMG SRC=gif/sailb2.gif ALIGN=absmiddle>
<IMG SRC=gif/sailb2.gif ALIGN=absbottom>
<IMG SRC=gif/sailb2.gif ALIGN=texttop>
in this order: baseline, absmiddle, absbottom, texttop.</P>
<P>These images are aligned
<IMG SRC=gif/sailb2.gif ALIGN=texttop>
<IMG SRC=gif/sailb2.gif ALIGN=absmiddle>
<IMG SRC=gif/sailb2.gif ALIGN=absbottom>
<IMG SRC=gif/sailb2.gif ALIGN=baseline>
in this order: texttop, absmiddle, absbottom, baseline.
```

Here is this section of the document:

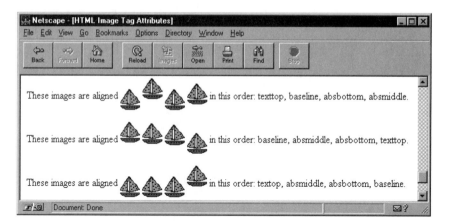

Notice how these alignment values affect the location of the baseline. If you use more than one image in a line be careful of mingling multiple alignment values between the images.

Images and Text-Only Browsers: ALT Attribute

Some browsers, such as Lynx, are not able to display images. Browsers that are able to display images usually offer readers the option of turning automatic image loading off. If you include many images in your document, these readers will miss the content associated with the images. The ALT option allows you to display text to those users who use a browser that cannot or will not display images.

With our kayak image, we may wish to substitute text indicating the content of the image for browsers that cannot display it, as follows:

```
<P><A HREF="#gear"><IMG SRC="gif/kayak.gif" ALT="[Kayak
Icon]"> kayaking gear</A>
<P><A HREF="#seakayak"><IMG SRC="gif/sea.gif" ALT="[Sea
Icon]"> sea kayaking</A>
<P><A HREF="#paddle"><IMG SRC="gif/paddle.gif" ALT="[Paddle
Icon]"> paddle information</A>
```

Users reading this document with a text-only browser will, instead of the embedded image, see the alternate text, such as "[Kayak Icon]." The following image shows how this section looks in Lynx.

```
                                           The Sport of Kayaking (p1 of 5)


                       THE SPORT OF KAYAKING


     Kayaking is an outdoor sport, practiced by adrenaline-junkies, in
     which enthusiasts paddle wild rivers and creeks in small, enclosed
     boats. Most people are a bit nervous the first time they kayak. Here,
     a first-time kayaker describes his experiences:


       I found kayaking to be a thrilling sport. At first, I was nervous
       about getting into such a small, tipsy craft, but then I discovered
       its extreme maneuverability.

     This document provides information on a number of kayaking topics:

     [Kayak Icon] kayaking gear

     [Sea Icon] sea kayaking

     [Paddle Icon] paddle information

-- press space for next page --
     Arrow keys: Up and Down to move. Right to follow a link; Left to go back.
     H)elp O)ptions P)rint G)o M)ain screen Q)uit /=search [delete]=history list
```

BORDER Attribute

BORDER specifies a width in pixels for the border that is placed around the image when it is linked. If this attribute is set some browsers will draw a border around the image even if it is not linked to anything. Let's look at an example:

```
<TD>BORDER=1<IMG SRC=../images/largesea.gif BORDER=1>
<TD>BORDER=5<IMG SRC=../images/largesea.gif BORDER=5>
<TD>BORDER=10<IMG SRC=../images/largesea.gif BORDER=10>
```

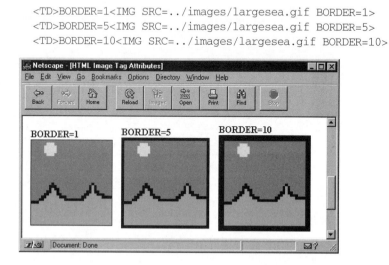

You can also hide the link border by setting the value to zero. You should do this only if the image itself offers a visual clue that it is linked to something (such as the image of a beveled button).

WIDTH and HEIGHT

These attributes allow you to specify the size of the image in pixels. Most image creation and manipulation programs can provide the size of the image. We will explain how to find the size of an image with Paint Shop Pro in the next chapter.

Setting the WIDTH and HEIGHT allows the browser to display documents with images more quickly by reserving space for the image without having to wait for the image to be downloaded to calculate the size. Additionally, a bug in some browsers that support JavaScript prevents JavaScript scripts from working correctly if there are images in the document that do not have a HEIGHT and WIDTH value set.

You can force the browser to stretch or shrink the image by specifying a size that is larger or smaller than the actual image. This can be a useful technique if you want to fill a certain amount of space, but the image you have is not large enough.

Avoid shrinking images in this fashion, since it will increase the amount of time that the document takes to load—the entire image will still have to be downloaded, and the browser will have to do extra work to shrink it. If you think you need to shrink an image, it is much better to load the image into an image manipulation program like Paint Shop Pro and save the image in the size you need.

HSPACE and VSPACE

These attributes allow you to create empty space around images. HSPACE creates horizontal space, and VSPACE creates vertical space. Both attributes may be set to a value in pixels. It's probably easiest to understand how these attributes work by looking at some examples.

```
<P>Testing 1 2 3
<IMG SRC=../images/sea.gif BORDER=1 ALIGN=MIDDLE>
Testing 1 2 3
<P>Testing 1 2 3
<IMG SRC=../images/sea.gif BORDER=1 HSPACE=20 ALIGN=MIDDLE>
Testing 1 2 3, HSPACE=20
```

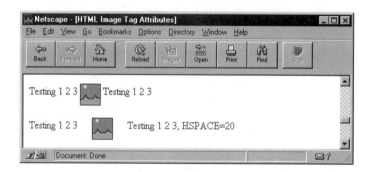

As you can see, the HSPACE attribute causes the browser to leave a space 20 pixels wide to the right and left of the image. Now let's review a VSPACE example:

```
<P>Testing 1 2 3<BR>
<IMG SRC=../images/sea.gif BORDER=1 ALIGN=MIDDLE>
Testing 1 2 3
<P>Testing 1 2 3<BR>
<IMG SRC=../images/sea.gif BORDER=1 VSPACE=20 ALIGN=MIDDLE>
Testing 1 2 3, VSPACE=20
```

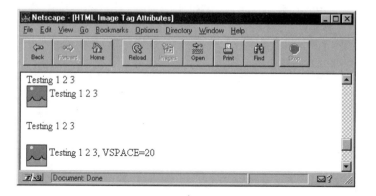

In this example, VSPACE created a space above the image. Had we had any text below the image, an equal amount of space would also have been reserved before displaying the text.

Although these attributes are in the HTML 3.2 standard, they were a fairly recent introduction and are not supported by many browsers.

Low-Resolution Image: LOWSRC

This is another attribute that was introduced by Netscape and that is only supported by Netscape Navigator (at least we were unable to find any other browsers that support it). It was designed to allow a low-resolution image to be quickly loaded and displayed while the final, high-resolution image was being downloaded. However, you can also use it to temporarily display any image before the image specified with the SRC attribute is displayed. There are a couple of restrictions you should keep in mind if you use this attribute:

- If you don't specify the height and width of the final image, the height and width of the LOWSRC image will be used for the final image, regardless of its actual height and width.

- If you do specify a height and width, the height and width will be used for both images regardless of their actual height and width.

To use it as it was designed, you would create a low-resolution version of your image (perhaps even a black-and-white version to reduce the size even more), and specify it with LOWSRC. For example, if we have a low-resolution image of Kelly Kayaker's picture in kelly-low.jpg, and a high-resolution version in kelly.jpg we would use:

```
<IMG SRC=kelly.jpg LOWSRC=kelly-low.jpg HEIGHT=200
WIDTH=300>
```

However, this attribute can be used to create other effects as well (somewhat akin to using a two-frame animated GIF, something we will describe later in this chapter). For example, you could create an embossed version of your image to be displayed first, and then display the real image over it. Or you could use it to display a logo, which is then replaced by a picture of a product (make sure that both images are the same height and width if you do this, though). You will find several examples of these and other ideas on the CD. Keep in mind that this attribute is supported only by Netscape Navigator, so any effects that you create with it will not be seen by readers using other browser.

Image Maps, Images with Clickable Spots

We've explained how to make images that are links. Now we'll show you how to do even fancier linking with images. Rather than making the entire image a single link, it is possible to make images with "hot spots" that have links. Readers can click on these spots to follow the link. For example, you could include the image of a map with hot spots that link points on the map to documents that describe those locations; or a picture of a car with each part of the car linked to a document describing how that part works.

Clickable images work by being associated with a coordinate map of the image that has links associated with specific coordinates. The association between the map and image is made by the server, so clickable images only work through a server. Here are the basic steps of making a clickable image:

1. *Get an image. The best images for this purpose should have well-defined sections and be in GIF format.*

2. *Decide what links you want to make to which sections of your image.*

3. *Make a coordinate map for your image. Different servers use different formats, so you will need to know the appropriate format for your server before you do this. You can make a map manually or with an application such as WebMap. We strongly recommend using an application to make the map.*

4. *Add information about your coordinate map to your Web server. If you are running your own server, you can do this yourself. If not, you'll need to ask the person in charge of your Web server to do it for you.*

> **5.** *Make a document that includes your clickable image. You specify the image as being clickable by including the ISMAP attribute with the IMG tag.*
>
> **6.** *Load your document in a browser and check it.*

Choosing Images for Image Maps

Not all images are suitable for use with image maps. In general, the more clearly the areas within the image are delineated from each other, the better the image is for use as an image map. Graphics with numerous buttons make good image maps.

Most photographs make poor image maps, since areas in photos are usually not well defined, making it difficult for users to know where to click to make the jump. If you really want to use photographs, consider incorporating several photographs in a single image and using each photograph as a separate hot spot.

If you wish to use a photograph for an image map, you should consider using an image processing program such as Paint Shop Pro or Adobe's Photoshop to create clear-cut areas in the image. However, remember that clickable areas in image maps are constrained to certain shapes, so that irregularly shaped areas will have to fit within one of these shapes.

Image Map Formats

There are two formats for image map files—one is for CERN-based servers and another for NCSA-based servers. Different servers use different formats for these maps, so you need to know which format your server uses (you should be able to get this information from your Web server administrator). To further complicate matters the allowable shapes for hot spots differ between these two formats: rectangles, circles and polygons for CERN, and rectangles, circles, points, and polygons with NCSA-based servers.

NCSA image maps are in the format:

```
#Comment lines may be included
default URL
rect URL x,y,x2,y2
circle URL x,y,r
poly URL x1,y1,x2,y2,x3,y3,x4,y4...
point URL x,y
```

CERN image maps are in the format:

```
#Comment lines may be included
default URL
rectangle (x,y) (x2,y2) URL
circle (x,y) r URL
poly (x,y) (x1,y1)....(xn,yn) URL
```

For example, here is a map file in NCSA format:

```
default http://oz.com/kayak.html
rect http://oz.com/kayak.html#resources 285,1 379,127
rect http://oz.com/kayak.html#paddle 192,0 283,125
rect http://oz.com/kayak.html#seakayak 102,1 191,127
rect http://oz.com/kayak.html#gear 1,0 101,127
```

And here is the same map in CERN format:

```
default http://oz.com/kayak.html
rectangle (1,0) (101,127) http://oz.com/kayak.html#gear
rectangle (102,1) (191,127) http://oz.com/kayak.html#seakayak
rectangle (192,0) (283,125) http://oz.com/kayak.html#paddle
rectangle (285,1) (379,127) http://oz.com/kayak.html#resources
```

The process of figuring out the coordinates for each area in your image map by hand can be very tedious. Fortunately, we have included a program on the CD that automates this process for you.

MapThis!

MapThis! is a freeware program by Todd Wilson that automates the process of image map creation. You can't beat its price or ease of use. It allows you to outline polygons, circles and rectangles on top of your GIF and PICT images and link a URL to each item. MapThis! also allows you to go back and delete these "hot spots," set a default URL for clicks outside of the "hot" areas and associate comments of arbitrary length with each object. Best of all, it knows about the formats for the NCSA, CERN and client-side maps.

You will find MapThis! in the Utilities folder on the CD. To install it simply drag its folder to your hard disk.

Running MapThis!

To start MapThis!, open the MapThis! folder and click the MapThis! icon:

Mapthis.exe

Using MapThis!

Let's see how to use MapThis! by going through an example. Rather than using separate images in our table of contents, let's combine our images into one and turn it into an image map. Before proceeding however, a word of caution should you decide to use an image map as a table of contents: remember to provide a corresponding text-based table of contents in addition to your image map. If you don't you will lose readers who are browsing with image loading turned off, and readers who are unable to view images.

The first step is to load our image into MapThis!. From the File pulldown menu, we choose New. This will open a dialog window:

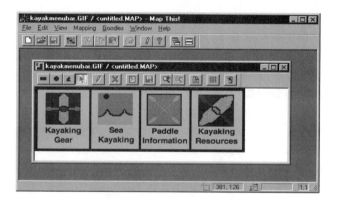

Choose the "Let's go find one" button, and then find and load your image file in the in the dialog window that appears. In our case, the file is named "kayakmenubar.gif." After it is loaded, we see it in the MapThis! window:

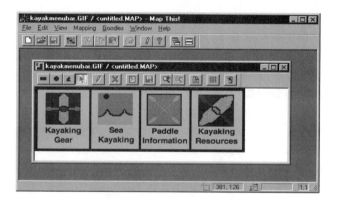

Our next step is to outline the hot spots in our map and link them to the appropriate URLs. Before we do this, we want to open up the Area List window, which shows us a list of the currently defined areas in our map. We open the window by choosing "Area List" from the View menu. And here it is:

Next we choose the rectangle from the menu bar, since our image has a rectangular section for each topic. Now we are ready to start making "hot spots." We outline each section of the image that we wish to link. As we create each outline, a settings box appears:

Next we choose the rectangle from the menu bar, since our image has a rectangular section for each topic. Now we are ready to start making "hot spots." We outline each section of the image that we wish to link. As we create each outline, a settings box appears:

Area #1 Settings

Type: rect   Position: (-7, -4) - (98, 123)

Dimensions: w=105, h=127

URL to activate when this area is clicked: (required)

http://ozone.com/kayak.html#gear

Internal comment about this area: (optional)

kayaking gear

| Delete | Up | Cancel |
| Help | Down | OK |

After we are done, we choose "Save" under the File menu. This will open an information window for the map:

```
Info about this Mapfile

       Filename: H:\HTML Treasure
                 Chest\HTML_Document_Treasure_Chest\Imag
    Image name: kayakmenubar.GIF

         Title: [kayakmenu                                ]

        Author: [Kelly Kayaker                            ]

   Default URL: [http://ozone.com/kayak.html              ]
    (Required)

   Description: [Kayak document menubar                   ]
               [                                          ]
               [                                          ]

           ┌─ Map file format: ────────────────┐
           │  ⊙ NCSA    ○ CERN    ○ CSIM        │
           └───────────────────────────────────┘

     [ Help ]          [ Cancel ]          [ OK ]
```

In this case we choose a map type of NCSA. When we click "Ok", a final Save window appears:

```
Save As                                         ? X

Save in:  [ Map Files            ▼ ] [↑] [▢] [▦]








File name:    [kayakncsa.map                    ]   [ Save    ]

Save as type: [All File Types (*.map,*.imp,*.htm,*.html) ▼]  [ Cancel  ]
File Format  ┌──────────────────────────────────┐
 ⊙ NCSA     │All File Types (*.map,*.imp,*.htm,*.html)│  [ Map Info... ]
            │ImageMap Files (*.map)             │
            │HTML Files (*.htm,*.html)          │
            │Older Map Files (*.imp)            │
            │All Files (*.*)                    │
            └──────────────────────────────────┘
```

Notice that a number of file types are available. We choose map. Here is how our finished map looks:

```
#$MTIMFH
#$-:Image Map file created by Map THIS!
#$-:Map THIS! free image map editor by Todd C. Wilson
```

```
#$-:Please do not edit lines starting with "#$"
#$VERSION:1.20
#$TITLE:kayakmenu
#$DESCRIPTION:Kayak document menubar
#$AUTHOR:Kelly Kayaker
#$DATE:Mon Jun 24 10:17:21 1996
#$PATH:H:\HTML Treasure
Chest\HTML_Document_Treasure_Chest\Images\
#$GIF:kayakmenubar.GIF
#$FORMAT:ncsa
#$EOH
default http://ozone.com/kayak.html
# kayaking gear
rect http://ozone.com/kayak.html#gear -7,-4 98,123
# Sea kayaking
rect http://ozone.com/kayak.html#seakayak 103,-1 192,126
# Paddle info
rect http://ozone.com/kayak.html#paddle 191,-11 283,126
# General kayaking resources
rect http://ozone.com/kayak.html#resources 285,-18 379,125
```

The process for creating a CERN-style map is essentially the same as that for the NCSA map. There is a slight difference in the procedure for the creation of a client-side image map (which is specified by clicking the CSIM button in the Save dialog window). In the last step, while specifying the file name, you must set the extension to "html" or "htm", and chose a file type of "All File Types" or "HTML Files." If you try to use "map" as an extension MapThis! will refuse to save the file. Once the settings are ready, MapThis! will then create the map file. In our example, the file looks like this:

```
<BODY>
<MAP NAME="kayakmenu ">
<!-- #$-:Image Map file created by Map THIS! -->
<!-- #$-:Map THIS! free image map editor by Todd C. Wilson -->
<!-- #$-:Please do not edit lines starting with "#$" -->
<!-- #$VERSION:1.20 -->
<!-- #$DESCRIPTION:Kayak document menubar -->
<!-- #$AUTHOR:Kelly Kayaker -->
<!-- #$DATE:Mon Jun 24 10:26:36 1996 -->
<!-- #$PATH:H:\HTML Treasure
Chest\HTML_Document_Treasure_Chest\Images\ -->
<!-- #$GIF:kayakmenubar.GIF -->
<AREA SHAPE=RECT COORDS="-7,-4,98,123"
```

```
HREF=http://ozone.com/kayak.html#gear ALT="kayaking gear">
<AREA SHAPE=RECT COORDS="103,-1,192,126"
HREF=http://ozone.com/kayak.html#seakayak ALT="Sea kayaking">
<AREA SHAPE=RECT COORDS="191,-11,283,126"
HREF=http://ozone.com/kayak.html#paddle ALT="Paddle info">
<AREA SHAPE=RECT COORDS="285,-18,379,125"
HREF=http://ozone.com/kayak.html#resources ALT="General
kayaking resources">
<AREA SHAPE=default HREF=http://ozone.com/kayak.html>
</MAP></BODY>
```

Notice that MapThis! has placed BODY tags around the map. Remember to remove these tags if you copy the map into an existing document rather than using it as a separate file.

Server-Side Clickable Images: ISMAP

Now we are ready to add the image to our document. We use the IMG element's ISMAP attribute to indicate that this is a "clickable image." ISMAP is an attribute that identifies an image as an image map. We place the image in an anchor tag that links it to the image map application in the server area. You will need to get the appropriate command for the image map program on your Web server from the person in charge of it. In our case, the line for the image map would be:

```
<A HREF="http://ozone.com/imagemap/kayakmenubar"><IMG
SRC="kayakmenubar.GIF" ISMAP></A>
```

You will need to get the appropriate command for your server from the person in charge of your Web server.

You will not be able to test a clickable image if you open a file locally with a browser. The server handles the mapping, so you can access the hot-spot functionality only through a server.

Client-Side Image Maps: USEMAP

With the ISMAP attribute you need to have a server in order to use or test standard image maps. With client-side image maps, the processing is done by the browser, so you can use them without a server. The HTML tags that support this functionality were introduced by Netscape and were first available with Netscape Navigator Version 2. This functionality is now part of the HTML 3.2 specification, and other browsers such as Internet Explorer, AOL Version 3, and Lynx (version 2.5 and above) support it as well.

The HTML extensions to support client-side image maps are composed of two parts: a new attribute, USEMAP, for the IMG tag, and new MAP and AREA tags.

The Map

MAP tags are used to contain a map and have one attribute: NAME, which is used to specify the name of the map so that the image can refer to it. The map itself is composed of a number of AREA tags. The AREA tag is in the form:

```
<AREA SHAPE=rect COORDS="x,y,x1,y1" HREF="destination">
```

or

```
<AREA SHAPE=rect COORDS="x,y,x1,y1" NOHREF>
```

The NOHREF tag indicates that clicks in this region should perform no action. An HREF tag specifies where a click in that area should lead. Note that a relative anchor specification will be expanded using the URL of the map description as a base, rather than using the URL of the document from which the map description is referenced. If you keep your maps in a separate document, you can use the BASE tag to change this if you wish.

The allowed values for SHAPE are RECT (rectangle), CIRCLE, POLY (polygon), and DEFAULT. DEFAULT specifies the destination for spots on the image that are not explicitly covered by the map. When you specify RECT, you will also need to include a

COORDS attribute to specify the rectangle's coordinates. The coordinates are in the form "x, y, x1, y1" where:

- x = left
- y = top
- x1 = right
- y1 = bottom

This is the same coordinate structure used in server-side map files. If two areas defined in a map intersect, the one that appears first will take precedence in the overlapping region. Any region of the image that is not defined by an AREA tag is assumed to be NOHREF.

Let's see how an entry in an NCSA map file would compare with a client-side map. Here is one of the lines from the NCSA kayak menu-bar map file:

```
rect file://localhost/kayak.html#gear 0,0 101,127
```

For our client-side map, the corresponding line would be:

```
<AREA SHAPE=rect COORDS="0,0, 101,127" HREF=kayak.html#gear>
```

As you can see in this example, the "map" portion of the document is composed entirely of tags. Browsers that are not able to handle client-side image maps will simply ignore that portion of the document. The map may be placed either in the document using the map or in a separate document (useful if you wish to use the map with a number of documents, such as in the case of a menu bar).

IMG and USEMAP

The USEMAP attribute is used to specify the location of the map and is specified in the same format as the source for an HREF. Adding a USEMAP attribute to an IMG element indicates that it is a client-side image map.

USEMAP takes a single argument—the name of the map. The name of the map should be specified in the same format as an HREF anchor. For example, let's say we have a map named "kayakmenumap" in a file "kayak.html":

Same file:

```
<IMG SRC=menubar.gif USEMAP="#kayakmenumap">
```

A different file:

```
<IMG SRC=menubar.gif USEMAP="kayak.html#kayakmenumap">
```

Notice that we do not need to contain our image in an anchor tag. Client-side image maps do not need to be linked to an external image map processing program since the processing is done by the browser.

Supporting All Users

People using nongraphical browsers cannot use image maps. Additionally, older browsers (including Version 1 of Netscape Navigator) do not include support for client-side image maps. Fortunately, by carefully planning the design of your image map, you can accommodate almost any level of browser.

The first thing to remember is that client-side image maps may be used in conjunction with server-side image maps. If you use the USEMAP attribute in an IMG tag, you can still include the ISMAP attribute. This allows the image to be processed as either a client-side or server-side image map. When both attributes are specified, the USEMAP attribute takes precedence, so the ISMAP will be ignored if USEMAP is supported. This allows you to provide a fallback for people with browsers that support server-side image maps but not client-side maps.

For browsers that do not have support for either type of image map, you can provide an alternative by placing a link to a text-based navigational list next to the image. For example:

```
<A HREF="kayak-nomap.html>Table of Contents</A>
<A HREF="http://ozone.com/imagemap/kayakmenubar"><IMG
SRC=menubar.gif USEMAP="kayak.html#kayakmenumap" ISMAP
ALT="[Menu Bar]"></A>
```

Background Images: BACKGROUND and BGPROPERTIES

The BACKGROUND attribute to the BODY tag allows you to specify an image to be used as a background for your document. The format for this attribute is:

```
<BODY BACKGROUND="background.gif">
```

Background images are displayed by tiling the image to fill up the background. Microsoft Internet Explorer also supports an additional attribute, BGPROPERTIES, that can be used to prevent the background from scrolling. It takes a single value: "fixed". For example:

```
<BODY BACKGROUND="background.gif" BGPROPERTIES=FIXED>
```

At the time this book was written, the BGPROPERTIES attribute was not supported by Netscape Navigator.

Not every image is suitable for a background. The best images are:

- Small. Your document won't be displayed until the image is loaded. A large image will delay the display.

- Noninterlaced. Interlacing increases the size of the image (only slightly), and the quick-loading effect that it offers for regular in-line images is lost on a background image.

- Compatible with the text color. This may seem obvious, but check and make sure that your text is visible on top of your image. If you use a dark image, the default text color may make your text difficult or impossible to read. Be sure to set a light text color in this case.

- Simple. While there are exceptions to this rule, most of the best background images are fairly simple and stick to a narrow color range. Busy backgrounds make it difficult to find a clearly visible text color.

Additionally, if you are using a textured image, make sure that it has been created so that the edges meet smoothly. Otherwise you will end up with seams where the "tiles" meet. In the chapter on Paint Shop Pro we will describe a technique to create a seamless background image.

If you plan to use a photograph or some other highly textured image as a background, compare the file size between JPEG and GIF. All the browsers we've found that support BACKGROUND also support JPEG, so you may be able to reduce your file size by using JPEG rather than GIF format.

Keep in mind that, although the use of a background image will usually prevent a background color from being seen, it is still advisable to set a background color when using a background image. The most important reason is that viewers looking at your document with image loading turned off will see the background color, but not the image. If you have set text colors to contrast with your background, they may not be compatible with the default background color. This happens frequently when light text colors are chosen to appear over a dark background image. If the background image is not loaded the text in these documents is then difficult or impossible to read over the common light background color.

From a design standpoint, setting a background color that matches the main color in your background image improves the chance that the general look of the document will be close to your vision even if the background image is not displayed. Note that you can use the Color Manipulation Device program described earlier in this chapter to preview a document color scheme and to review the look of the text colors against the image background.

We've included a number of images that are suitable for backgrounds in the background folder. Netscape offers a number of GIF-format images suitable for backgrounds on its server. You can find these images at the URL:

```
http://home.netscape.com/assist/net_sites/bg/backgrounds.html
```

GIF89a Animations

We think GIF89a animation is the simplest method for incorporating animation in a document. Although browser support for this format was limited (at the time this book was written the club included Version 2 and above of Navigator, and Version 3 and above of Internet Explorer), its ease of use and compatibility with other browsers make it a winner.

There are many advantages to using GIF89a animations over animation through server push or client pull. Some of them include:

- Everything is in one file. Once the image file is loaded, no further network connections are needed (vs. multiple connections for client pull, or a lengthy connection for server push).

- Small file size. The spinning globe we will use as an example takes only 17kb.

- Unlike animation that is done with client pull, there is no need for multiple HTML files. It's all contained in a single image file.

- No need for access to the CGI directory. These are just images and can be used like any other image. If the viewing browser doesn't support animation, only the first "frame" will be displayed.

- No additional overhead if you reuse the image in a document. Once the image is loaded, you can use it over and over in the same document, and it doesn't need to be reloaded over the network.

GIF Construction Set

GIF Construction Set from Alchemy Mindworks provides an easy way to construct GIF89a animation files. This program is distributed as bookware. No, that's not a typographical error! After an evaluation period if you decide to use this software, you need to purchase and read[1] *The Order* by Steven William Rimmer. Since the book with shipping and handling is around $10, this is a difficult deal to beat! Information on obtaining the book is included in the GIF Construction Set folder.

You'll find GIF Construction set in the gifcon folder on the CD. To install it, simply drag the folder over to your hard disk. Now let's see how to use it by creating a spinning-globe animation.

We have ten small GIF images showing a globe in different steps of the rotation. If you would like to try this yourself you can find the individual images in the spinning-globe folder, which is in the Images folder on the CD. Our goal is combine these images into a single GIF89a file along with the appropriate control information. We start by clicking on the GIF Construction Set icon:

Gifcon.exe

---

1. Yes, Vivian purchased and read the book. She even enjoyed it. What a deal—a great software package and a fun read all for around $10!

The main window will then appear:

To start a new GIF file for your animation choose New from the File menu:

Header Block

A GIF image (both animated and plain) begins with a header block. GIF Construction Set automatically places a header block in the file when you start a new GIF image. GIF Construction Set allows you to modify the following header block information:

Screen width and depth

The dimensions in pixels of the screen on which you expect the image to be displayed. This is not necessarily the same as the size of the image in the file, but if is not the same it may affect where the image is placed on the screen. To get the best results, set this size to the size of the largest image included in your file.

Background

The color of the area around the images, if the image is smaller than the screen size.

Global Palette

Tells viewing programs whether there is a global palette in the file. GIF Construction Set checks this flag and prompts you accordingly as it adds images to your file.

You update the Header block information by clicking on the Edit button while the Header block is chosen:

Since we want to make sure that the screen size is set to the size of the largest image in our file, we wait until we have added all the image before updating this information.

Loop Block

The next item in the file should be a Loop block. You add this block by clicking the Insert button and choosing Loop from the button bar that appears:

Insert Object ☒
Image
Control
Comment
Plain Text
Loop
Cancel

The Loop block controls the number of times the animation will be repeated. Earlier versions of Navigator with GIF animation support ignored this setting. However, we've found that the newer versions do follow it. Constant looping can be very distracting, so unless you really need to have a continual loop it is best to set this value to one or some other small number.

Image Import

Now we're ready to start adding our images to the file. Each image should be preceded by a Control block. We add Control blocks and images to the file in the same fashion as Loop blocks—click the Insert button and choose the appropriate item from the button bar. Note that the images you add to your file do not have to be in GIF format—GIF Construction Set will make the necessary conversions if you add an image in one of the other formats that it supports. Some of the formats it can handle are JPEG, PNG, BMP and PCX.

If you are using a global palette, the Import Image function will check to see if the palette for the image being imported matches the global palette. If it does not, it offers you a number of options:

Use a local palette

A dangerous choice since it means that the palette for this image may differ from the palettes of other images in the file. Since you can display multiple images at the same time, it may cause some serious problems.

Use a local grey palette

Converts the image to greyscale. May cause problems for the same reasons that a local color palette is dangerous.

Remap this image to the global palette

This is akin to the mapping you may do with images and the Netscape color palette. In fact, you may wish to use a Netscape palette as your global palette to avoid dithering in Netscape browsers. Colors are mapped to the closest match in the palette. A poor choice for photographs (see the Netscape color palette for more information).

Dither this image to the global palette

Dithers the image as it maps it onto the global palette. If you are using photographs, this is the best choice.

Use this image as the global palette

This choice is available only for the first image added to the file.

Use it as it is

A dangerous choice, as it may result in weird color shifts if the image's palette differs too much from the global palette.

There is also a 15-bin quantize option that may produce more attractive images if extensive color mapping is required. However this choice will slow down the import process quite a bit (it more than doubled the image load time on our system).

Since our images are fairly simple drawings, we use the default "Dither this image to the global palette" for all of the images that we add to our file. Here is how our window looks when we are done adding our images:

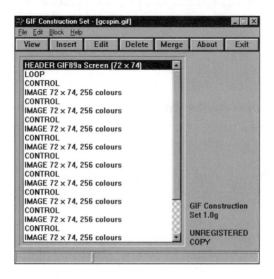

As you can see, the size of each image is listed. We find the largest image in the list (actually in this case all of our images are the same size) and use this information to update our header block.

We make one more adjustment. We want our spinning globe to have a transparent background. Even if the original GIF images are saved with transparent backgrounds, the transparency is not carried over to the new file. We have to add it by setting it in our file's control blocks. We do this by editing each control block and checking the Transparent box.

Now we are ready to build our animated GIF image. To do this we simply choose "Save" from the File menu. It brings up a dialog box to provide a filename for the output file. We choose gcspin.gif for our output file. That's it! You can see our final globe by looking at the animated-gif.html document.

Tips and Techniques

Our spinning-globe images were fairly small, so our final image was also relatively small. However, if you want to create an animated image using a larger image you can end up with a huge file. If you are changing only part of the file in each frame, you can minimize file size by using cropped images and then placing them in the file. We used this technique to create the animated banner at the top of the HTML Treasure Chest. The final image is composed from two images: the full banner and an overlay with the words "for Windows 95". We "overlay" our Windows 95 image over the full banner by editing the image itself (double-click on the image you want to edit in the main GIFcon list)

Edit Image

Image

Image width: 297

Image depth: 100

Image left: 125

Image top: 20

☐ Interlaced

WINDOWS 95

Palette

☐ Local palette   Load

256 colours   Save

Show

Help   View   Cancel   OK

The overlay is created by setting the location for the upper left corner of the image. Rather than using the default, which would simply place it at the upper left of the screen, we set the value for our image left and top to 125 and 20 respectively. These are values in pixels by which we want the image to be offset from the default location. We used Paint Shop Pro to find the offset location (we'll explain how to find the coordinates in an image in the chapter on Paint Shop Pro).

We encourage you to experiment with both the Image and Control block settings. You can achieve many interesting effects through creative adjustments to the values in these blocks.

Sound

Audio is a difficult problem for Web designers. Some of the problems associated with sound are similar to those associated with images—large file size and multiple formats. Table 5–5 lists some commonly used audio file formats and their associated extensions.

TABLE 5–5 Common Audio Sound Extensions

Description	Extension
AIFF sound	.aiff
μLAW sound	.au
MIDI sound file	.mid
Real Audio	.ra
WAV sound file	.wav

Unfortunately, the situation with audio is even more complicated than the one with images. Built-in audio support in Web browsers is much more inconsistent than that for images. Although most browsers can use an external viewer to play an audio file, it is often up to the user to get the viewer program and configure the browser to use it. Additionally, there has been a proliferation of plug-ins that support custom audio formats. These plug-ins offer greater flexibility in format support, but many are still not in wide use or available on many platforms. In other words, just choosing the audio format to use with your documents can be a nightmare. Let's look at the most common formats and their pros and cons:

μlAW (.au)

This format was developed for use on Sun Microsystems computers and was popularized on UNIX systems. If a browser has built-in support for audio, it is likely to support this format. However, recording quality is mediocre, and this format is not suited for music. It is a good choice for plain voice recordings.

MIDI

Musical Instrument Digital Interface. MIDI is a communications protocol that was created to allow electronic musical instruments to communicate with each other. Microsoft Internet Explorer has built-in support for MIDI files, and plug-ins are available for other browsers.

WAV

An audio format developed for use with Microsoft Windows. WAV files can be recorded at 11 kHz, 22 kHz, and 44 kHz, in 8- or 16-bit mono and stereo formats. WAV files use approximately 10mb/min for 16-bit samples with a sampling rate of 44 kHz, although significant size reductions may be made by reducing the sampling rate.

AIFF

Audio Interchange File Format. This format was developed by Apple Computer for the storage of music and other high-quality sound. It was used primarily on Apple and SGI systems, although many browsers that support sound now provide multiplatform support for AIFF as well.

Real Audio (ra)

RealAudio by Progressive Networks is a proprietary real-time streaming audio format (in plain English this means that the sounds can be played before the entire sound file is downloaded). It is part of the new wave of audio formats that are supported by browser plug-ins and custom server extensions. Your documents will have to be served from a system that has a RealAudio server extension in order to use this format's ability to start playing the sound before the entire sound file has been downloaded.

Sound Issues

There are many issues to consider when preparing sound file for inclusion in your Web documents. They boil down, though to the same issues that need to be considered when including images—support and size. A daunting number of supported (or should we say somewhat supported?) formats are available for the storage of sound files on the Web. If you are lucky, you are preparing your sound for distribution via an Intranet and have an inkling about the formats that are supported by the browsers used by your readers. However, if you're like most of us, you'll have to make an educated guess. Unfortunately, sound is a fairly new frontier on the Web, with vendors coming out with new and improved schemes for storing, transferring and playing audio files all the time.

If you want to get serious about creating your own sound files, you should become familiar with issues such as sampling rates and multiple channels (stereo vs. mono), since these things greatly affect the size and quality of the resulting file. Addressing these issues in greater detail goes beyond the scope of this book. However, numerous books are available that cover the various sound formats and the pros and cons associated with each. Find one and read it.

However if you don't want to become a sound engineer and only want to prepare simple voice recordings, you can stick with the au format.

Internet Explorer Sound Support: <BGSOUND>

Microsoft Internet Explorer includes built-in support for wav, au and MIDI sound files. You can include them in your documents with BGSOUND. Sounds included with this tag will automatically be played when your document is loaded. The tag has two attributes:

SRC

This is used to specify the location of the sound file.

LOOP

Used to specify the number of times that the sound file should be played. Values may be any positive number, INFINITE or −1 (equivalent to INFINITE).

For example:

```
<BGSOUND SRC=bgsound.au LOOP=1>
```

Embedded Objects: <EMBED>

The EMBED tag allows the insertion of arbitrary objects such as audio or Shockwave files directly into an HTML page. This tag was introduced by Netscape, and at the time this book was written was supported only by Netscape. The standards committee was looking into alternative methods for the inclusion of external objects, so this tag may end up being similar to BGSOUND in being supported by only one browser.

Netscape embedded objects are supported by application-specific plug-ins. EMBED has three predefined attributes, which are listed in Table 5–6.

TABLE 5–6 Default EMBED Attributes

Attribute	Description
SRC	Specifies source URL. Required.
HEIGHT	The object's image will be scaled to fit the specified height and width.
WIDTH	The object's image will be scaled to fit the specified height and width.

Many other attributes are available but depend on the plug-in for the object being embedded. In general, these attributes come in the form:

```
ATTRIBUTE_NAME=<ATTRIBUTE_VALUE>
```

Since we are reviewing methods for including sounds in this section, we will only go over the attributes associated with the Live Audio sound plug-in that comes with the Navigator. These attributes are listed in Table 5–7.

TABLE 5–7 Embed Audio Attributes

Attribute	Description
LOOP	Specifies whether the object should be played repeatedly. It may be set to TRUE, FALSE or a number.
ALIGN	Controls text alignment around the object in a similar fashion to the ALIGN attribute for images. It may be set to TOP, BOTTOM, MIDDLE, LEFT, and RIGHT.
VOLUME	For audio objects, set the volume level. It may be set to a value between 1 and 100, with 100 being the loudest.
AUTOSTART	Used to start playing an audio object automatically when the document is loaded. May be set to TRUE or FALSE.
CONTROLS	There seems to be only one supported value for this attribute at this time—"console". Since it is the default, it is safe to leave this attribute out.

It is important to remember that all but the three predefined attributes are specific to the plug-in being used. You will need to consult the vendor's documentation for the selected plug-in to determine what attributes have been defined for use with it.

Alternate Objects: <NOEMBED>

The NOEMBED tag is analogous to the use of the NOFRAME tag in frame documents and the ALT attribute with the IMG tag. NOEMBED is used to hide alternate text or a link from browsers that understand EMBED. For example, if you have a embedded an audio file in your document with the EMBED tag, people using browsers that do not support EMBED will not be able to hear it. As far as they are concerned, your document does not have any sound, since browsers that do not support EMBED will give no indication that the tag and associated information are in the document. NOEMBED allows you to provide an alternative for these browsers. For example, if we have an audio file named "hello.au" we could use a combination of EMBED and NOEMBED to make it available:

```
<EMBED SRC=hello.au HEIGHT=0 WIDTH=2 AUTOSTART=TRUE LOOP=1>
<NOEMBED><A HREF=hello.au>Listen to me say
hello!</A></NOEMBED>
```

When Navigator encounters this section of the document, it will play the sound file and ignore the text contained in the NOEMBED tag. Other browsers will simply display the linked text, and users can then click on the link to download the sound in the traditional manner.

Background Sound Example

Let's look at an example. We have a short hello message that we would like to play automatically when our document is loaded. If you've been paying attention, you probably realize that it is impossible to guarantee that this will happen in all browsers. However, we can do our best to cover the browsers that do offer some built-in audio-playing capabilities. Although there are tag wars going on between browsers, fortunately for the most part the tags do not conflict with each other.

Our audio file contains a simple voice message, so we choose the μlaw format. We store it in a file named bgsound.au. We add it to our document by inserting the following lines:

```
<BGSOUND SRC=bgsound.au LOOP=2>
<EMBED SRC=bgsound.au AUTOSTART=true VOLUME=100 WIDTH=0
HEIGHT=2 LOOP=false>
```

Internet Explorer understands the first line, and Navigator Versions 2 and above understand the second. Notice that our EMBED tag includes attributes of WIDTH=0 and HEIGHT=2. Through some experimentation we discovered that this prevents the browser from displaying the console icon[2] (it does leave a small space where the icon would be placed, but if you place the tag at the end of a paragraph, it should not be noticeable). Either the width or the height may be set to 2 (if they are both set to 2, the space will appear as a grey dot). If they are both set to 0 or 1, the browser will display the console.

Now that we've covered the newer versions of the two most popular browsers, we would still like to offer readers using a browser that does not support sound a way to hear our message. This can be done in the traditional manner, with a link to the sound file:

```
<A HREF=bgsound.au>Hear me say hello!</A>
```

This link will be redundant for Navigator and Internet Explorer users, since the sound will have been played already. You can hide this section of your document from Navigator users by placing it in a <NOEMBED> tag:

```
<NOEMBED><A HREF=bgsound.au>Hear me say hello!</A></NOEMBED>
```

NOEMBED will not prevent the text from being displayed in Internet Explorer, so there will be some redundancy.

Video

Video and animations are two of the most dramatic and eye-catching elements that you can include in your Web documents. The two most common formats used on the Web are Quicktime and MPEG (Moving Picture Expert Group). However, Internet Explorer includes built-in support for the Windows Video format, also known as Audio-Video Interleaved or AVI, so it may increase in popularity. Table 5–8 contains a list of these formats and the file extensions normally associated with them.

---

2. The LiveAudio documentation describes the attribute HIDDEN, that is supposed to provide this functionality in the future. However, at the time this book was written it had not been implemented.

TABLE 5–8 Common Video File Formats

Description	Extension
QuickTime movie	.mov , .qt
MPEG movie	.mpeg or .mpg
Audio-Video Interleaved	.avi

Xing Technology (http://www.xingtech.com/) has developed a new format for video files that offers vastly improved compression ratios over other formats. Since Xing also has plug-ins for many platforms, this may become a popular video storage format.

Quicktime

Quicktime is a format originally developed by Apple, which allows users to view and edit digital video, animation, sound, text, music and other dynamic information. From a technical point of view, Quicktime supports two kinds of files: image files and time-based movie files. Apple maintains a Quicktime Web site at:

```
http://quicktime.apple.com
```

MPEG

MPEG is a standard for digital video and audio compression. MPEG is expected to become the industry standard for delivery of interactive television. Note that older versions of MPEG do not support digitized audio. These MPEG files using the older standard sometimes come with accompanying sound files in WAV format. Quicktime also supports MPEG compressed video.

On the CD we have provided examples of movies in both Quicktime and MPEG formats, so that you can compare the two.

In the next section we describe three aspects of video usage: preparing video for Web use, incorporating video in Web documents, and viewing video within Web documents.

Preparing Video

While the actual process of making high-quality video is beyond the scope of this book, we mention one critical aspect for Web publishing. Many tools for creating and editing Quicktime movies may create documents that reference other movie documents and resources. In the Macintosh world, this is called a multifork file. Since this is a Mac-specific implementation, it is not supported by the Web protocol. Therefore, to create Quicktime movies that contain all the necessary data for Web use, you must make sure that your movie is "self-contained" and "flattened."

Creating a "self-contained" movie usually involves selecting this option when saving the movie file.

Flattening combines all resources used by the movie into one data fork. Some applications will include flattening as an option when saving the movie. Otherwise, you must use a separate tool. Once you have flattened and made your movie self-contained, it is ready to be incorporated into Web documents.

Incorporating Video

Incorporating video in your Web documents is similar to the inclusion of other multimedia elements—somewhat chaotic. As with sound, the tags to allow video to be included in a document vary between different browsers. The traditional method of simply setting up a link with the <A> tag to the video file should work with any browser that is configured to display video format used to store your file. For example, suppose Kelly wanted to include a link to a Quicktime movie on kayaking, called kayaking.mov. She would write her link as follows:

```
<A HREF="kayaking.mov">My kayaking movie</A>.
```

IMG DYNSRC Attribute

Of course the traditional method also means that the video clip will be played by an external viewer and will not be incorporated in the browser window. Microsoft Internet Explorer supports an extension to the IMG tag that allows you to include an alternate AVI-format video clip in your document. The format is:

```
<IMG SRC="url.gif" DYNSRC="url.avi" ALT="[My video clip]">
```

If the browser supports the format of the video included with the DYNSRC attribute, the video will be displayed. If not, the plain image will be loaded (or, in the case of a browser that does not support images, the ALT text will be displayed).

Two additional IMG attributes are supported by Internet Explorer for use with video:

LOOP

Sets the number of times the video should be played. May be set to a positive number, INFINITE or –1 (which has the same effect as INFINITE).

START

Determines when the browser should begin playing the video. Value may be set to FILEOPEN (start as soon as the clip is loaded) or MOUSEOVER (start when the mouse cursor is moved over the image). It is allowable to set both values at the same time: "START=FILEOPEN, MOUSEOVER"

Viewing Video

If you are using one of the popular Web browsers, all you need in order to view video is the appropriate "helper" application. If your browser is properly configured, it will automatically download the video with the correct viewer.

A document named video.html is provided on the CD that includes a number of videos. The Quicktime video that is part of this document was made with a black-and-white digital video camera called QuickCam, made by Connectix. Although it is a short clip—only about eight seconds long—it takes up 880 kb of disk space. If it were color, the clip would take up even more space. This should drive home the point that video storage requires large amounts of disk space.

We translated the clip into MPEG format, and now it only takes up about 180 kb. If you view the clip, you will see that we've lost both quality and sound!

In sum, if you plan to incorporate video into your Web documents, you must ensure that you have adequate disk space. In addition, you'll probably also want to have a fast server machine and a fairly high-bandwidth network connection. Otherwise, Web clients trying to retrieve video documents risk having to wait a long time while the video is transferred (which they may have to do anyway, if their end of the connection is slow).

The Good, the Bad and the Ugly

Turning a Web document into a multimedia presentation can be fun, but it is easy to get carried away. Here are some guidelines to keep your documents under control:

- Be nice to your readers. If you have a large image, offer either a thumbnail or a plain text link to it. On a related note, for video and sound as well as images, it is a good idea to include the size of the multimedia element next to the link that will be used to retrieve it.

- Remember to use the ALT attribute, so that readers without a graphical browser are not left out.

- If is often possible to reduce an image's storage requirements by reducing the number of colors in its palette. You can do this with Paint Shop Pro. Reducing the number of colors also reduces the likelihood that all of the available colors on your reader's system will get used up.

- In general, you should try to offer your images in GIF format.
- Interlaced images will allow readers with a browser that supports this format to see what the image looks like more quickly.

In toc.html on the CD you can see the versions of the kayak table of contents we've gone over in this chapter.

Desktop digital video has only recently become widely available. This means that the technology is rapidly evolving. It also means that there are many factors that can affect the quality and effectiveness of video within Web documents.

First, digitized video takes up a significant amount of disk space. If you plan to make extensive use of video, you need to make sure you have enough disk space available. You can reduce disk-space usage by using higher compression rates, though the resulting quality of the video will suffer.

In the network's Web environment, other factors will also affect the quality of video playback. Some of these factors are:

- The power of the server machine. A more powerful server will serve large files faster.
- The speed of the network connection. With large video files and slow network connections, downloading will take a long time, and may even time out!
- The power of the client machine. A more powerful client will play movie files faster.
- The browser plug-in or "helper" viewer application used. These vary in how well they implement and support the video standards.
- The options set by the user in the viewer application. Different settings will affect playback quality and speed.

IN THIS CHAPTER YOU WILL LEARN HOW TO USE PAINT SHOP PRO TO:

- CREATE TRANSPARENT BACKGROUNDS
- CREATE THUMBNAIL VERSIONS OF YOUR IMAGES
- CREATE INTERLEAVED GIF IMAGES
- MAKE RAISED LETTERS USING MASKS
- ADD DROP SHADOWS TO YOUR IMAGES

PAINT SHOP PRO

In a perfect world, we would all have systems with a gazillion megabytes of memory, superfast processors and a complete set of high-end commercial illustration tools like Adobe's PhotoShop and Illustrator. But this is the real world, where most of us have to survive with limited budgets. Fortunately, in the real world we have Paint Shop Pro. Even better for you, it's here on the CD. If you decide to use it, you'll still have to pay the registration fee of $69—but you have 30 days to try it out without paying a single penny.

What can this terrific program do for you? How about making thumbnail copies of your images (one or a whole batch), creating images with transparent backgrounds, adding drop shadows, and making slick background images? Paint Shop Pro has everything you need to make sure that your images are in a Web-ready format. It comes with a cornucopia of filters so you can add all sorts of special effects to your images. What's more, it can accept Adobe-compatible plug-ins, so you can get even more filters, and more effects if you wish. We know you must be anxious to get started, but first we need to tell you about this chapter.

This chapter will introduce you to the basic controls in Paint Shop Pro. However, since this is a book on HTML, and not Paint Shop Pro, we focus on the use of Paint Shop Pro to create some of the popular effects used in Web images. For a full introduction to Paint Shop Pro, you should refer to the on-line documentation available through the help menu in the program.

Installing Paint Shop Pro

You will find the Paint Shop Pro in the Utilities folder on the CD. To install it on your hard disk, simply drag the executable to your hard disk and click on it.

Starting Paint Shop Pro

After the installation is completed, you can access Paint Shop Pro by clicking on its icon in the folder. It will pop up a registration warning message while it is loading:

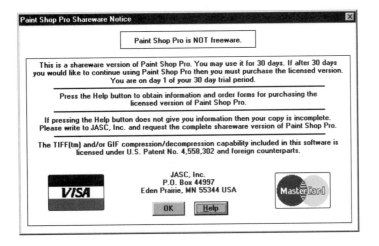

After you click the OK button the main window will open. In addition to the main window, a number of floating toolboxes will appear as well. These toolboxes are used to tell the program which tool should be used. Figures 6–1 and 6–2 provide a quick reference for the Select and Paint Toolboxes.

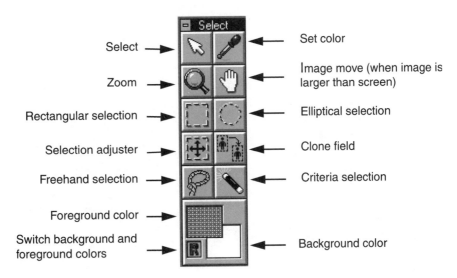

FIGURE 6–1 *Select Control Toolbox*

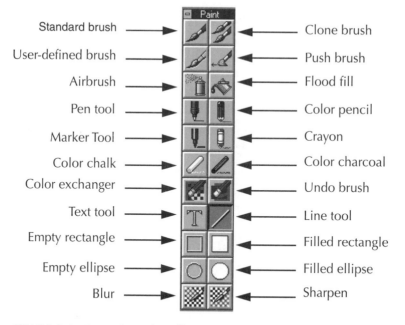

Standard brush	Clone brush
User-defined brush	Push brush
Airbrush	Flood fill
Pen tool	Color pencil
Marker Tool	Crayon
Color chalk	Color charcoal
Color exchanger	Undo brush
Text tool	Line tool
Empty rectangle	Filled rectangle
Empty ellipse	Filled ellipse
Blur	Sharpen

FIGURE 6–2   Paint Control Toolbox

In addition to these floating toolboxes, a number of other display options through the View menu are available:

- The Histogram window displays a graph of image colors by luminance (brightness).
- The Tool Control Panel is a small floating panel that provides controls for the current tool. For example, if Zoom is the current tool, it will display controls for Zoom level. If the tool is switched to one of the brushes, the Control Panel will switch to controls for brush size and style.
- Toolbar display. If you want to maximize screen size for image viewing, you can remove the toolbar display.

After you load an image, you will see information about it in the status bar at the bottom of the main window:

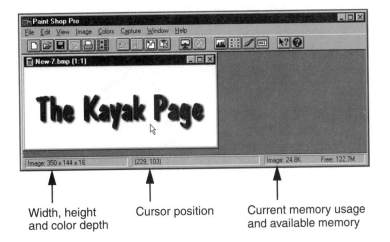

Width, height and color depth | Cursor position | Current memory usage and available memory

You can use the information about the height and width of the image to set the HEIGHT and WIDTH attributes for the IMG tag.

Deformations and Filters

Paint Shop Pro comes with a great collection of deformations and filters. These are special processing modules that allow you to easily add special effects to your images. Paint Shop Pro even allows you to add other plug-in filters and create your own filters (you can find more information on creating your own filters in the on-line help). You will find them under the Image menu:

Here are the choices for the default deformations and filters:

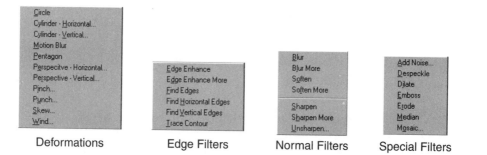

| Deformations | Edge Filters | Normal Filters | Special Filters |

You can use filters on selections, entire images, or masked sections of an image. If you are new to filters, we recommend using the Deformation Browser and Filter Browser to quickly review how each filter will modify an image.

We'll explain how to use specific filters in the sections on creating special effect for Web images later in this chapter. For more information on filters, consult the on-line help.

Converting Between Formats

As we've mentioned, graphics in Web pages should be stored in GIF or JPEG format. What do you do if you already have hundreds of image stored in some other format? You could open each one manually and then save it in the desired format—or you could take advantage of Paint Shop Pro's easy Batch Conversion function to convert a whole directory full of images in one quick sweep. You'll find Batch Conversion under the File menu (shortcut: <ALT-F>-T). When you start it, a window like this one will appear:

Batch Conversion		
Input:		OK
File **N**ames:	Di**r**ectory:	Cancel
[*.*]	H:\HTMLTR~1\...\Pictures	Select **A**ll
green-blue-back.GIF	h:\	Help
green-grey-back.GIF	htmltr~1	
green-grey2-back.GIF	HTML_Document_Trea	
green-purple-back.GIF	Images	
	Pictures	
File **T**ype:	Dri**v**e:	
All Files	h: dec-b	
Output:		Options
File **T**ype:	Directory:	
JPG - JPEG - JFIF Compliant	h:\workarea	Suppress error messages during conversion
Sub-Type:	[Change]	
None		

As you can see, you have the option of choosing a single file, or every file in a directory. You can also choose a separate output directory for the files that have been converted. This is important, especially if you are doing something like converting a set of images in GIF87 format to GIF89/Interlaced, since the filenames will conflict with each other if you stick to a single directory. In our case, we want to convert a set of GIF files into JPEG format. As a note of warning, for the best resulting image quality it is better to switch to JPEG from another 24-bit format such as TIFF or Photoshop rather than GIF, which is an 8-bit format.

Our originating directory contains only GIF images, so, after setting the directories and choosing our output file format, we start the conversion process by clicking on the "Select All" button. If your directory contains a mix of images and other files, you can choose multiple files by holding down the SHIFT key and clicking on the files that you wish to convert. If you do this, you should click the OK button rather than the Select All button to start the conversion.

In our case the conversion process automatically tries to convert all of the files in the directory to JPEG. Since JPEG is a 24-bit format, and our starting format is only an 8-bit one, we get a warning each time it starts a conversion:

Paint Shop Pro

(?) This image needs to have the color depth increased to 16.7 million colors before it can be saved to this file type. Should the image be changed?

[Yes]   [No]

We simply click on OK to complete the conversion. You will get a warning message anytime the conversion is between two formats with the different storage bit-levels. If you prefer not to see this warning message, you can turn it off by setting your preferences. To do this, choose "Preference" from the File menu (shortcut <ALT-F>-F), and then pick General from the Preference menu. Choose the "Save" tab from the set of tabs in the window that appears:

General Preferences

| General | Loading | Saving | Misc |

ASK before changing the image to comply with selected file format and subformat, during...

☑ File-Save As
☐ File-Batch Conversion

ASK to save changes to images that have been altered, during...

☑ File-Exit
☑ Window-Close All

DPI to be written to the file when using the format:

PCX   TIFF
300   300

WPG   JPEG
300   72

JIF/JPG Compression Level
37

OK
Cancel
Help

Under the box that starts with "ASK before changing the image", make sure that "File-Batch Conversion" is **not** checked.

After the conversion is completed, Paint Shop Pro will display a window with a log of the conversion activity. You can view the status of your conversions in the window or save it to a file for your records:

Batch Processing Status (File 4 of 4)

Reading h:\HTML Treasure Chest\HTML_Document_Treas
..OK.
Saving h:\workarea\green-grey2-back.jpg
..OK.
Reading h:\HTML Treasure Chest\HTML_Document_Treas
..OK.
Saving h:\workarea\green-purple-back.jpg
..OK.
Batch conversion complete.
4 File(s) successfully converted.

Close   Save Log

Creating Interlaced GIF Images

The simplest method for creating interlaced GIF images is to use the batch conversion process. Choose GIF for the output format, the subtype box beneath the primary type field will contain a list of the various types of GIF formats that Paint Shop Pro supports. Simply choose "Version 89a - Interlaced" as the subtype:

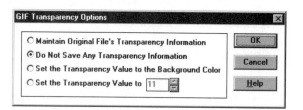

Creating Transparent Backgrounds

As we mentioned in the section on transparent backgrounds, Paint Shop Pro can save an image with transparent color information. The procedure is fairly simple:

- Load your image into Paint Shop Pro.
- From the File menu, chose "Save As".
- In the dialog box that appears choose "GIF - Compuserve" from the List of File Types, then "GIF 89a - Interlaced" or "GIF 89a - Noninterlaced" from the Sub-Format menu.
- Click the Options button. The following dialog box should appear:

You can choose to leave the current transparency information alone (if any exists), remove the transparency information, set the transparency color to whatever is currently set as the background color (look in your Select menubar to find the current background color), or set a specific background color (you will need to know which colors are in which location of the palette to use this option[1]).

- Click OK, and then OK again in the Save As dialog box.
- Enter the filename you wish to use, and you're done.

Making Thumbnails

If you plan to incorporate many images in your documents, one thing you will undoubtedly need to do is to create a thumbnail version of some of your images. Let's see how to make a thumbnail copy of Kelly's image. First we load the image by choosing Open from the File menu and entering the name of the file. Then we get the following screen:

---

1. To find the index value for a particular color choose Edit Colors from the Colors menu and click on the color for which you wish to find the index value. The value will appear in the lower righthand side of the window.

To make a thumbnail version of our image, we choose "resize" from the Image menu:

Resize ☒

Select the new size...

○ <u>3</u>20 x 200
○ <u>6</u>40 x 350
○ 6<u>4</u>0 x 480
○ <u>8</u>00 x 600
○ <u>1</u>024 x 768

◉ C<u>u</u>stom Size:

72 x 56

☑ <u>M</u>aintain Aspect Ratio
o<u>f</u> 1.2911 to 1

[OK] [Cancel] [<u>H</u>elp]

Be sure to check the "Preserve Aspect" box, and then set either one of the values in the Custom Size boxes (the other value will automatically be updated as long as Preserve Aspect Ratio has been set). Click OK, and choose Save As from the File menu to save the resulting image to a new file (be careful not to do a plain Save, since this will overwrite your original image.

Creating Drop Shadows and Highlights

Adding a drop shadow is an easy way to add a three dimensional effect to your images. The following sections explain how to create text with a drop shadow and images with drop shadows.

First a few notes about the use of drop shadows. **It is safer to save images with drop shadows with transparency turned off**. Why? To create the shadow effect, the program blends the shadow color with the current image background color:

As a result if drop shadows are used in combination with transparent backgrounds, the image background should be the same color as the background color in the document. If the document has a different background color, the shadow will appear with a halo of color in the image's background color. This halo is due to the pixels in the shadow that are in shades that approach the image's background color but are not quite the same. Since transparency is set to only one color, these pixels still show up.

Avoid banded shadows. Like real shadows, image shadows go from a dark shade close to the object being shadowed to a lighter shade as the shadow gets further from the object. Typically this is done by the use of progressively lighter shades of the shadow color. However, since Web images in GIF format are stored in an 8-bit (or less) format, there are usually only a few shades of each color available in the color palette. The resulting image can end up looking banded or streaked as multiple shades get mapped to a single shade.

To avoid this problem, keep your shadows small—the larger they are, the more shades will be required to create the dark to light gradient, and the more likely that a banded look will appear. If you have a large shadow, stick with the 8-bit palette rather than trying to minimize file size by reducing to a smaller palette. Try dithering when you reduce your colors—it is more likely to retain the original effect, although it is worthwhile to save the image using both nearest color and dithering and then compare the image in a few browsers.

Note that even if the image does not appear banded in Paint Shop Pro, it may still appear banded in a browser (see the section in the Multimedia about the Netscape color palette for an explanation), so it is essential to check your images in a browser rather than relying on the way that they appear in Paint Shop Pro.

Drop Shadows with Text

Creating text with a drop shadow is a simple process. Open a new image with the background color set to whatever you wish to use for the background color in your document, and the foreground color set to black (or some other dark color). Check the status bar and make sure that the image is in 24-bit (16 million) mode. If it isn't use the Increase Color Depth choice from the Color menu to set it to the correct level. If it isn't set correctly, the filters will not work.

First we create the shadow. Use the Text tool to enter the text:

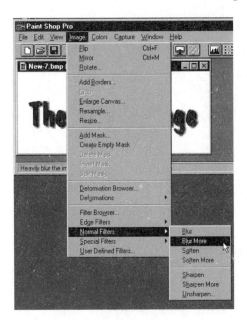

Place the text slightly below the location where you wish your final text to appear. Now choose "Blur More" from the "Normal Filters" submenu under the Image menu:

You can enlarge the shadow by repeatedly applying this filter. We usually apply it only once to keep the shadow small.

The foreground color should be reset to whatever color you wish to use for your text. Do not use the same color that you used for the shadow, since that would cause the shadow to blend with the text. Enter the text by choosing the text tool from the Tool Toolbox and clicking on the image. It should remember your font settings and text. Place the new text over the blurred text you created in the previous step, but be sure to offset it enough so that the lower and left or right (depending on the direction that you want the shadow to be oriented) edges of the blurred text are visible.

Reduce the colors and save the image GIF format in a non-transparent mode. We recommend GIF over JPEG, because JPEG will introduce spottiness in the background. That's it!

Drop Shadows for Objects

Adding a drop shadow to an object is a bit more complicated than adding a shadow to text. It is done through the use of masks. In this section we will go through the steps to do this.

Open your image. The object should have clearly defined edges, and the image itself should have a solid background. For easy mask creation, the ideal background color is white. If your image does not have a white background, you can use Paint Shop Pro to adjust it. For the purposes of this section, we will assume that your background is white.

We use an image named owl, which has been saved in Photoshop format in our example. Ideally, you should start with an image that is stored in a 24-bit format. However, if you only have an 8-bit source, simply switch to 24-bit format after opening the file.

Our next step is to create a mask. Masks allow you to modify a portion of the image while "masking off" the rest of it. Paint Shop Pro can use a number of different criteria to determine which sections of the image should be included in the mask:

source luminance, any value but 0 (in other words, anything in the image that is not black) , or selection. In our case, we want to use the "any value but 0" criteria. However, we do have a problem, since our background is white, and this criterion is looking for black areas to mask. We get around this problem by choosing "Negative Image" from the Color menu. Now our background is black, and our image's colors have been reversed. We add a mask to our image by choosing "Add Mask" from the Image menu:

Add Mask Channel ☒

Source Window

| This Window ▼ |

OK

Create mask from

○ Source luminance

◉ Any non-zero value

○ Current selection

Cancel

Help

☑ Invert mask data

After this step, there won't be any visible indication of the areas that are masked, but the letter "M" will appear in the title bar next to the image name to indicate that there is a mask in this image.

However, we need to modify the mask, and the only way we can do this is to separate it from the image. We do this with the "Split Mask" command under the Image menu. We actually need two copies of the mask, so we create a duplicate copy by repeating the Add Mask/Split Mask commands. The masks will then appear as separate images.

We make one of the mask images active and apply the Blur More filter to it several times. Now we need to offset the portion of the mask that is to become the shadow, so that it will show up behind the original image. We do this with the clone selection tool, by selecting the image and then cloning it so that it is offset below and to the right of the original image location. If the original image area is not covered by the cloned image, use one of the paint tools to remove the part of the old image that shows.

Now we have a shadow, but if we were to apply the shadow directly to our original image, it would cover part of the image. To avoid this problem, we apply the second copy of the mask to our blurred mask by choosing Add Mask from the Image menu and choosing our second mask copy as the source:

Add Mask Channel

Source Window

mask24.bmp

OK

Create mask from

Cancel

○ Source luminance

● Any non-zero value

Help

● Current selection

☐ Invert mask data

Now our mask is ready to apply to the original image. However, as you may recall, we had inverted the colors in the original image to create the mask. Before applying our newly created mask, we revert the image back to the original version. We then apply the mask with the "source luminesce" box checked. Source luminescence preserves the shading (luminescence) in the mask. This will preserve the feathering at the edges of the shadow.

Now our workspace looks like this:

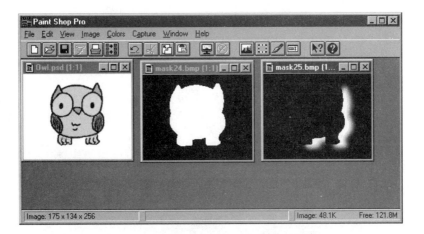

Our final step is to add the shadow. We do this by adjusting the brightness in the masked area. We choose Brightness/Contrast from the Adjust submenu under the Colors menu and adjust Brightness to -40. This will cause the masked area to get darker, thus creating a shadow.

Notice that the preview box will show the whole image with the adjustment rather than only the masked area.

Reduce the colors in the image, using the same criteria as for text with a dropped shadow, and save it in GIF format.

Reducing the Color Palette

If you read the previous chapter on Multimedia, you know that keeping your images small is an important part of Web graphic design, and that one of the ways to reduce image size is to minimize the number of colors in the color palette. Paint Shop Pro makes palette shrinkage a snap. The first step is to find out how many colors are being used in your image. There is a handy command called (is this obvious enough?) "Count Colors Used" under the Color menu. It will tell you exactly how many colors are being used in your image:

If the number is greater than 256, you have two options—save the image as a JPEG (leaving the palette alone) or reduce the number of colors in the image. If your image has a solid background, reducing the number of colors will probably produce a better-looking picture, since JPEG introduces variations in solid-color areas. When you reduce the color, you have a number of choices:

- map the existing colors to the closest color in the palette
- dither colors in the palette to simulate the colors in the image that are not in the palette

While both methods can produce attractive results, they do have limitations. Dithering can result in a spotty-looking image, while mapping can result in a weird blocky effect. The best result depends on the image, and we frequently check the image using both methods before deciding which way to save the image.

To pick either method, choose "Decrease Color Depth" from the Color menu. Pick the color depth you wish to use for your image. You will be presented with a dialog box that allows you to choose the method for doing the reduction:

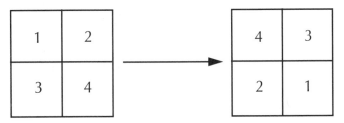

After you've made your choices, click OK. Then save your file, and you're done!

Creating Seamless Backgrounds

Textured backgrounds can dress up your Web pages. However because browsers tile the background image to fill the window, you can end up with a shower-wall look unless you take precautions to create "seamless" background images. You can do this by dividing your image into quarters, rearranging the quarters, and then blurring the seams between the quarters. Figure 6–3 shows how the grids should be rearranged.

FIGURE 6–3   Grid Exchange for Seamless Backgrounds

The original image should be a square. We like to start with a 144 by 144 pixel image. Avoid images with strong geometric patterns, as it will be difficult to clean up the seams. We start our example with a simple looped pattern we made with the marker. Our first step is to create an empty image that is the same size as our original. It does not matter what the background color in the new image is set to, since we will be covering it with blocks from the original image.

Since our image is 144 by 144, our next step is to create a selection box that is a quarter of the size of this area: 72 by 72 pixels. We do this by dragging a box from the top corner and watching the measurements in the center of the status bar. You may find it easier to create a box that is approximately the right size, and then adjust the sides using the selection adjuster.

Once you have a box that is the correct size, use the selection adjuster to make sure that it is pushed up against the upper left corner. Now copy the selection by choosing Copy from the Edit menu (shortcut <CTRL-C>). Switch to the empty image and Paste the image as a new selection.

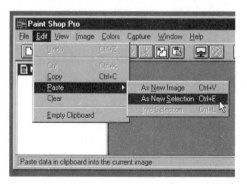

Push the selection into the lower right-hand corner of the new image.

Switch back to the original image; make sure the selection adjuster tool is chosen (this is important—if one of the other selection tools is set, you will loose your selection box and have to recreate it). Move your selection box into one of the other corners, copy it and then paste it as a new selection into the new image. Push it into the appropriate corner as described in Figure 6–3. Repeat this process until all four quarters have been copied into the new image.

Now you should have an image with four visible tiles. The seams between the tiles must be removed without modifying the edges of the image. Since the adjustments will vary, depending on the type of image being used and the amount of variation in the seams, we provide general guidelines here:

- If the image has a fine texture, the best bet is to use the clone brush. Click the right mouse button on a location fairly close to the seam, and then paint over the seam. You may need to do some touch-up with the smudge and push brushes.
- If there are strong figures in the image (such as lines or loops), it may be useful to draw some new lines and loops over the seam with the appropriate tool.

After the seams have been eradicated from the new image save it and check its size. Background images should be fairly small. If your image is too large, you can reduce the image size by reducing its dimensions or reducing the number of colors in the palette. Now check the image as a background in a document.

Creating Logo Backgrounds

In this section we explain how to create a background using a logo or some text. In this case, the logo or text is on a plain background, so there is no concern about seams. If you use a logo or some text for a background, you need to minimize the number of colors and use a fairly muted set of colors, so that the text in your document will show up on top of the background.

One of the easiest ways to do this is to emboss the image. This flattens out the colors and gives a raised appearance to the edges. We will demonstrate with a textual background for our kayak page. We first create an image containing the words "The Kayak Page" in a thick black type on a white background. Because we are going to be using filters, we create the image in 24-bit mode.

Plain words are pretty boring, so we decide to place them diagonally. This can be done by either rotating the image or using the Skew filter. Since the Skew filter also changes the proportions appropriately, we use it in this example:

We skew our image 30 percent vertically. Notice that the image size is automatically increased to accommodate the extra vertical height required to fit the words on the page. Next we emboss the image by choosing the Emboss filter under the Special Filters submenu in the Image menu.

After embossing, the image is fairly dark, and there is also a wide variation in shades used in the image. We need to minimize the shading variation and lighten the picture to make it easy to find a text color that will appear clearly on top of the background. This is done by adjusting the contrast and brightness through the Adjust submenu under the Color menu:

Brightness/Contrast

% **Brightness**
40

% **Contrast**
-40

OK   Cancel   Help

Our preference is to increase the brightness by 40 while setting the contrast to -40. Finally, we convert the file to 4-bit through the Decrease Color submenu under the Colors menu, save it and check it in a browser.

Getting More Help

Many of the techniques described in this section were adapted from techniques that we learned in PhotoShop. Although we were unable to locate any books specifically about Paint Shop Pro, you will find that many of the techniques described in PhotoShop books (and there are many of them) can easily be adapted to Paint Shop Pro.

Paint Shop Pro can also use PhotoShop-compatible plug-ins, so you can extend its functionality even further by loading more filters. You will find that Paint Shop Pro can be used to manipulate your images in many other ways as well. Don't forget that one of the best sources for information about this useful tool is the Help menu.

Finally—don't forget to register it if you choose to use it. At $69, it is a bargain!

CREATING INTERACTIVE AND DYNAMIC DOCUMENTS

What's In This Chapter

In this chapter we describe how to create interactive and dynamic documents. We first describe how to create documents that contain tags supporting user input (via forms). We describe how to write scripts (or programs) that process user input and send new output to users back through the Web server, via the Common Gateway Interface (CGI). We then discuss dynamic documents. Such documents can be created on the fly to contain tailored information, such as the current date and time. Similarly, with the use of Java and VRML, documents can contain nonstatic information, such as animations and executable programs.

Introduction

By definition, Web documents are interactive. If a document contains a hyperlink, users can individually select links and choose their own pathway through the information.

The Web also supports other ways for users to interact with documents. HTML Version 2.0 and higher provides support for several kinds of user interactions. For example, Web documents can contain graphics with clickable regions and support keyword searches of databases. Documents can also cause a program to be executed, with the input to the program supplied by the user. The output from the program is then displayed to the user, typically in a new Web document. We call these kinds of documents highly interactive documents.

In a typical scenario, user input and output is processed in the following manner. A Web document uses special set of HTML tags, called forms, to collect user input. This document also specifies the name of the program on the Web server that should process the user input. After the user has entered the desired input, it is then packaged by the browser and sent to the server. The Web server recognizes that this particular browser request contains a user query and specifies a program. Accordingly, the server ships the user input to the responsible program and continues being a Web server. In turn, the program is run using the input from the user. If the program has output—for example, a new Web document—the program sends the output to the server, which then ships it back to the requesting browser. In this way, the Web documents returned to users are specifically tailored to users' input. Figure 7–1 illustrates this process.

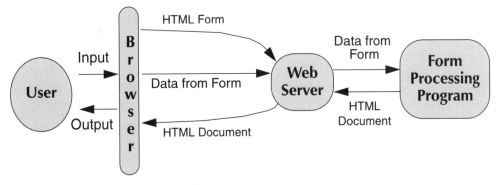

FIGURE 7–1   Flow of Information for Forms.

In this chapter we first describe markup tags that support higher levels of interaction with the user. We then describe the latest in Web technologies for supporting the creation of dynamic pages.

Forms

Our description begins with the FORM tag. As with all HTML elements, forms depend on browsers, and their support varies wildly from browser to browser. This is one area where testing your documents in several browsers is especially important. We will display many of our examples in at least two browsers to give you some idea of the variety you can expect.

Although all of the newer browsers we tested support forms in some fashion, many older browsers don't. When you use form elements in a document, you should warn your readers that they may not be able to access all the features by including a line stating that forms support is required.

Forms: <FORM>

The form element is an HTML tag that is used to demark a data input form (or fill-in-the-form). A region using forms is enclosed within the <FORM> </FORM> pair of markup tags. A Web document can contain several forms, but the form element itself cannot be nested within other form elements. However, forms can be embedded within other HTML tags. Similarly, within a forms region, the usual HTML formatting tags can be inserted.

The form element allows three possible attributes. They are ACTION, METHOD, and ENCTYPE. We explain ACTION and METHOD in the following example.

Suppose we wish to author a user-survey questionnaire within a Web document. We begin our form as follows:

```
<HTML>
<HEAD>
<TITLE>Testing Forms</TITLE>
</HEAD>
<BODY>
<H1>User Survey</H1>
<FORM METHOD="POST" ACTION="http://ozone.com/cgi/survey.cgi">
</FORM>
```

The ACTION attribute specifies the destination URL to which the form should be submitted, once it has been completed by the user. If no URL is specified, the URL of the current document containing the form is used. Here, our destination URL is:

```
http://ozone.com/cgi/survey.cgi
```

In this example the file "survey.cgi" is a CGI script that parses and collates users' responses. We have located the program in the folder called "cgi." The actual location of CGI scripts or programs is dependent on how the server is set up and must be discussed with your server administrator.

The method used to transmit the user's response is defined by both the access method contained in the URL and the value of the METHOD attribute. Thus, the value contained in the METHOD attribute must be compatible with the access method defined in the URL. (Confused? Don't worry, it will become clear after you've gone through the CGI section.) The method attribute specifies the way in which the data from the user is encoded; the program that receives the user input naturally expects the user data to be encoded in this manner.

The default METHOD is GET. However, for most applications, we recommend the POST method. The reason for this preference will become clear in the section on CGI scripts. Note that the value of the METHOD attribute is case sensitive on some servers!

As we will describe, a form is generally submitted by the user once the "Submit" button or "Return" key is pressed. When a form is submitted, the destination URL receives a string containing the selections and text entry made by the responding user. The method you choose (GET or POST) determines how the data is sent to the server. The selection of a method is a server-side issue and must be discussed with your Web server administrator. In the section on CGI scripts we explain how to use CGI scripts to decode data sent via forms.

Each field within a form is defined by the following nested elements: INPUT, TEXTAREA, SELECT, and OPTION. These are described next. These fields must use the NAME attribute to identify the value selected by the user when the form is completed and submitted by the user. Thus, the submitted contents usually contain a stream of name/value pairs. The name is equal to the NAME attributes of the various elements within the form. The value is equal to the entries made by the responding user.

Input: <INPUT>

The Input tag is a nested element within a form, denoted by <INPUT>. It specifies the kind of input field presented to the user. The contents of the input field are then modifiable by the user.

The Input tag uses the following, optional attributes: NAME, TYPE, CHECKED, ALIGN, MAXLENGTH, SIZE, SRC, and VALUE. A summary of these attributes may be found in Table 7–1.

TABLE 7–1   Input Attributes

Attribute	Description
NAME	The name of the particular form item. This attribute is required for most input types. When parsing a user's input, the NAME value is used to provide a meaningful identifier for a field.
CHECKED	Indicates that a checkbox or radio button is selected.
ALIGN	When an image is used, this specifies the vertical alignment of the image. The syntax is the same as that of the <IMG> tag.
MAXLENGTH	Indicates the maximum number of characters that can be entered by users in a text field. If this attribute is not set, there is no limit on the number of characters.
SIZE	Specifies the size of the field and depends on its type.
SRC	Denotes URL for an image. This is used only with IMAGE type.
VALUE	Contains the initial value displayed to users. This attribute is required for radio buttons.
TYPE	Defines the type of data used in the field. The default is free-text input. The following types are definable: CHECKBOX, RADIO, HIDDEN, IMAGE, TEXT, PASSWORD, SUBMIT and RESET.

Input TYPE Attribute

The TYPE attribute is used to specify the type of data used in an Input field. The other attributes that are applicable to a particular field depend on the field's TYPE attribute. For example, the MAXLENGTH attribute specifies the number of characters that may be entered in a field. It should only be used with fields that allow text entry (such as TEXT), since it has no meaning with other types such as RADIO or CHECKBOX. If no type is specified, TEXT is used.

CHECKBOX Type

A checkbox is an item where several values can be selected at the same time. This type is submitted as separate name/value pair for each selected value. The default value for checkboxes is *on.*

You should always set both a NAME and a VALUE for each checkbox. Since each checkbox will cause the form to return two pieces of information to you, there are two ways you could set up checkboxes that are grouped together:

- set a unique *name* for each checkbox
- set a unique *value* for each checkbox.

The more common choice is to use the same name while setting a unique value for each checkbox in a group. It is vital that you do at least one of these things; otherwise, you will not be able to distinguish what was selected in the different boxes. For example:

```
<B>Why do you browse the Web?</B><BR>
<input NAME ="browse" TYPE=checkbox>Fun
<input NAME ="browse" TYPE=checkbox >Work
<input NAME ="browse" TYPE=checkbox>Research
<input NAME ="browse" TYPE=checkbox>Education
```

In this example no value is set, so all of the checkboxes would be returned with the name that we assigned along with the default value. Thus the name/value pair that is returned for any checkbox in this group would be "browse/on". There is no way to tell the difference between the boxes. One way to set up this set of checkboxes would be:

```
<B>Why do you browse the Web?</B><BR>
<input NAME="browse" VALUE="fun" TYPE=checkbox>Fun
<input NAME="browse" VALUE="work" TYPE=checkbox>Work
<input NAME="browse" VALUE="research" TYPE=checkbox>Research
<input NAME="browse" VALUE="education" TYPE=checkbox>Education
```

Now each checkbox will be submitted with a unique value. Here we see how this section looks:

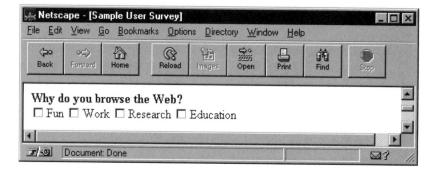

Be careful to use different names for different groups of checkboxes. Otherwise, if the same value is used in two groups, it will be impossible to tell which set of checkboxes returned the data. In the following example we have a couple of true/false questions. Since we use values of true and false for the questions, we make sure that there is a different name for each set of checkboxes:

```
<p>I like cats.
<input NAME="cats" VALUE="true" TYPE=checkbox>True
<input NAME="cats" VALUE="false" TYPE=checkbox>False
<P>I like dogs.
<input NAME="dogs" VALUE="true" TYPE=checkbox>True
<input NAME="dogs" VALUE="false" TYPE=checkbox>False
```

You can also define the initial setting for a checkbox by including the CHECKED attribute. When this attribute is set, the checkbox will appear to be selected when the form is first displayed or after the reset button is chosen. The reader can deselect the box by clicking on it.

RADIO Type

The RADIO type defines an item where only one value can be selected from a set of possibilities. A set is defined as the group of radio boxes with the same NAME attribute. Only the name and the selected value are returned. Note that you must set a value for each radio box. Here is a sample set of radio boxes:

```
What is your gender?
<INPUT NAME="gender" VALUE="male" TYPE=radio>Male
<INPUT NAME="gender" VALUE="female" TYPE=radio>Female
```

Let's see how this looks:

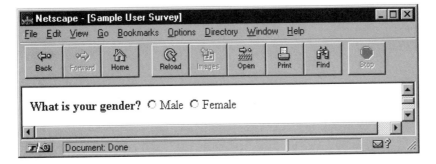

You can also set a default box by using the CHECKED attribute. However, you should be careful never to set more than one CHECKED radio box in the same name set. For example, if we add a CHECKED attribute to our document:

```
What is your gender?
<INPUT NAME="gender" VALUE="male" TYPE=radio>Male
<INPUT NAME="gender" VALUE="female" TYPE=radio CHECKED>Female
```

it will look like this:

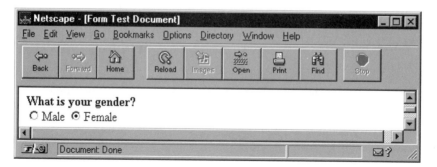

A reader can switch the value by checking one of the other boxes.

HIDDEN Type

No field is presented to the user (although a user looking at the source will be able to see that the field is there), but the contents of the field are returned in the submitted data. You might wonder what use there could be for an invisible field that does not allow user input. The primary use for this field is record keeping for programs that may parse user input from forms. For example, if you are using the same program to process input for a number of forms, you could use a hidden field to tell the program which type of form is being submitted:

```
<HIDDEN NAME="type" VALUE="websurvey">
```

TEXT Type

This enables single-line text entry fields; it is used in conjunction with the MAXLENGTH and SIZE attributes. As you may recall, MAXLENGTH allows you to specify the number of characters that may be entered in the field, and SIZE allows you to specify the size of the field on the form.

Be careful to set MAXLENGTH to a value equal to or greater than SIZE. Otherwise, readers will be presented with an entry box that cannot be filled out completely.

Let's take a look at an example. Here is our document:

```
<P><B>First Name:</B> <INPUT NAME="fname" TYPE=text
MAXLENGTH=30 SIZE=30></P>
<P><B>Last Name:</B> <INPUT NAME="lname" TYPE=text
MAXLENGTH=30 SIZE=30></P>
<P><B>E-mail Address:</B> <INPUT NAME="eaddr" TYPE=text
MAXLENGTH=50 SIZE=50></P>
```

In Netscape Navigator, this source looks like this:

If you need a multiline text entry, use TEXTAREA (see below).

PASSWORD Type

Password is the same as text, except the text is not displayed to the user. Like text, you can use the SIZE and MAXLENGTH attributes with this field.

```
<P><B>Enter a password to be used to retrieve survey
results:</B><BR>
<INPUT NAME="password" TYPE=password MAXLENGTH=50 SIZE=50></P>
```

This section in Netscape Navigator looks like this:

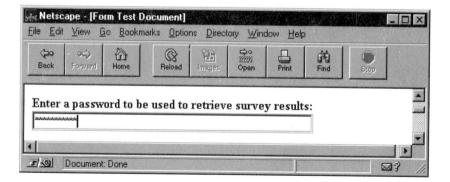

Do not allow the nonechoing characteristic of this field to lull you into a false sense of security. Although the reader (and anyone peeking over the reader's shoulder) will not be able to see whatever is typed in the field, the information is still exchanged with the server in a nonsecure fashion. You cannot rely on this field to provide real security.

SUBMIT and RESET Types

The SUBMIT button is used to submit the form's contents, as specified by the ACTION attribute. RESET resets the fields to their initial values. Both buttons may be used with the VALUE attribute to set the text that is displayed in the button. If you do not use the VALUE attribute, the buttons will be displayed with either SUBMIT or RESET. For example, we might end our survey with the following:

```
<P>Thank you for responding to this questionnaire.
<INPUT TYPE=SUBMIT>
<INPUT TYPE=RESET>
</FORM>
```

This looks like:

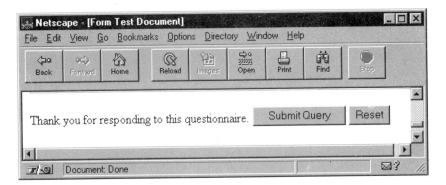

Now let's see how the addition of the VALUE attribute changes the buttons:

```
<P>Thank you for responding to this questionnaire.</P>
<P><INPUT TYPE=SUBMIT VALUE="Finished - Submit">
<INPUT TYPE=RESET VALUE="Restart - Clear All Fields"></P>
```

Here's how it looks now:

IMAGE Type

If you do not like the look of the plain button used with SUBMIT, you may use the IMAGE type along with an image as an alternative to SUBMIT. The image type defines an image field that can be clicked on by the user with a pointing device, causing the form to be immediately submitted. The coordinates of the selected point are measured in pixel units from the upper left corner of the image. These are returned (once the form is submitted) in two name/value pairs. The x-coordinate is submitted under the name of the field with an x value appended, while the y-coordinate is submitted under the value of the field with a y value appended.

Let's look at an example now. We have the image of a submit button that we prefer over the standard submit button. Our image is in the file SUBMIT.GIF, located in the GIF folder.

```
<P>Thank you for responding to this questionnaire.</P>
<TABLE BORDER=3><TR><TD><input NAME="submit" TYPE=IMAGE
SRC="GIF/SUBMIT.GIF" ALIGN=TOP></TABLE></P>
```

Here is how this looks:

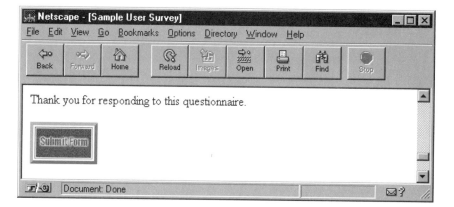

Notice that we took advantage of the beveled look of wide table borders to create a beveled button.

The standard way of submitting forms is with the SUBMIT button, described earlier. While the IMAGE type provides a method for using a fancy button, there is no corresponding method to reset your form. Resetting may be done only with the RESET type. Thus, if you need to have a RESET button, you should probably stick with the SUBMIT type.

Textarea: <TEXTAREA>

The TEXTAREA tag is a nested element within a form. It is used when we wish to let users define more than one line of text. The tag creates a multiline text input region, which can contain pre-specified text (which is set with the VALUE attribute). The end tag, </TEXTAREA>, is required, even if the form is initially blank. The TEXTAREA tag uses two arguments, ROWS and COLS, to specify the height and width of the text box.

The following example displays a scrollable box into which the user can type text. The box begins with the following text:

```
<P>Please enter any additional comments here:
<TEXTAREA NAME="comments" ROWS=2 COLS=60>
</TEXTAREA></P>
```

This source looks like this in Netscape Navigator:

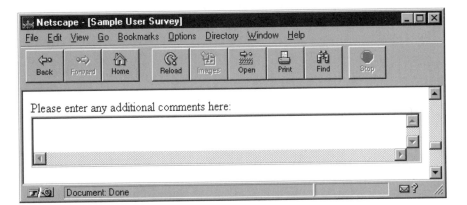

If you want to include default information, it should be placed within the <TEXTAREA> and </TEXTAREA> tags. Note that default information can be erased by the user. If default information is not erased, it will be returned as data by the form.

TEXTAREA Attribute: WRAP

If your readers are using Versions 2 and above of Netscape, an additional attribute, WRAP, is available with TEXTAREA. This attribute controls how word wrapping for text input should be handled. The default condition for TEXTAREA is for text to scroll until the person entering the data enters a carriage return. With WRAP, you can change this behavior. The following values may be used:

OFF

The default setting. No wrapping. Lines are sent exactly as typed.

VIRTUAL

The display word-wraps, but long lines are sent as one line without new lines.

PHYSICAL

The display word-wraps, and the text is transmitted at all wrap points.

Select: <SELECT> and Option: <OPTION>

The SELECT and OPTION tags are used to create enumerated lists of values. In other words, the SELECT element allows the user to choose one (or possibly more) items from a list. The items, which are specified with the OPTION element, are generally displayed in a compact manner as a pulldown list. SELECT may be used with three attributes:

MULTIPLE

This attribute allows the user to choose more than one option

NAME

This is the name of the field. This attribute should always be included.

SIZE

This attribute is used to specify the number of items that should be displayed. If no size is specified, typically only one option is displayed.

For example, in our survey we might have the following:

```
<P><B>Please select your occupation from the following
list</B>
<BR><SELECT NAME="occupation">
<OPTION>Unemployed
<OPTION>Student
<OPTION>Administrative
<OPTION>Professional
</SELECT><P>
```

In Netscape, the reader would see something like this:

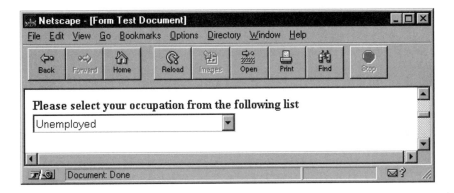

Note that some browsers will display the first choice in the box, while others leave the box empty until the reader makes a choice. When the reader clicks on the select box, the list of options will be displayed:

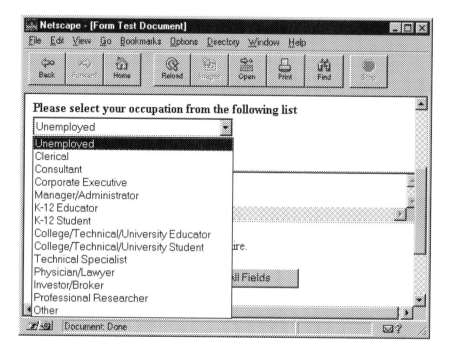

Size Attribute

The SIZE attribute allows you to tell the browser the number of options you wish to be displayed. For example, if we add the attribute SIZE=3 to our SELECT tag:

```
<SELECT NAME="occupation" SIZE=3>
```

It will be displayed like this:

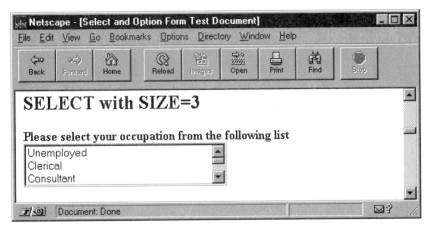

To illustrate the importance of checking your documents in as many browsers and platforms as possible we check this on a Macintosh:

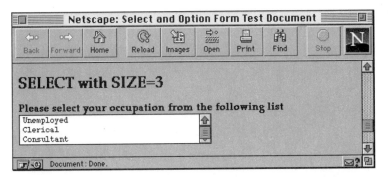

Notice that on the Macintosh SIZE=3 does not provide enough space for the scroll bar to be displayed properly. Should you decide to use the SIZE attribute, make sure that you choose a size large enough to accommodate the scroll bar.

Multiple Attribute

The MULTIPLE attribute allows readers to choose more than one option. We could modify our example to use the MULTI-PLE attribute:

```
<BR><SELECT NAME="occupation" MULTIPLE>
```

Now let's see how this changes the display for this field:

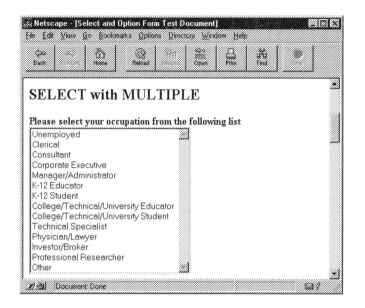

As you can see, all of the options are displayed. You can use the SIZE attribute to limit the number of options displayed at one time if your list is very long.

Option

The OPTION element can occur only within a SELECT element. It represents one choice in a list of alternatives. Once the user has selected an option from the list, it becomes the visible element in the pulldown list. Two attributes may be used with OPTION:

SELECTED

This attribute causes the option to be selected until the user chooses another option.

We strongly advise using the SELECTED attribute no more than once with each group of options. In our tests with different browsers we found that even if the MULTIPLE attribute was used with the SELECT tag, specifying

SELECTED with more than one option did not have the desired effect. For example, with Netscape, we found that all the options with SELECTED attributes would appear as being selected when the form was displayed, but the information returned by the browser when the form was submitted included only the last option with the SELECTED attribute.

VALUE

Specifies a value to be returned if the option is chosen. If no value is specified, the content of the OPTION element is returned. For example, we may want to place the results of our form directly into a database in which occupations are given a single-letter code. We can have the form return the appropriate code letter by using the VALUE attribute:

```
<P><B>Please select your occupation from the following
list</B>
<BR><SELECT NAME="occupation">
<OPTION VALUE="U">Unemployed
<OPTION VALUE="S">Student
<OPTION VALUE="A">Administrative
<OPTION VALUE="P">Professional
<OPTION VALUE="O">Other
</SELECT><P>
```

The Complete Form

Our complete survey example, with three questions and a text-entry box, can be found on the CD in form2.html.

HTTP File Upload: ENCTYPE

Netscape browsers Version 2 and above support a new attribute, ENCTYPE, that allows you to write forms that take files as input. An example of such a form would be:

```
<FORM ENCTYPE="multipart/form-data"
ACTION="http://ozone.com/cgi/form" METHOD=POST>
<P>Send this file: <INPUT NAME="inputfile" TYPE="file">
</FORM>
```

Meta Information: <META>

We introduced the META tag in Chapter 2 and promised to explain more about it later. It's time now. As we said before, the META tag is used to include "meta information" in your document. As you may recall, META is one of the few tags allowed in the head portion of the document. The head of a document has a special purpose—among other things it can contain information that can be downloaded without having to retrieve your entire document (there is a special HTTP method, HEAD to do this). While Web surfers may not care about retrieving the information from the head portion of a document, many of the programs that work behind the scenes make use of this capability to learn about a document without wasting the time to download the entire thing.

For example, it is possible to write a program to retrieve the TITLE information in a document without having to get the whole document. But what if you would like more than the TITLE of a document? Wouldn't it be great if a cataloging program could get index information about a document without having to retrieve it in its entirety? How about checking to see if the document has been updated recently? This is where META comes in. It is a versatile tag, although spotty support for it limits its usefulness. It is used for two purposes:

- specify additional HTTP headers for the page
- specify additional document header-related information.

META has three attributes:

HTTP-EQUIV

The Hypertext Transfer Protocol (HTTP) is used by Web servers to send HTML documents on the Internet. This attribute is used to specify one of the predefined HTTP response headers. Note that you can cause problems if you incorrectly override one of the default values such as Content-Type.

HTTP header names are not case sensitive. If not present, the NAME attribute is used to identify this meta-information and it should not be used within an HTTP response header. Examples: Refresh, Expires, Keywords, Reply-to, Content-Type

NAME

Meta-information name. Assumed equal to the value HTTP-EQUIV if not set explicitly. Examples: Author, Description, Copyright, and Keywords.

CONTENT

Used to set the information content to be associated with the given name and/or HTTP response header.

Here is an example of a set of META tags that could be used to set up cataloging information:

```
<META NAME="Author" CONTENT="Kayaker, Kelly">
<META NAME="Copyright" CONTENT="Kelly Kayaker,1996">
<META NAME="Keywords" CONTENT="Kayaking, Ozone, Paddles">
<META NAME="Resource-Type" CONTENT="Document">
```

You can find more information on using the META tag to provide cataloging information for search engines in the last chapter of this book.

As we said before, support for this tag is spotty—not all browsers and servers pay attention to it, so even if you take the time to add it to your documents, there is no way to guarantee that the information you include will be used.

Forcing Document Reload

As we mentioned before, the META tag is quite versatile. With some browsers it may be used to force a document to be reloaded from the server rather than read from cache. This is done by setting the HTTP "Expires" header line to the current (or a few minutes in the future) time and date. For example, if today were April 10, 1996, I would include:

```
<META HTTP-EQUIV="Expires" CONTENT="Wed, 10 Apr 1996
00:00:00 -0000">
```

Browsers that support this (Netscape Navigator is one such browser) will check the time and should not cache the page at all.

Another use for the META tag is described later in this chapter in the section on Client Pull.

HTML Tags: ISINDEX, ISMAP, USEMAP

Three additional HTML tags supporting user input are ISINDEX, ISMAP and USEMAP. ISMAP and USEMAP are attributes that can be used with the IMG tag to make images with "hot spots." They are described in the multimedia chapter.

ISINDEX: <ISINDEX>

The ISINDEX element in a document signals to the browser that the requested document also serves as an index document. This tag was created before the FORM tag, and you can frequently use FORM to accomplish the same thing as ISINDEX.

ISINDEX should be placed in the HEAD portion of a document. The presence of the ISINDEX tag indicates that the user can perform a keyword search. From a user's point of view, the browser displays a text-entry box in which the user may type search keywords. As with FORM, the use of the ISINDEX tag requires close interaction with the Web server and its administrator, since it will return information to a CGI program.

We have added the ISINDEX tag to a short HTML document to illustrate the way some browsers provide a search box. Here is our document:

```
<HTML>
<HEAD>
<TITLE>ISINDEX Test Document</TITLE>
<ISINDEX>
</HEAD>
<BODY>
<H1>ISINDEX Test Document</H1>
</BODY>
</HTML>
```

Different browsers may present the search box in different ways. Let's see how this looks in Netscape Navigator:

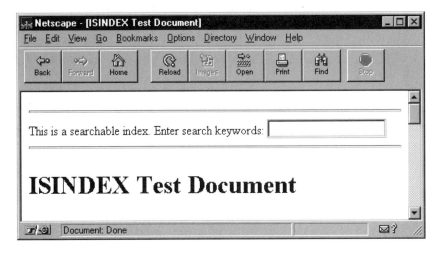

and in NCSA Mosaic:

Netscape places the input box in the main window and off-sets it with some horizontal rules. Contrast this with NCSA Mosaic, which creates a special section of the window for the input box.

PROMPT Attribute

PROMPT attribute to ISINDEX was originally introduced by Netscape and is now part of the HTML 3.2 specification. It allows you to change the default message (i.e., "This is a searchable index. Enter search keywords:").

```
<H1>PROMPT Attribute</H1>
<H2>ISINDEX</H2>
<P>Here is the default prompt:
<ISINDEX>
<P>Here it is with the PROMPT attribute:
<ISINDEX PROMPT="Enter the name of a river: ">
<HR>
```

Notice that we have violated the HTML standard in this example by placing the ISINDEX tag in the body of our document rather than in the head. Although most browsers can handle this, some do not. Thus, it is preferable to stick to the standard and place ISINDEX in the head section of your document.

In this example, we have set the prompt to "Enter the name of a river:"

PROMPT Attribute

Here is the default prompt:

This is a searchable index. Enter search keywords:

Here it is with the PROMPT attribute:

Enter the name of a river:

What happens in NCSA Mosaic? Remember that Mosaic sets up a special section of the window for the input box. How does it handle an ISINDEX tag in the middle of a document?

Here is the default prompt: Here it is with the PROMPT attribute:

Search Index:

As you can see, it does not display anything when it runs across the ISINDEX tags. This is fully in keeping with the HTML specification, although it looks bad. However, if we had created a document that adhered to the standard, we would not have this problem. Just one more reason to try to follow the specification!

ACTION Attribute

Netscape takes ISINDEX one step further by supporting an ACTION attribute. This attribute is similar to the ACTION attribute for forms—it is used to specify where the input should be sent. However, unlike ACTION and the FORM attribute, it is not part of the HTML specification and is not widely supported. If you want to specify the return location for your input, use the BASE tag. It is part of the specification and is supported by many browsers.

ISINDEX Data Flow

If everything has been set up correctly, the browser will capture the user input and send the query to the server. The browser does this by adding a question mark at the end of the document URL, followed by the list of desired keywords. These keywords are separated by the plus (+) sign.

Documents containing the ISINDEX tag are often generated dynamically by a CGI script on the server, so there is no confusion about searchability. Since the document is generated on the fly by the script, the user may access it only through the CGI script's URL. The data provided by the user is then returned to the script for processing. We realize that this can be confusing, so let's look at an example.

Suppose we encounter a searchable Web document on the server OZONE.COM that lists the addresses of kayak stores throughout the world. The document is generated by a CGI script named "findkayak". This particular CGI script has been written so that it returns a query form when it gets an empty request. Thus, when we access the document through the path:

```
http://ozone.com/cgi-bin/findkayak
```

it does not see a query, so it returns a form asking for search keywords. As a user, we can look for store locations within California by entering "California" in the keyword box. The query is sent by the browser to the server, as follows:

```
http://ozone.com/cgi-bin/findkayak?California
```

This passes the user input "California" back to the CGI program, which then processes the query and returns the matches from the database.

If you choose to add the ISINDEX tag to a document manually, you should be careful to add it only if the document is really set up for searches. Since it is unlikely that a static HTML document would be able to process a database query, you will probably need to use it in conjunction with the BASE tag. By setting a location with the BASE tag, the query can be directed to the correct search location. For example, rather than having our query document for the kayak stores be generated by the CGI script, we could create a static document named kayak-stores.html and include:

```
<ISINDEX>
<BASE HREF=http://ozone.com/cgi-bin/findkayak>
```

This will cause the user data to be sent to the findkayak CGI script rather than to the static kayak-stores.html document.

Please note that in order for any ISINDEX query to work, the document or script receiving the query must already be configured to perform keyword searches, and its Web server must already possess search-engine software.

ISINDEX vs. FORM

Much of the functionality offered by ISINDEX is also available through FORM. ISINDEX is good for short keyword searches, but since it uses only a single input field, it does not provide a way to add modifiers to the search as you can do with a form. Additionally, if you want to place your input box in a specific location in your document, forms provide this ability in a standard-conformant manner. Since forms offer more flexibility, you should review your requirements to make sure that ISINDEX rather than a FORM is the most appropriate way to submit your data.

CGI Scripts

The Common Gateway Interface, or CGI, is a standard developed to allow external computer programs to interface with information servers, such as Web servers (Figure 7–2).

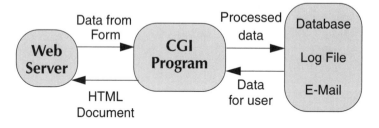

FIGURE 7–2 CGI Data Flow

Essentially, the standard allows a Web browser to execute a program on a Web server. This program then sends back information to the server, which returns it in a format readable by the browser. The implementation of CGI scripts requires close interaction with the Web server and its administrator.

Some things you might use a CGI program to do include:

- Process the information from an order form and return a confirmation along with the total cost of the order
- Provide an interface to a searchable database, and return the result of a search to the client in HTML
- Process input from a guestbook, including logging information to a database or file, and return a message to the client
- Provide the current hit count as part of a page each time someone accesses that page

CGI programs can be written in any programming or scripting language. In the Windows 95 environment some of the most popular options are Perl, Visual Basic and C. The examples provided in this chapter and on the CD are written in Perl.

CGI programs are executed on a server through the use of URLs. The URL in the ACTION attribute points to the desired Web server and the executable program. For example, the URL

```
http://ozone.com/cgi-bin/guestbook.cgi
```

requests that the CGI program named "guestbook.cgi" in the folder named "cgi-bin" be run. The METHOD attribute specifies the method for sending the user's input to the program that will be run. Thus, a form tag using this URL along with the POST method would be:

```
<FORM METHOD=post
ACTION="http://ozone.com/cgi-bin/guestbook.cgi">
```

Upon receiving the form's output, the server hands off control to the executable program. This program is run with the user's input. The server then returns the output from the program to the browser, usually as another Web document.

If you choose to keep your documents on a commercial Web provider's system, odds are high that the provider will have some CGI programs available for your use. It is also likely that your provider will not allow you to load your own CGI programs on the server. This is because there are many security problems inherent in the use of CGI programs, and it is difficult for a provider to be sure that a foreign CGI program meets strict security standards. Given these limitations, we will now show you the rudiments of creating CGI programs. You should have some programming background if you wish to use the information in the following sections about CGI.

Redirect Script

This script is about as simple as they come. It does one thing—redirects the browser to another document:

```
#!h:\win95cd\perl\per15\bin\perl.exe
#
print "Location: http://ozone.com/index.html\n\n";
```

Anyone accessing this script will automatically be redirected to the new URL, http://ozone.com/index.html. Although this script is about as simple as you can get, it can also be quite useful for automatically shifting readers to another location if you move your site, or in combination with a search it may be used to send the reader to a specific document.

Notice the "\n\n" at the end of the last line in the script. This creates an empty line after our Location command. The empty line is important, because it lets the server know that you are done sending the first set of commands. Of course in this case that's all we send. In most CGI scripts, you will probably create an HTML document. If you forget the blank line before you start sending the document, you may not get any errors, but your script may not do anything.

Time Stamp CGI Script

Let's look at a simple Perl script that demonstrates how you can embed the current date and time in a document. You can find a copy of the script in time.pl, which is located in the CGI Scripts folder.

```
#!h:\win95cd\perl\perl5\bin\perl.exe
#
# Print the current time on the server.
print "HTTP/1.0 200 OK\n";
print "Content-type: text/html\n\n";
print "<HTML><HEAD><TITLE>Time and Date</TITLE></HEAD>\n";
print "<BODY><H1>Time and Date</H1>\n";
($sec, $min, $hour, $day, $mon, $year, $wday, $yday) =
localtime(time);
$mon++;
print "<P>Date and time: <strong>";
print "$mon/$day/$year $hour:$min</strong>\n";
print "<P>Click your reset button to update the time.";
print "</BODY></HTML>";
```

Move the script onto a computer with the Perl interpreter that is running a Web server. Load the document by using the following URL:

```
http://your.site/cgi-bin/time.pl
```

and you will see a document with the current date and time. For example:

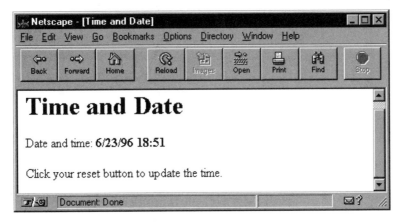

If you keep hitting the "Reload" button, you will see the contents correspondingly updated. This kind of approach can be used to create documents on-the-fly.

Environment Variables

CGI programs use *environment variables* to exchange information with a Web server. The CGI specification states that the following variables should be set for all requests:

SERVER_SOFTWARE

The name and version of the information server software answering the request (and running the gateway).

Format: name/version

Example: Netscape-Communications/1.12

SERVER_NAME

The server's hostname, DNS alias, or IP address as it would appear in self-referencing URLs.

Example: ozone.com

GATEWAY_INTERFACE

The revision of the CGI specification to which the server complies.

Format: CGI/revision number

Example: CGI/1.1

The following environment variables depend on the request being fulfilled by the gateway program:

CONTENT_LENGTH

The length of the content as given by the client. Used with data sent by a POST command to determine how many characters are in the input stream.

CONTENT_TYPE

For queries which have attached information, such as HTTP POST and PUT, this is the content type of the data.

Example: application/www-form-urlencoded

PATH_INFO

The extra path information, as given by the client. In other words, scripts can be accessed by their virtual pathname, followed by extra information at the end of this path. The extra information is sent as PATH_INFO. This information should be decoded by the server if it comes from a URL before it is passed to the CGI script.

Example: /index.html

PATH_TRANSLATED

The server provides a translated version of PATH_INFO, which takes the path and does any virtual-to-physical mapping to it.

Example: /webdocuments/index.html

QUERY_STRING

The information that follows the "?" in the URL that referenced this script. Additionally, information from ISINDEX, ISMAP, and forms with the GET method can be found here.

REQUEST_METHOD

The method with which the request was made.

Examples: GET, HEAD, POST

SERVER_PROTOCOL

The name and revision of the information protocol this request came in with.

Format: protocol/revision number

Example: HTTP/1.0

SERVER_PORT

The port number to which the request was sent.

Example: 80

SCRIPT_NAME

A virtual path to the script being executed, used for self-referencing URLs.

Example: /cgi-bin/guestbook.pl

REMOTE_HOST

The hostname making the request.

Example: ozone.com

REMOTE_ADDR

The IP address of the remote host making the request.

Example: 10.0.0.51

AUTH_TYPE

Authentication method used to validate the user. Only applicable if the server supports user authentication, and the script is protected.

REMOTE_USER

The name of the authenticated user. Only applicable if the server supports user authentication, and the script is protected.

REMOTE_IDENT

If the HTTP server supports RFC 931 identification protocol, this variable will be set to the remote user name retrieved from the server.

If any header lines are received from the client they are placed into environment variables with the prefix "HTTP_" followed by the header name. Any "-" (dash) characters in the header name are changed to "_" (underscore) characters. Note that the server may exclude any or all of these headers if including them would exceed system environment limits. Possible variables include:

HTTP_ACCEPT

The MIME types that the client will accept. Each item in this list should be separated by commas.

Format: type/subtype, type/subtype

Example: text/html,image/gif,image/jpeg

HTTP_USER_AGENT

The browser the client is using to send the request. If you wish to provide custom pages for specific browsers, this is the variable to check. You can find a listing of the strings returned by many browsers at the Browsercap site. The URL for this site is listed in Appendix C.

Format: software/version library/version.

Example: Mozilla/3.0b3 (Win95, I)

Environment Variable Script

Let's look at a simple CGI script that prints the predefined environment variables. We write our script in Perl. Perl is an interpreted language and is one of the most popular languages for CGI scripting. While it is primarily used on UNIX, it is also available for many other platforms as well. We've included a copy of Perl and this script on the CD, so that you can try this example yourself. Here it is:

```
#!h:\win95cd\perl\perl5\bin\perl.exe
#
#Simple script to print out the environment variables
print "Content-type: text/html\n\n";
print "<HTML><HEAD><TITLE>Environment Variables</TITLE></HEAD>\n";
print "<BODY><H1>Environment Variables</H1>\n";
print "SERVER_SOFTWARE: $ENV{'SERVER_SOFTWARE'}<BR>\n";
print "SERVER_NAME: $ENV{'SERVER_NAME'}<BR>\n";
print "GATEWAY_INTERFACE: $ENV{'GATEWAY_INTERFACE'}<BR>\n";
print "SERVER_PROTOCOL: $ENV{'SERVER_PROTOCOL'}<BR>\n";
print "SERVER_PORT: $ENV{'SERVER_PORT'}<BR>\n";
print "REQUEST_METHOD: $ENV{'REQUEST_METHOD'}<BR>\n";
print "PATH_INFO: $ENV{'PATH_INFO'}<BR>\n";
print "PATH_TRANSLATED: $ENV{'PATH_TRANSLATED'}<BR>\n";
print "SCRIPT_NAME: $ENV{'SCRIPT_NAME'} <BR>\n";
print "QUERY_STRING: $ENV{'QUERY_STRING'} <BR>\n";
print "REMOTE_HOST: $ENV{'REMOTE_HOST'} <BR>\n";
print "REMOTE_ADDR: $ENV{'REMOTE_ADDR'}<BR>\n";
print "AUTH_TYPE: $ENV{'AUTH_TYPE'}<BR>\n";
print "REMOTE_USER: $ENV{'REMOTE_USER'}<BR>\n";
print "REMOTE_IDENT: $ENV{'REMOTE_IDENT'}<BR>\n";
print "CONTENT_TYPE: $ENV{'CONTENT_TYPE'}<BR>\n";
print "CONTENT_LENGTH: $ENV{'CONTENT_LENGTH'} <BR>\n";
print "HTTP_ACCEPT: $ENV{'HTTP_ACCEPT'}<BR>\n";
print "HTTP_USER_AGENT: $ENV{'HTTP_USER_AGENT'}<BR>\n";
read(STDIN, $buffer, $ENV{'CONTENT_LENGTH'});
print "Form input: $buffer\n";
print "</BODY></HTML>";
```

Notice that the first thing our script prints is "Content-type: text/html." This is the MIME type for the document and is the first thing a CGI program normally returns to the server. Next, we print the typical opening for an HTML document—the HTML, HEAD and TITLE tags. In the body of our script we simply echo each environment variable.

Here is an example of what this script returns when we run it on the server included on the CD:

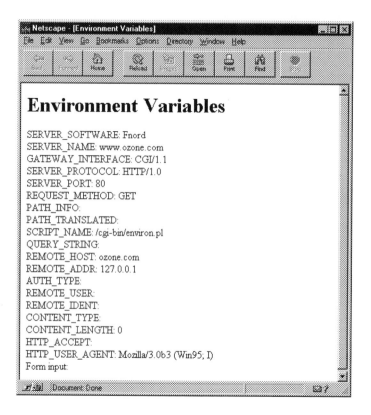

Notice that many of the variables do not have a value. Since we loaded our script directly, it did not get any input. As you can see, all the variables associated with input are empty. Now let's see how those variables get filled in. First we need to look at the different ways that forms may return data to our CGI program.

POST vs. GET

As previously mentioned, two methods can be used to send data from a form. These methods are POST and GET. The way in which the server receives the encoded results of the form depends on which method is specified in the form. With GET, the data are appended to the URL, much like the data sent through the ISINDEX tag. With POST, the program receives the user's data from standard input.

If you are confused about which method to pick, you can follow this guideline

- if your input is short, GET is probably easier
- if you don't know how much input you will receive, use post

Why? The maximum length of a URL is limited by the browser and the server. If you use GET, you run the risk of losing part of the data if the information returned by your form exceeds the length that the browser and server can handle. With the POST method there is no length limitation, since user data come from standard input. The drawback (although small) to using POST is that you will need to determine the length of the input using the CONTENT_LENGTH environment variable.

We therefore recommend using the POST method if the number of user input parameters is large, or if there is a <TEXTAREA> in your form. With the POST method you do not run the risk of the URL length exceeding what the browser or server can handle. Of course, you can always write your script such that it handles both methods.

POST Method: METHOD="POST"

If you use the POST method, your CGI script or program receives the encoded form input in its standard input stream. The server will not send an end-of-file (EOF) at the end of the data input. Therefore, you must use the CONTENT_LENGTH environment variable, which specifies how much data should be read from standard input, to determine how much data is in the input stream. If you haven't already gotten our message, this is the method we recommend.

GET Method: METHOD="GET"

If you use the GET method, your CGI program receives the encoded form input in the QUERY_STRING variable, which follows the "?" in the URL that calls the script.

Recall that in the above ISINDEX example the query from the browser was sent to the server as:

```
http://ozone.com/cgi-bin/findkayak?California
```

If we use the GET method in this example, "California" will be placed in QUERY_STRING.

Form Data Format

We have now told you where to find the output data from a form. Next, you need to decode this data. Recall that each form item should have a NAME tag. When the user enters information in that particular form item, this information is encoded in the form data. The name of the information is simply the NAME of the item tag, while the value is the information entered by the user.

Form data is then returned to the user as name/value pairs. Each pair is separated by the ampersand (&) character, while each pair of name and value is separated by the equal (=) character. For example, let's look at a form with two input fields, one with the name "kayaktype" and a value of "sea kayak", and one with the name "paddletype" and a value of "dihedral". The returned data would look like:

```
kayaktype=sea+kayak&paddletype=dihedral
```

Notice that the space character becomes the plus character. This is because these data are also URL encoded (see Chapter 3 for more information on URLs).

Let's look at a specific example now. We'll use an abbreviated version of the form that we developed in the previous section. Here is the completed form with answers checked off.

```
Netscape - [Form Test Document]                    _ □ ✕
File  Edit  View  Go  Bookmarks  Options  Directory  Window  Help

 ⇦o      o⇨       ⌂         ⟳         🖼        ⇨o      🖨       🔍       ⬣
Back   Forward   Home     Reload    Images     Open    Print    Find     Stop
```

User Survey

What is your gender?
○ Male ⦿ Female

Why do you browse the Web?
☑ Fun ☐ Work ☐ Research ☐ Education

Please select your occupation from the following list

College/Technical/University Educator ▾

Please enter any additional comments here:

Please send a copy of the results to me.

Thank you for responding to this questionnaire.

    Submit Survey   Restart - Clear All Fields

```
Document: Done
```

The output from these answers looks like this:

```
gender=female&browse=fun&occupation=College%2FTechnical%2FUniv
ersity+Educator&comments=Please+send+a+copy+of+the+results+to+
me.
```

Each pair of values is separated by the "&" character. The first item in a pair is the NAME, as specified in the form, and the second is the VALUE, as selected by the user. The name/value pairs are separated by equal (=) signs, and spaces in the input fields are replaced with plus (+) signs. Reserved characters such as "<", ">", "+", "=", ";" and "&" will be translated to their corresponding URL encoding. For example, "=" would be returned as "%3D".

The basic process in a CGI script that processes posted form data is:

- Split up the elements separated by ampersands (&).
- Split up the individual elements on the equal sign, so that you have name/value pairs.
- Translate special characters such as "+" for a space, and URL-encodings, %nn to the appropriate character.
- Decide how to respond to the user.

Now we know what the output looks like, but where did we find it? Let's go back to our environment variable printing script again. Almost at the end of the script you should see:

```
read(STDIN, $buffer, $ENV{'CONTENT_LENGTH'});
```

This line takes the input from a form that has been submitted through a POST action and stores it in a variable named "$buffer." It does this by reading characters from the input stream (in Perl it is called STDIN). It knows how many characters to read by referencing the environment variable CONTENT_LENGTH.

Serving Documents Based on Browser Type

We've discussed the importance of knowing the capabilities of your reader's browsers. However, creating documents for the lowest common denominator can be frustrating if you want your documents to have the visual appeal offered by newer and vendor-specific HTML tags. If you're willing to maintain multiple sets of documents, you can use a CGI script to automatically direct your readers to the appropriate document. You do this by checking the HTTP_USER_AGENT variable with your CGI script, and then serving the appropriate document based on its value. Let's look at a simple script that directs Navigator users to one set of documents and everyone else to another. We take advantage of the fact that all versions of Netscape browsers send "Mozilla" as part of the HTTP_USER_AGENT variable.

```
#!h:\win95cd\perl\perl5\bin\perl.exe
#
#Simple script to print out the environment variables
print "Content-type: text/html\n\n";
if ($ENV{'HTTP_USER_AGENT' =~/Mozilla/$ENV{'HTTP_USER_AGENT'){
    print "Content-type: text/html\n\n";
    (output netscape document)
}
else {
    print "Content-type: text/html\n\n";
    (output plain document)
}
```

Of course, before this will work, the reader must access your documents through the CGI program rather than directly. For example, if our script is named "docdirect.pl", the URL for the document might be:

```
http://ozone.com/cgi-bin/docdirect.pl?kayak.html
```

Security

CGI scripts are one of the most vulnerable aspects of the Web. These scripts are susceptible to tampering by malicious users, and transmitted data can be snooped on. We urge you to consult with Web administrators during implementation, because Web security is an area of active development.

Sources for CGI Programs and Scripts

As we said before, odds are high that you won't be able to use your own CGI scripts if you are storing your documents on a Web service provider's system. Since many service providers have their own custom CGI scripts that allow you to access the functionality offered by a CGI without having to do the coding yourself, you may find this a preferable route over a write-your-own script. However, if you're running your own server or you have a service provider who is willing to allow you to run your own scripts, you may still wish to bypass the time and effort required to write your own scripts. Fortunately, there are many sources for prewritten scripts. Some of them are even free. An especially popular freeware repository is Matt's Script Archive at http://worldwidemart.com/scripts/.

You will also find listings for many commercial scripts that provide services like shopping carts and database interfaces by looking in any popular Web search engine.

Creating Dynamic and Animated Documents

The Web was originally conceived as a document distribution system. As you might imagine, this was soon not enough. People want to be able to send documents that contain customized information, or change dynamically. They want to be able to send animations. Lately, they even want to send programs that are executed on the browser's computer! In the fast-changing world of the World Wide Web, it is impossible to predict what tomorrow will bring. But we can give you a taste of some of the exciting dynamic capabilities, including Server Push and Client Pull, Server-Side Include, Sun's Java, Netscape's JavaScript, and VRML.

Server Push

Netscape defined a couple of methods to repeatedly send new data from a Web server to a browser. These methods are only guaranteed to work with Netscape's server and client, although we have found support for them in other browsers such as Microsoft's Internet Explorer.

The first method, server push, keeps open the connection between a server and a browser so that the server can keep sending new data to the browser. Server push is not supported by fnord, so if you want to implement server push, you will need to purchase a full-featured Web server or buy space from a service provider that supports server push. Server push provides a more seamless way to do animation than client pull, since it allows only a small portion of a window to be redrawn.

However, since Server push requires a network connection to remain open, it is a fairly resource-intensive way to accomplish animation. It is preferable to provide animation with Java or a similar facility.

Client Pull

In the second method, client pull, the client requests new data from the server after a prespecified interval. This works by including a directive in the document that tells the browser to wait a specified number of seconds, and then to reload the document or fetch a new one.

You do this by placing a <META> tag with the appropriate settings in the HEAD portion of your document, as in the following example:

```
<META HTTP-EQUIV=Refresh CONTENT=1>
```

This HTTP header tells the browser to "Refresh" after 1 second. You could place one of these directives in a CGI program that generates a dynamic document to have the document automatically refresh itself. For example, we could modify our time.pl script as follows:

```
#!h:\win95cd\perl\perl5\bin\perl.exe
#
# Print the current time on the server.
print "HTTP/1.0 200 OK\n";
print "Content-type: text/html\n\n";
print "<HTML><HEAD><TITLE>Time and Date</TITLE>";
print "<META HTTP-EQUIV=Refresh CONTENT=5>";
print "</HEAD>\n";
print "<BODY><H1>Time and Date</H1>\n";
($sec, $min, $hour, $day, $mon, $year, $wday, $yday) =
localtime(time);
$mon++;
print "<P>Date and time: <strong>";
```

```
print "$mon/$day/$year $hour:$min</strong>\n";
print "</BODY></HTML>";
```

Notice that the META tag is placed in the head portion of the document. The addition of this directive would cause the script to be retrieved every five seconds and thus create a continually updated clock.

You can also use the CONTENT attribute to direct the browser to load another document rather than the current one. If we wanted the browser to refresh after 1 second with a new document called newdoc.html, we would use the following tag:

```
<META HTTP-EQUIV=Refresh
CONTENT="1;URL=http://your.site/newdoc.html">
```

This is a useful feature if you move your site and would like to leave a notice behind about your new location, and then automatically have readers transferred to the new location.

If you plan to use client pull in your documents, you should keep the following guidelines in mind:

- The URL in the CONTENT field must be fully qualified, containing the name of the server site and the name of the document.

- The <META> tag must be contained within the <HEAD> portion of your document.

- The Refresh directive is one time only. If you want the document to be repeatedly refreshed, you must embed the appropriate <META> tag within each newly loaded document.

Client pull is a useful feature for displaying documents with changing content. For example, a stock trader may wish to view a document containing updated stock prices every five minutes. Client pull can even be used to implement a "low-tech" animation. Each frame of the animation contains a refresh directive and a URL pointing to the next frame in the animation. Of course, given network delays, this won't be a movie-quality production!

Server-Side Include

Server Side Includes provide a method for substituting information on the fly in a document, and were originally supported by the NCSA server. They are useful for including information that may be shared among many documents, such as a copyright notice. Server-side include statements are placed in comments, so that documents that include them will not show the commands when being served by a server that does not have support for them.

A typical server-side include statement looks something like this:

```
<--#command argument(s) -->
```

For example, the command to include a file named "mycopyright.html" would be:

```
<#include file="mycopyright.html">
```

However, before you become too eager to make use of this capability, we have to tell you that it is completely dependent on the Web server in use. Some servers do not have any built-in support for this capability, while other server administrators may not choose to turn it on. Server-side includes vastly increase the load on the server, because they require the server to read every document and check for include commands. Some servers try to reduce the load by only supporting server-side statements in documents with special extensions such as "shtml".

Additionally, it is important to remember, if you do include files in your documents through server-side includes, that the files not contain complete HTML documents, since they will be embedded within another document. If you use a full document, you will end up with duplicate TITLE tags and other tags that may cause problems.

Because server-side includes are so dependent on the server, you should refer to the documentation provided with your server or by your server provider for a full description of these commands.

Java and APPLET

Java is an object-oriented programming language developed by Sun Microsystems specifically to allow programs to be incorporated into Web documents. These programs, called applets, are then run locally on the browser's computer. The applets can be stand-alone applications or they can be embedded within HTML documents using the APPLET tag:

```
<APPLET CODE="myapplet.class" WIDTH=X HEIGHT=Y>
```

Also developed by Sun Microsystems, HotJava is a Web browser that knows how to run these applets. At the time this book was written the HotJava browser was freely available for various kinds of UNIX platforms and Windows 95 and NT. A port to Macintosh system 7.5 was due soon. In addition, Netscape has added support for Java applets in new versions of Netscape Navigator (Version 2.0 and later). Other browser manufacturers such as Microsoft have announced plans to support it as well.

An overview of the Java language is beyond the scope of this book. However, you can find additional information about Java, a free Java Developer's Kit, and demonstration applets at http://java.sun.com.

The ability to send running programs within Web documents, adding untold spice and life, clearly adds enormous potential to the kinds of documents that will become available. Only time will tell to what extent this approach will catch on.

JavaScript

JavaScript is an interpreted language developed by Netscape. An early version of this language was called LiveScript, and you may still occasionally see references to it under the old name. We have already described a few simple JavaScript functions that can be incorporated in your documents even if you don't want to learn the whole language. For those of you who would like a more thorough explanation on the use of JavaScript, we provide a JavaScript tutorial and some example scripts in the next chapters.

VRML: Virtual Reality Markup Language

The Virtual Reality Modeling Language is a developing standard for delivering interactive three-dimensional scenes with Web hyperlink. Like the Web, these can be delivered across the Internet, making it a kind of HTML for Virtual Reality. Plug-ins are available to add VRML capabilities to existing browsers, such as Navigator. It is widely expected that the next generation of Web browsers will understand and interpret VRML.

With VRML, 3-D interactive scenes can be displayed. As with Virtual Reality, users can explore and interact with these scenes in order to gain a sense of a new environment. More information and demonstrations are available at:

```
http://www.sdsc.edu/vrml
```

Macromedia's Shockwave

Macromedia has created a plug-in for browsers that allows Director movies to be played on the Web. This plug-in is part of the Shockwave extensions for Director. If your readers will be using browsers that have been configured with the Shockwave plug-in, adding multimedia elements with Shockwave is a great way to add snap to your pages. Since Director movies can include both animation and sound, it is a much cleaner method for incorporating these elements into a document than some of the more traditional methods that require browsers to launch an external application.

However, the drawback is that before a reader can see your creation, the reader must have downloaded the Shockwave plug-in and installed it in their browser. Since it does take an extra step (and a machine with a fair amount of memory), it may be awhile before the average Internet user has a browser with the Shockwave plug-in. Of course, if you decide to go this route and are worried about losing readers, you can encourage people to install Shockwave by adding a link to the Macromedia plug-in page.

You can find more information about Shockwave at:

```
http://www.macromedia.com
```

The Good, the Bad and the Ugly

Test your forms with as many browsers as possible. Some form tags are not supported as universally as others, and if you use default values (such as CHECKED or SELECTED) you may find that different browsers will return different data if users leave the defaults alone. For example, when using SELECT in a form, be sure that you do not specify more than one option with the SELECTED attribute. If you try to specify more than one, you will probably find that some browsers will only return one anyway.

- Do not place an ISINDEX tag in a document unless you are certain that it has been correctly set up for searches.
- Never set the CHECKED attribute for more than one item in a set of radio boxes.
- Make sure that you set a value for every radio box.
- Don't forget to include name and value attributes for your input tags. If you don't, how will you decode the user's data?

- Remember to include a submit button in your forms even if you only have one input field in your form. Some browsers such as Netscape automatically submit the form if there is only one field, so you may be tempted to leave the submit button out. If you do this, readers using browsers like Lynx will not be able to use your form.
- When using client pull, keep in mind the additional network overhead that will result.

IN THIS CHAPTER YOU WILL

- LEARN ABOUT THE DIFFERENCE BETWEEN JAVA AND JAVASCRIPT
- LEARN BASIC JAVASCRIPT CONSTRUCTS
- FIND TABLES DESCRIBING JAVASCRIPT OBJECTS, PROPERTIES, METHODS, STATEMENTS, AND EVENT HANDLERS

INTRODUCING JAVASCRIPT

What's In This Chapter

In this chapter we introduce Netscape's JavaScript language. We explain the differences between JavaScript and Java and introduce you to the language.

Using This Chapter

A complete JavaScript tutorial would fill an entire book—and it would be a book for programmers. Since we had to have some space for HTML, and since this book is for designers as well as programmers, our goal here is to provide information that will be of use to programmers and people without any programming experience.

The first part of this chapter presents basic concepts and language structure. The second half of this chapter summarizes the most commonly used JavaScript objects. If you are a programmer, we recommend going through the entire chapter and then reviewing the sample JavaScript scripts in the next chapter. If you are not a programmer, but would like to incorporate the features offered by one of these scripts, you should first read the section introducing JavaScript and then go directly to the section in the next chapter describing the script you wish to use.

Introduction

As mentioned in the previous chapter, the age of static HTML documents has passed. Now, we want our documents to contain running animations. We want them to contain live, interactive content. In short, we want our documents to contain real applications.

Traditionally, applications are written in programming languages such as C or C++, then compiled to run on specific platforms, such as the Macintosh or Windows. This means that you need to compile an application for every target platform. And as applications become more full-featured, they take up increasing amounts of disk space. In an environment requiring high-performance, networked computing on multiple platforms—like the Internet—the traditional approach simply won't work. There is too much overhead in creating applications for multiple platforms, and users don't have the patience to wait for large applications to download.

Enter Java and JavaScript. While the Java programming language, designed by researchers at Sun, was not intended for the Internet, it proved to be a natural fit. JavaScript, a scripting language developed by Netscape, came along later to make the power of Java accessible to nonprogrammers.

To better understand JavaScript, we must first describe Java. Unlike other programming languages, Java is both *compiled* and *interpreted*. This means that the programmer's Java source code is first compiled into what is known as Java Bytecode. This Bytecode isn't native machine code, but is closer to machine code and is platform independent. Then, when the client downloads the Bytecode, it is efficiently translated by the Java Interpreter into native code for the particular machine. This means that each client, no matter what its platform is, only needs the Java Interpreter to run the Java application. Similarly, a programmer can write a Java application for the Internet, called an applet, which can be embedded in HTML documents. When downloaded by the client browser, the applet is interpreted by a Java-aware browser, such as Netscape 2.0 or HotJava, and run on the client.

JavaScript is a scripting language based on Java. While Java is like C++, JavaScript is more like Perl, AppleScript, or Hyper-Talk (the scripting language behind Hypercard).

JavaScript scripts are directly embedded as text in HTML documents, using the <SCRIPT> tag. When a JavaScript-aware browser, like Netscape 2.0, encounters the tag, it interprets the script that follows. *Interprets* means that the computer translates the script as it is run. Thus, programs written in JavaScript are distributed without first being translated into native code.

In addition, Netscape Web servers now support server-side JavaScript. These scripts are also embedded in HTML documents but are first interpreted by the server when the document is requested. The results of interpreting and running the script are then sent to the client. This chapter does not describe server-side JavaScript, since currently only Netscape Web servers support server-side JavaScript.

Programming for the Web

What does programming for the Web mean? For most of the examples in this book, any necessary processing is done by the server. For example, if you wished to check the input sent from a form, you would use a CGI application that would perform the check *on the server* and return the results to the browser.

This results in a slow and cumbersome interaction. With Java and JavaScript, you can create programs that will take care of some of these actions on the browser's machine, without going out on the network.

Java vs. JavaScript

Since Java and JavaScript are both intended for the creation of dynamic and interactive documents for the Web, how does one decide which of these languages to use? Let's look at some strengths and weaknesses of each language.

It is much easier to start working in JavaScript than in Java. From a programming standpoint, JavaScript is a much simpler language than Java. It is a scripting language that you insert directly into HTML documents. To write JavaScript, all you need is a browser that supports JavaScript (Navigator Version 2.0 and above and Internet Explorer Version 3 and above are two such browsers), and a text editor. Essentially, the tools that you use to author plain HTML documents should also work for authoring documents that contain JavaScript.

Also, future versions of JavaScript will enable you to control the appearance and behavior of Java applets and Netscape plug-ins. In essence, your scripts can act as the glue for applets and plug-ins.

Unfortunately there are also problems with JavaScript. Among them:

- Limited browser support reduces the number of readers that can use the features you offer with JavaScript.

- It is not always easy to integrate a non-JavaScript alternative in your documents for readers who view the document with browsers that are not JavaScript aware.

- Some browsers that are not JavaScript aware do not always recognize the JavaScript portion of the document as being a script that should not be displayed. As a result they may display the script as part of the document (we will show examples of this problem later in this chapter).

With Java on the other hand, you can create multiplatform stand-alone applications, or applets for the Web. These applets can be more cleanly integrated with regular HTML documents. Since only the Java Bytecode is distributed, Java applets may be incorporated in HTML documents through the use of a few specific tags. Although browsers that are not Java aware will not understand these tags, they will not display the tag or its contents. As a full-fledged, object-oriented language, Java also provides much more functionality and much faster performance than JavaScript.

On the down side, if you lack experience with languages such as C++, learning Java requires commitment. In addition, you will need a development environment so that you can compile your Java applications or applets before distributing them. Although Sun's Java Developer's Kit (JDK) is free, you may prefer to purchase a third-party development environment that provides more features than Sun's JDK.

In the final analysis, JavaScript has an important niche in Web documents. For example, JavaScript can:

- Perform data validation. It can, on the client, quickly check the validity and integrity of form data entered by the user.
- Create special features such as scrolling messages on the status bar.
- Perform the functionality of a simple database by sending data to the client and searching the data in response to user queries.

For advanced development issues, it will probably be necessary to use Java rather than JavaScript.

Some Concepts

Before presenting our examples, we define some important concepts in JavaScript:

- **Objects** are tangible elements in the browser environment. Examples of objects include windows, frames, documents, and forms. Objects in JavaScript follow a hierarchy that is based on the structure of the HTML page. The topmost object is the window. Subobjects in the window are the location (the current URL), the history list, and the current document. The document object has many subobjects, including the document's forms and links. Finally, the form has its many subobjects, including text fields, text areas, and checkbox, radio, password, submit, and reset buttons.
- **Properties** describe the attributes of objects, such as the background color of a document.
- **Methods** are functions (or procedures) associated with objects, such as writing some text to a document or frame, or opening and closing a window.
- **Event handlers** signal user events that occur on the client. Important events include loading a document, clicking the mouse button, or submitting a form.

We describe the more commonly used objects, properties, methods, and handlers in this chapter.

Starting Your Script: <SCRIPT>

JavaScript scripts are delineated from the rest of your document through the <SCRIPT></SCRIPT> tags. You should also use the optional LANGUAGE="JavaScript" attribute to specify the language used in the script. At present the JavaScript-aware browsers will correctly choose JavaScript as the language to interpret, since it is the only scripting language supported. However, it is likely that other scripting languages will be supported in the future, making it important to let the interpreter know which language is being used.

Scripts consist of a series of statements that optionally are terminated with a semicolon. If you wish to put more than one statement on a line, you must separate them with a semicolon. Your script should be placed in the HEAD portion of your document to insure that it is completely loaded into memory before anything tries to use it. Let's look at a simple script that simply prints out a few lines. Here it is:

```
<HTML>
<HEAD>
<TITLE>JavaScript Demo Document</TITLE>
<SCRIPT LANGUAGE="JavaScript">
// My simple JavaScript script
{
document.write("<TITLE>A New Title</TITLE>")
document.write("<H1>Simple JavaScript Document</H1>")
document.write("<P>This is a simple JavaScript")
document.write("demonstration.</P>")
}
</SCRIPT>
</HEAD>
<BODY>
</BODY>
</HTML>
```

Notice that our entire script is in the head portion of the document. Now look in the body portion of the document. As you can see, it is empty. Yet, when we load the document into Netscape Navigator, here is what is displayed:

What happened? Our script is interpreted when the document is loaded, and the document.write commands in the script cause their arguments (which are lines of HTML) to be displayed in our document. As used here, the *document* object refers to the currently loaded document, and the *write* method specifies that the argument should be displayed in the document.

There are a few important points to consider here. Although we included a TITLE tag in our document, the title that is displayed is the one that our script produced. If you try loading this script yourself (you can find it in simple-script.html on the CD), you will find that the original title flashes on the title bar but is quickly replaced by title printed by the script. Had we included some lines of text in the body of the document, they too would have been replaced. In practice, our script has created a new HTML document and loaded it over the one that was there. However, although it appears to be a plain HTML document, there is a significant difference. This brings us to our second point.

If you were to try to print this document from the browser, it is likely you would get a blank piece of paper. This is because output that is generated by JavaScript cannot be printed by the current version of Netscape (Version 2.01). This behavior may change in future versions of Navigator or may not be a problem in other JavaScript-aware browsers. Nevertheless, you should not count on readers being able to print out a copy of a document generated by HTML. For example, don't generate a confirmation message from a form, and tell your readers to print it out and mail it in.

Basics

This section covers basic JavaScript constructs. JavaScript is a loosely typed language. This means that variables are not associated with a specific data type when they are created. The type is set when the variable is used, and for the most part, conversion between types is done automatically.

Although JavaScript does not explicitly type variables, it does distinguish between certain value types. These types include:

- Numbers (5, 3.14, and so on)
- Boolean values (true or false)
- Strings ("Kayaking is fun" and so on)
- null. This is a special keyword that denotes a null value. Since JavaScript is case sensitive, it must be in lower-case letters.

As we stated before, you do not need to specify the type. When a value is used, JavaScript automatically analyzes it to determine its type.

Literals are fixed values and may be integers, floating-point (real) numbers, logicals (true or false), or strings. Some examples include:

- 245
- 5.13242
- true
- "Ozone Books"

Converting Strings to Numbers

Although JavaScript is loosely typed, there are times when it is necessary to do explicit type conversion. For example, input from forms is considered to be in strings. If you are trying to get numerical input from a form, you will need to convert the strings into numbers.

JavaScript provides several special functions for converting strings to numbers. If the string cannot be converted, the functions will return an error value.

eval

Usage: eval(*variable_name)*

Evaluates a string representing any JavaScript literal or variable, converting it to a number. For example:

```
var test = "a - 36 * 100"
x = eval(test)
```

would assign the variable "x" the numerical value associated with the string contained in the variable "test". There is an important difference in the result from eval based on the type of input provided. Consider the following two sets of statements:

```
a = "1"
b = "2.1"
eval(a + b)

a = 1
b = 2.1
eval(a + b)
```

In the first set of statements, the values for a and b are strings. Eval provides the concatenated result—12.1. In the second set of statements, a and b have numerical values, and eval returns 3.1. If any variable in the string being evaluated has a string value, the entire set of variables will be treated as strings, so if we have:

```
a = 1
b = "2.1"
eval(a + b)
```

eval will return 12.1.

Eval will also evaluate JavaScript expressions. For example:

```
h = "<P><B>Hello</B>"
g = "<P><B>Good-bye</B>"
var evalstring = "if (a < b) {x = h} else {x = g}"
document.write(eval(evalstring))
```

In this example, "Hello" will be displayed if the value of a is greater than b, and "Good-bye" will be displayed if the value of b is greater than a.

parseInt

Usage: parseInt(*variable_name*)

Converts a string to an integer. For example:

```
x = parseInt(mystring)
```

parseFloat

Usage: parseFloat(*variable_name*)

Converts a string to a floating-point number.

```
x = parseFloat(mystring)
```

Variable Names

Variables in JavaScript are created with the "var" statement. To create a variable named "Kayak" that contains the string "Best rivers", you would use the var statement as follows:

```
var Kayak = "Best rivers";
```

As you can see from this example, you do not need to explicitly tell JavaScript that the variable will hold a string. Although you do not specify a type when you create a variable, the variable name itself must conform to certain rules. Specifically, variables:

- Must start with a letter ("A" through "Z" and "a" through "z") or underscore ("_")
- May have digits (0-9) in any position but the first one.

Remember that JavaScript is case sensitive. For example, the variable "Kayak" is considered to be a different variable than "KAYAK".

Special Characters

Special characters are included in strings through the use of special escape sequences. You can use the escape codes in Table 8–1 to represent special characters in JavaScript.

TABLE 8–1   *Special-Character Escape Codes*

Escape Code	Description
\b	backspace
\f	form feed
\n	new line character
\r	carriage return
\t	tab character

If you wish to include a quotation mark in a string, you will need to escape it with a backslash. For example, to create a variable named kellstring containing the string:

"Kelly said "Kayaking is the best sport.""

you would use:

```
var kellstring = "Kelly said \"Kayaking is the best sport.\""
```

Assignment Operators: =, +=, -=, *=, /=

Assignment of a value to a variable is done with the "=" sign. JavaScript also offers additional assignment operators, as listed in Table 8–2.

TABLE 8–2   *Assignment Operators*

Operator	Equivalent Statement using "="
x = y	x = y
x += y	x = x + y
x -= y	x = x - y
x *= y	x = x * y
x /= y	x = x / y
x %= y	x = x % y

Arithmetic Operators

JavaScript arithmetic operators take numeric values (which may be literals or variables) as their operands and return a single numerical value. JavaScript supports the standard arithmetic operators:

- addition: +
- subtraction: -
- multiplication: *
- division: /

In addition to the standard operators, the following operators are also available:

Modulus: %

Usage: x % y

It returns the remainder of dividing x by y. For example, 17 % 3 would return 2.

Increment: ++

Usage: x++ or ++x

It adds one to its operand. If it is used as x++, it returns the value before incrementing. Thus if x is 5, "y = x++" would result in y being set to 5 and x being set to 6. If it is used as ++x, it returns the value after incrementing. For example if x is set to 5, "y = ++x" would cause both x and y to be set to 6.

Decrement: --

Usage: var-- or --var

It subtracts one from its operand. If it is used as x--, it returns the value before decrementing. For example, if x is 5, the statement "y = x--" would result in y being set to 5 and x being set to 4. If it is used as --x, it returns the value after decrementing. Thus if x is 5, "y = --x" would result in both x and y being set to 4.

Unary negation: -

> **Usage:** -x
>
> This operand returns the negation of its operand. For example, y = -x.

Logical Operators

JavaScript has support for a number of logical operators. These operators take boolean values as expressions and return a boolean value. Logical operators supported by JavaScript include those in Table 8–3.

TABLE 8–3 *Logical Operators*

Name	Operator	Usage	Description
And	&&	*expr1 && expr2*	Returns true if expr1 and expr2 are both true, and returns false otherwise
Or	||	*expr1 || expr2*	Returns true if either expr1 or expr2 is true. Returns false if both expr1 and expr2 are false.
Not	!	*!expr*	Returns the negated value of expr. If expr is false, it returns true; if expr is true, it returns false.

Comparison Operators: ==, >, >=, <, <=, !=

A comparison operator compares its operands and returns a logical value based on whether the comparison is true or not. The operands may be numerical or string values. When used on string values, the comparisons are based on the standard lexicographical ordering. Comparison operators are listed in Table 8–4.

TABLE 8–4   Comparison Operators

Name	Operator	Usage	Description
Equal	==	*expr1* == *expr2*	True if the operands are equal.
Not equal	!=	*expr1* != *expr2*	True if the operands are not equal.
Greater than	>	*expr1* > *expr2*	True if left operand is greater than right operand.
Greater than or equal to	>=	*expr1* >= *expr2*	True if left operand is greater than or equal to right operand.
Less than	<	*expr1* < *expr2*	True if left operand is less than right operand.
Less than or equal to	<=	*expr1* <= *expr2*	True if left operand is less than or equal to right operand.

Concatenation Operator: +

The concatenation operator (+) can be used to join string values together. It returns a string that is a union of the strings being concatenated. For example,

```
"Ozone " + "Books " + "and Raging Wahine Adventure"
```

returns the string:

```
"Ozone Books and Raging Wahine Adventure"
```

The concatenation assignment operator (+=) can also be used to concatenate strings. For example, if the variable ozone contains "Ozone ", and the variable books contains "Books", then the expression:

```
ozone += books
```

evaluates to "Ozone Books" and assigns this value to the ozone variable.

Operator Precedence

The precedence of operators determines the order of their application when evaluating an expression. The default precedence may be overridden through the use of parentheses.

The precedence of operators, from lowest to highest is:

- comma (,)
- assignment (=, +=, -=, *=, /=, %=, <<=, >>=, >>>=, &=, ^=, |=)
- conditional (?:)
- logical-or (||)
- logical-and (&&)
- bitwise-or (|)
- bitwise-xor (^)
- bitwise-and (&)
- equality (==, !=)
- relational (<, <=, >, >=)
- shift (<<, >>, >>>)
- addition (+), subtraction (-)
- multiply (*), divide (/), modulus (%)
- not (!), negation (-), increment (++), decrement (--)
- call "()", member ([])

Creating New Objects

The *new* operator is used to create new objects. For example:

```
var lastname = new makeArray(maxentries)
```

creates a new object named "lastname" using the parameters defined in the makeArray function. You can find a copy of this function in the section on "this" later in this chapter.

Statements

JavaScript statements consist of keywords used with the appropriate syntax. The following statements are available in JavaScript:

- break
- comment
- continue
- for
- for...in
- function
- if...else
- return
- var
- while
- with

We describe these statements later in this chapter.

Comments

Comments allow you to make notes in your script. Like the comments in most programming languages they are ignored by the interpreter. Comments on a single line should be preceded by a double slash (//). Comments that span multiple lines should be preceded by a "/*" and followed by a "*/".

For example:

```
//This is a single-line comment
x = y;
/*This is a multiline comment.
This line is part of the comment
This is the last line of the comment */
```

Note that the interpreter will also ignore HTML comment lines.

JavaScript Objects

Netscape's JavaScript is an object-based scripting language that can be embedded in HTML documents. As an object-based language, JavaScript contains *objects* in a hierarchy that is based on the structure of the HTML page. These objects have properties and associated methods. In addition, scripts can be run in response to events triggered by the user.

Using the Tables

The tables that follow contain the most useful JavaScript objects. Each object is listed with the properties, methods and event handlers that may be used with that particular object. To determine what a particular property, method, or event handler does, simply check the table in the appropriate section.

Remember that, unlike HTML, JavaScript is case sensitive, so you must use the correct capitalization for the interpreter to recognize your commands. For example, onLoad is not the same as Onload.

In JavaScript, the topmost object is the window. Every window always has the following subobjects: *location* (the current URL), *history*, and *document*. Table 8–5 shows these objects and their properties, methods, and event handlers.

TABLE 8–5 *Window Objects*

Object	Properties	Methods	Event handler
window	defaultStatus, status, window, frames	alert, close, confirm, open, prompt, set-Timeout	onLoad, onUnload
location	hostname, href, pathname, protocol		
history	length	back, forward, go	
document	alinkColor, bgColor, fgColor, forms, lastModi-fied, links, location, title	clear, close, open, write	

Document Object

The document object allows you to manipulate the current document (Table 8–6). Depending on the actual loaded document, the document object has many subobjects, including the document's forms and links:

TABLE 8–6   Document Objects

Object	Properties	Methods	Event handler
link	target		onClick, onMouseOver
form	action, method, name, target	submit	onSubmit

Form Object

The form object may have its many subobjects, including text fields, text areas, and checkbox, radio, submit, and reset buttons (Table 8–7).

TABLE 8–7   Form Objects

Object	Properties	Methods	Event handler
text fields	defaultValue, name, value	focus, blur, select	onBlur, onChange, onFocus, onSelect
textarea	defaultValue, name, value	focus, blur, select	onBlur, onChange, onFocus, onSelect
checkbox	checked, default-Checked, name, value	click	onClick
radio	checked, default-Checked, length, name, value	click	onClick
button	name, value	click	onClick
submit	name, value	click	onClick
reset	name, value	click	onClick

Built-in Objects

The objects described so far are "client" objects. JavaScript also supports three built-in (aka common) objects. There are no event handlers associated with these objects (Table 8–8):

TABLE 8–8 Built-In Objects

Object	Properties	Methods
Math	E, LN2, LN10, LOG2E, LOG10E, PI, SQRT1_2, SQRT2	abs, acos, asin, atan, ceil, cos, exp, floor, log, max, min, pow, random, round, sin, sqrt, tan
String	length	anchor, big, blink, bold, charAt, fixed, fontcolor , fontsize, indexOf, italics, lastIndexOf , link, small, strike, sub, substring, sup, toLowerCase, toUpperCase
Date		getDate, getDay, getHours, getMinutes, getMonth, getSeconds, getTime, getTimeZoneoffset, getYear , parse, setDate, setHours, setMinutes , setMonth, setSeconds, setTime, setYear, toGMTString, toLocaleString, UTC

Math Object

The Math object provides a way to manipulate mathematical expressions. Note that we do not describe the properties and methods associated with this object, since they are common mathematical functions.You may find it convenient to use the "with" statement in functions that utilize many Math objects, since this removes the need to type "Math." at the beginning of every math object. For example:

```
with (Math){
x = round(i);
y = abs(x);
i = PI * y;
}
```

String Object

The String object is used to store character sequences.

Date Object

The Date object provides storage and manipulation of dates. Dates are stored internally as the number of milliseconds since January 1, 1970 00:00:00.

Properties

Objects have *properties* that describe their attributes (Table 8–9).

TABLE 8–9 *Object Properties*

Property	Applies to	Description	Syntax
defaultStatus	window	default message in status bar	window.defaultStatus
frames	window	array of objects containing frame windows	window.frames[*]
status	window	message in status bar	window.status
hostname	location	hostname of URL	location.host
href	location	entire URL	location.href
pathname	location	file path portion of URL	location.pathname
protocol	location	protocol portion of URL	location.protocol
alinkColor	document	color of anchor link on mouse-down	document.alinkColor
bgColor	document	color of document background	document.bgColor
fgColor	document	color of document foreground text	document.fgColor

TABLE 8–9 Object Properties (Continued)

Property	Applies to	Description	Syntax
forms	document	array of objects containing document forms	document.forms[*]
lastModified	document	last modification date	document.lastModified
linkColor	document	color of hyperlink	document.linkColor
location	document	complete URL of document	document.location
title	document	title of document	document.title
vlinkColor	document	color of visited links	document.vlinkColor
action	form	destination URL for form being submitted	formname.action
method	form	method for sending form input to user	formname.method
target	form, link	destination of completed form or clicked-on link	document.*.target
checked	checkbox, radio	selection state of checkbox or radio element (true or false)	name.checked
name	form, text, textarea, radio, checkbox, button	a string containing name of element	*.name
value	form, text, textarea, radio, checkbox, button	a string containing value of element	*.value
length	string	The length of the string	string.length

Methods

Objects can have associated *methods* (or procedures). These methods describe actions that the object can take, such as opening or closing a window (Table 8–10).

TABLE 8–10 *Object Methods*

Method	Applies to	Description	Syntax
alert	window	display an Alert dialog box	alert("message")
confirm	window	display a Confirm dialog box	confirm("message")
close	window	close window	window.close()
open	window	open new window	window.open("URL", "window name")
prompt	window	display a Prompt dialog box	prompt("message")
setTimeout	window	evaluate an expression after a certain amount of time	timeoutID=setTimeout(expression, msec)
back	history	load previous URL in history	history.back()
forward	history	load next URL in history list	history.forward()
go	history	load a URL in history list	history.go()
close	document	close output stream	document.close()
open	document	open output stream	document.open()
write	document	write expression	write(...)
writeln	document	write expression followed by a newline character	writeln(...)
submit	form	submit form	formname.submit()
blur	password, text, textarea	remove focus	*.blur()

TABLE 8–10 Object Methods (Continued)

Method	Applies to	Description	Syntax
focus	password, text, textarea	give focus to current object	*.focus()
select	password, text, textarea	select input area of object	*.select()
click	button, checkbox, radio, reset, submit	simulate mouse click	*.click()
toLowerCase	string	converts string to lowercase	string.toLower-Case()
toUpperCase	string	converts string to uppercase	string.toUpper-Case()

Event Handlers

JavaScript is mostly event driven. This means that script execution is triggered by user events on the client. These user events apply to specific elements in the browser environment. Events include loading a document, clicking the mouse, or submitting a form. A script can use *event handlers* to cause specific JavaScript functions to be run in response to recognized user events (Table 8–11).

TABLE 8–11 Event Handlers

User Event	User action	Event handler	Applies to
blur	removes focus from form element (opposite of focus)	onBlur	text fields, text areas, selections
click	clicks on button or link	onClick[a]	buttons, links
change	changes value of form element	onChange	text fields, text areas, selections
focus	selects element for input (opposite of blur)	onFocus	text fields, text areas, selections
load	loads page	onLoad	documents
mouseover	moves mouse over link	onMouseOver[b]	links
select	selects input field	onSelect	text fields, text areas
submit	submits form	onSubmit	form submit buttons
unload	leaves page	onUnload	documents

a. Examples using onClick events may be found in the Frame chapter.
b. Examples using onMouseOver events may be found in the URL chapter.

Statements

JavaScript statements provide a method for connecting and using objects and functions in your script. A statement is composed of keywords and may span multiple lines. This section contains a list of the keywords that may be used in a statement.

You may include multiple statements on a single line by separating them with semicolons.

break

For use in a while or for loop. It terminates the current loop and transfers program control to the statement following the terminated loop.

Syntax

```
break
```

Example

This function decrements the variable *i* in a while loop. Since the condition for this loop is always true, the loop would never end were it not for the break. The if statement in the loop checks to see if *i* equals 7, and if it does, break will terminate the loop, and *i*'s value will be printed.

```
function breaktest(){
    var i = 10
    while (true){
        i--
        if (i==7) {
            break
        }
    document.write(i)
    }
}
```

continue

To be used in a while or for loop. It causes statement execution to jump from the current to the next iteration of the loop. In a while loop, this will cause it to go to the condition check; in a for loop it will go to the update expression.

Syntax

```
continue
```

Examples

This function decrements the variable *i* in a while loop and prints the value of *i* on each iteration of the loop. The if statement in the loop checks to see if *i* equals 7, and if it does, continue will cause the loop to jump to the next iteration. Since the print command comes after the if statement, it will not be executed if continue is called. Thus, this function will print all the numbers except 7 between 9 and 1.

```
function continuetest(){
    var i = 10
    while (i>0){
        i--
        if (i==7) {
            continue
        document.write(i)
        }
    }
}
```

for

Creates a loop based on three expressions:

1. An expression used to initialize a counter variable
2. A condition that is evaluated on each pass
3. An expression used to update the counter variable

All of these expressions are optional and should be enclosed in parentheses and separated by semicolons. They are followed by the block of statements to be executed in the loop.

Syntax

```
for ( [expression1]; [condition]; [expression]) {
    [statements in the loop]
}
```

expression1 can be a statement or variable declaration.

Example

This loop will print out the numbers from 1 to 5.

```
for (var x=1; x <=5; x++) {
    document.write{x}
}
```

for...in

Iterates a variable over all the properties of an object obj. For each distinct property, it executes the statements in the loop.

Syntax

```
for (var in obj) {
    [statements in the loop]
}
```

Example

The following function prints all the members in the tele-
phone-extension example from the JavaScript chapter.

```
function printbook(){
    for (counter in lastname) {
        document.write("<P>"+ lastname[counter])
        document.write(" " +extension[counter])
    }
    document.close()
}
```

function

This is used to create a JavaScript function name. It may
include parameters, which can be strings, numbers, and
objects. Parameters are passed by value, so any changes
made to them are not reflected globally.

Functions can be set to return a value by including a
return statement specifying the value to return.

Syntax

```
function functionname( [parameter1]  [, parameter2] [...,parametern])
{
     [statements]  }
```

Examples

This function compares two input strings and returns true
if they are equal.

```
function compstring(InString1, InString2) {
    if (InString1 == InString2) {
        return true;
    } else {
        return false;
    }
}
```

if...else

Executes statements if the condition is true. The else
clause is optional and is executed if the condition is false.

Syntax

```
if (condition) {
    [statements]
} [else {
    [statements]
}]
```

Example

If MyString equals "Hello", "World" is appended to it. If not, the string is set to "Go away".

```
if ( MyString == "Hello" ) {
    MyString = MyString + "World"
} else {
    MyString = "Go away"
}
```

return

Specifies the value to be returned by a function.

Syntax

```
return expression
```

Example

The following function returns its argument, InStr, appended to the string "Hello ".

```
function AddHello(InStr) {
    return "Hello " + InStr
}
```

this

A keyword used to refer to the current object.

Syntax

```
this[.propertyName]
```

Example

We use "this" in our phone-book makeArray function:

```
function makeArray(n) {
this.length = n
for (var i=1; i <= n; i++)
        this[i] = null
        return this
}
```

var

Creates a variable and may initialize it to a value. Variable names can be any legal identifier, and the value can be any legal expression. The scope of a variable is the current function or, for variables declared outside a function, the current application.

To create a variable outside a function, you can simply assign a value to a variable name. However, it is good style to use var. It is required in functions when there is a global variable with the same name.

Syntax

```
var varname [= value] [..., varname [= value] ]
```

Examples

Create a variable named myvar:

```
var myvar
```

Create a variable named myvar and initialize it to 1:

```
var myvar = 1
```

Create variables named i and j and initialize them to 10:

```
var i,j = 10
```

while

Creates a loop that evaluates the expression condition, and if it is true, executes statements. The loop terminates when the condition is false.

Syntax

```
while (condition) {
    [statements]
}
```

Examples

This will print the numbers from 1 through 5. It is functionally equivalent to the example we used for the for loop.

```
var x=1
while (x <=5) {
    document.write{x}
    x++
}
```

with

Establishes a default object for the statements. Any property references without an object are assumed to be for the object. Note that the parentheses are required around object.

Syntax

```
with (object){
    statements
}
```

Examples

```
with (Math){
    x = round(i);
    y = abs(x);
    i = PI * y;
}
```

Conditional Expressions

A conditional expression can have one of two values based on a condition. The syntax is

```
(condition) ? value1 : value2
```

If condition is true, the expression has the value of value1, otherwise it has the value of value2. You can use a conditional expression anywhere you would use a standard expression.

For example, here is a use of a conditional expression in our phone-book database:

```
form.result.value = (foundMatch) ? ext[i] : "No match found"
```

This statement assigns the value in the variable ext[i] to the variable form.result.value if foundMatch is true. Otherwise it assigns "No match found" to the variable.

The Future

There are still many areas in JavaScript that are unfinished—both in the development of the language specification and in the interpreter. For example, one of the rumored additions to the language will be the ability to separate JavaScript scripts into separate files, which would be included in documents through the use of an SRC attribute for the SCRIPT tag.

We have tried to present the most current information about JavaScript available at the time this book was written. However, since this is a rapidly changing field, we recommend referring to the on-line documentation at Netscape for the latest information. You will find it at:

```
http://home.netscape.com/comprod/products/navigator/
version_2.0/script/script_info/index.html
```

- HOW TO CREATE A FORM-CHECKING APPLICATION IN JAVASCRIPT
- HOW TO USE JAVASCRIPT TO CREATE A SCROLLING MESSAGE ON THE STATUS BAR
- HOW TO BUILD A SIMPLE DATABASE AND SEARCH ENGINE
- HOW TO CREATE AN ANIMATION WITH JAVASCRIPT

JAVASCRIPT EXAMPLES

In the last chapter we reviewed the basic concepts and constructs and provided an introduction to the most commonly used JavaScript objects. In this chapter we put that information to use. This chapter contains four complete JavaScript examples:

- Simple database look-up
- Scrolling status bar message
- A forms checker
- Basic animation

We will explain how we created these scripts and how they may be customized for your use. Programmers may use this information to create new scripts, while those of you without a programming background should be able to copy the scripts from the CD and make the appropriate changes for your own use.

Simple Database Look-Up

This example shows how you can use JavaScript to provide simple database look-up functionality—all on the browser.

Ozone Books has been growing rapidly and the company is finding it hard to keep the current list of employee telephone extensions on everyone's desk. Kelly decided this problem can be neatly solved by JavaScript. She authored an HTML document, named phones.html, that contains a simple form. When someone wants to find out the telephone extension of a new employee, she loads Kelly's document, then types in the name of the employee.

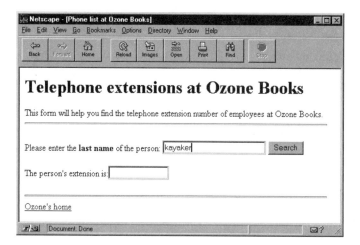

The JavaScript in phones.html contains a list of employee names and their extensions. When the user enters a query, the JavaScript searches its list and displays for the user the appropriate extension.

```
Netscape - [Phone list at Ozone Books]                        _□×
File  Edit  View  Go  Bookmarks  Options  Directory  Window  Help
  ⇦⊙     ⊙⇨     ⌂      Ⓡ      🖼      ⇶°     🖶      🔎      ●
  Back   Forward  Home   Reload  Images   Open    Print    Find    Stop
```

Telephone extensions at Ozone Books

This form will help you find the telephone extension number of employees at Ozone Books.

Please enter the **last name** of the person: [kayaker   ] [Search]

The person's extension is: [5555   ]

Ozone's home

```
□🔊  Document: Done                                          ☑?
```

Conveniently, all of the processing takes place on the browser, so employees can store a copy of this document on a local disk for use even when they are not connected to the network. Moreover, when the master list needs to be updated, only one file needs to be changed, phones.html.

Let's look at the complete document, phones.html. Here are some things you should notice. First, we embed the JavaScript within the <SCRIPT></SCRIPT> tags and place it in the HEAD of the document. This way, the script is fully loaded before the user can enter information into the form. Second, comments in the script are preceded by "//". Here is the full document:

```
<HTML>
<HEAD>
<TITLE>Phone list at Ozone Books</TITLE>
<SCRIPT LANGUAGE="JavaScript">
//Maximum number of entries allowed in the phone book
var maxentries = 5

// make an empty array of n items
function makeArray(n) {
  this.length = n
  for (var i=1; i <= n; i++)
      this[i] = null
      return this
}
```

```
// make a phonebook listing object
function phoneentry(lname, ext) {
    this.lname = lname;
    this.ext = ext;
}
var phonedb = new makeArray(maxentries)
phonedb[1]= new phoneentry("KAYAKER","5555")
phonedb[2] = new phoneentry("BIKER","5556")
phonedb[3] = new phoneentry("HIKER","5557")
phonedb[4] = new phoneentry("CAVER","5558")
phonedb[5] = new phoneentry("SWIMMER","5559")

// Has input been entered by user?
function notempty(inputStr) {
  if (inputStr == "" || inputStr == null) {
      alert("Please enter a last name before clicking
Search.")
      return false
  }
  return true
}

// search thru lastname database to find match
function search(form) {
  var foundMatch = false
  var inputStr = form.entry.value
  if (notempty(inputStr)) {
      inputValue = inputStr.toUpperCase()
      for (var i in phonedb) {
          if (i!="length") {
              if (inputValue == phonedb[i].lname) {
                  foundMatch = true
                  break
              }
          }
      }
  form.result.value = (foundMatch) ? phonedb[i].ext : "No
match found"
  }
}
</SCRIPT>
</HEAD>
<BODY BGCOLOR=#FFFFFF>
<H1>Telephone extensions at Ozone Books</H1>
<P>This form will help you find the telephone extension
number of employees at Ozone Books.
```

```
<HR>
<FORM METHOD=post NAME=testform>
Please enter the <b>last name</b> of the person:
<INPUT TYPE="text" NAME="entry" SIZE=25 MAXLENGTH=25>
<INPUT TYPE="button" VALUE="Search"
ONCLICK="search(this.form)">
<P>The person's extension is:<INPUT TYPE="text" NAME="result"
SIZE=14>
</FORM>
<HR>
<A HREF="http://www.ozone.com">Ozone's home</A>
</BODY>
</HTML>
```

Let's briefly walk through the script. Using "this", the statement that refers to the current object, the script defines a new object type named phoneentry:

```
function phoneentry(lname, ext) {
    this.lname = lname;
    this.ext = ext;
}
```

It has two items: lname, which will be used to store the employee's last name, and ext, which will store the phone number. We make an array of these objects called *phonedb* via a call to the new operator:

```
var phonedb = new makeArray(maxentries)
```

Five elements of this array are then assigned values with the last name and phone number of each of five employees. For example:

```
phonedb[1]= new phoneentry("KAYAKER","5555")
```

We do not want our readers to have to worry about case matching in their queries, so we store all our names in upper case. When we do the comparison, we use the "toUpperCase" string method to convert the reader's query to upper case:

```
inputValue = inputStr.toUpperCase()
```

The function *notempty* returns true if the string is nonempty. Otherwise it returns false and pops up an alert box to the user. This is a useful general function. The next function, *search*, contains the meat of the script. It takes as an argument the form with the search query. It extracts the query string from the form and uses the notempty function to make sure that a query has been entered. It then checks the input string against each last-name entry in the phone database.

Did you notice that the query form has two text input fields? The first field is used for the user's query. The second field is used by JavaScript to print out the extension or an error message if no match is found. Setting output to a text field is probably the simplest way for JavaScript to provide output. Unlike other methods, in which JavaScript outputs a whole document, updating a text field allows the rest of the information in the window to remain intact.

The text field for the output message is named "result", so the command used to send the result of the query is:

```
form.result.value = (foundMatch) ? phonedb[i].ext : "No
match found"
```

Notice that this is a compound statement. If an entry was found, the field value is set to that value. If no entry is found, it is set to the string "No match found."

Finally, the HTML part of the document contains some text and a form into which the user enters the name to search on. The form includes a button field, which is a field type specific to JavaScript, and allows custom buttons to be created. In this case:

```
<INPUT TYPE="button" VALUE="Search"
ONCLICK="search(this.form)">
```

Thus when the button "Search" is clicked, the function *search* is run. Results from the search are immediately displayed in the last form box.

Customizing the Database

If you wish to customize the script, you would replace each of the *phonedb* values with your own information. If you have more or less than 5 entries in your list, you will need to change the value for the maxentries variable to the number of entries you wish to have in your database. Thus, if your phone list has 10 entries, your script contains:

```
var maxentries = 10
```

The version of the script on the CD also includes some extra functions that allow you to print out a copy of the database and a copy of all the items associated with the phonedb array. If you wish to extend the functionality of this script for your own uses, you may find these functions helpful in understanding how data is stored and retrieved.

Scrolling Status Bar

Now let's look at a script that scrolls a message across the browser's status line. Our scripts also include a stop button. Since we have found that scrolling messages can be quite annoying (especially when you want to see the messages that are normally displayed in the status bar), we like to offer our readers the ability to stop the message if they prefer.

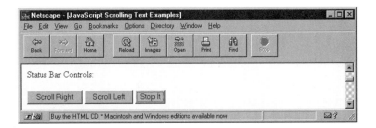

The document you will find on the CD, scrollcontrol.html, actually contains four scripts: left status bar scroll, right status bar scroll, left frame scroll, and right frame scroll. Since they are all very similar, we will go over the left status bar scroll here.

```
<HEAD>
<SCRIPT LANGUAGE="JavaScript">
// Print scrolling text on status bar
function scrollstatusleft(countdown, iteration) {
    var phrase1  = "Buy the HTML CD";
```

```
    var phrase2  = "Macintosh and Windows editions available
now";
    var separator = " * ";
    var scrollmsg= phrase1 + separator + phrase2;
    var timewait = 60;
    if ((countdown < scrollmsg.length) &
!(document.forms[0].stopit.value=="true")){
        var tmpcount = scrollmsg.length-countdown;
        window.status=
scrollmsg.substring(tmpcount,scrollmsg.length) +  separator +
scrollmsg.substring(0, tmpcount);
        countdown++;
        var cmd="scrollstatusleft(" + countdown + "," +
iteration +  ")";
        cmdtimer=window.setTimeout(cmd,30);
    }
    else {
        if ((--iteration >= 1) &
!(document.forms[0].stopit.value=="true")){
            var cmd="scrollstatusleft(0 ," + iteration + ")";
            cmdtimer=window.setTimeout(cmd,120);
        }
        else {
            window.status=scrollmsg;
        }
    }
}
// Done with the code -->
</SCRIPT>
<TITLE>JavaScript Scrolling Status Bar Example</TITLE>
</HEAD>
<BODY bgcolor="#FFFFFF" >

-- Additional text removed for brevity --

<P>Status Bar Controls:
<form>
<input type=button
onclick="document.forms[0].stopit.value=false;
ScrollTime=window.setTimeout('scrollstatusleft(0,4)',0)"
value="scroll left">
<input type=button
onclick="document.forms[0].stopit.value=true;" value="stop
it">
<input type=hidden name=stopit value="false">
</form>
```

Now let's see how we made the message appear. We placed our message on the status bar by setting the value of the status property for our window to the message that we wished to display. For example:

```
window.status=scrollmsg;
```

Since we want the message to scroll slowly enough for our readers to see and read it, we need to use a timer to adjust the speed of the scroll. The timer method is setTimeout. This method takes two arguments: the command to be evaluated, and the number of milliseconds to pause before the command should be executed. For example:

```
cmdtimer=window.setTimeout(cmd,120);
```

executes the command in the string "cmd" after 120 milliseconds.

Customizing the Status Bar Script

Now let's look at how the script may be customized for your use. As it currently stands, this script allows two phrases, although it is fairly simple to add additional ones should you desire. We split our phrases between different variables because JavaScript has problems with very long string assignments (although in this case, our strings are short enough to have been assigned in a single shot). The variables for the phrases are *phrase1*, and *phrase2*.

```
var phrase1  = "Buy the HTML CD";
var phrase2  = "Macintosh and Windows editions available now";
```

To add your own phrases, simply replace the text between the quotation marks with your own phrases. For example, if you wish to use "Late-breaking news..." as your first phrase, the line for phrase1 would become:

```
var phrase1  = "Late-breaking news...";
```

You should not place carriage returns or quotation marks in the phrases you create.

You can also customize the separation characters, which are kept in the variable *separator*.

```
var separator = " * "
```

As with the phrases, replace the text between the quotation marks with your preferred separation characters. Remember to leave spaces so that your phrases do not get pushed up against the separation character(s).

Next, copy the script (everything from <SCRIPT> to </SCRIPT>) into the HEAD portion of the document where you wish to use it.

We let our readers turn the message on and off through the use of forms. However, if you prefer to have a message begin as soon as the document is loaded, simply grab the command for the type of message that you want (the command is attached to the onclick attribute) and add an "onLoad" attribute to the BODY tag with that command. For example:

```
<BODY
onLoad="ScrollTimer=window.setTimeout('scrollstatusleft(0,3)',
0)">
```

This script takes two arguments. The first should always be set to 0, since it is used by the script as a countdown timer. The second argument is the number of times the banner should be displayed. Notice that we have set the banner to display 3 times. We chose to have the banner run a finite number of times because a problem with Version 2.0 of the Netscape browser caused it to run out of memory if the banner was allowed to loop indefinitely. It may also annoy readers if they completely lose control over the status bar and their view of the messages that normally appear there. If you prefer to have it run indefinitely, you can simply remove the check for loopnum.

That's it! To check your script, just load it into Netscape 2 or higher. If you made any errors, the browser will pop up a window with a message describing the error.

Animation

Doing animation with JavaScript is fairly easy, but also rather ugly. This is due to JavaScript's lack of a method for updating specific areas of a window. As a result, the whole document must be reloaded (this is similar to client pull animations). The resulting animation tends to be very jerky.

Given these limitations, we recommend using an animated GIF or a Java applet if you want to include animation in your document. We include this script here primarily as a learning tool. However, if you do decide to use JavaScript to add animation to your documents, we recommend using it in combination with frames. By placing your animation in a frame of its own (sized to the animation), only a single frame needs to be updated rather than the entire window. The other benefit this combination provides is a side-effect of the fact that at the time this book was written, the only browsers[1] that supported frames also supported JavaScript. By using a <NOFRAME> tag in your top-level frame document, you can provide users with a non-JavaScript, nonframe alternative—something that is difficult to do without frames.

Now let's look at an example. You may recall from our previous discussions about animation that we have a sequence of GIF images that can be used to create a spinning globe. Our images are in files named globe1.gif through globe10.gif. As with any animation method that requires a separate image file to be loaded for each frame of the animation, we strongly recommend that you give your files the same name followed by a number. This allows you to step through the images with a counter rather than having to build different file names (along with the appropriate order) into your script.

---

1. At the time this book was written the browsers that supported JavaScript and frames were Navigator Version 2 and above, and Internet Explorer Version 3 and above.

The first thing we do is to create an HTML document that lays out the frames in our window. We plan to display our globe in a square frame on the top left of the window. Our main document will be displayed in a frame to the right of our animation, and we leave the frame below the animation empty. Our initial document looks like this:

```
<HTML>
<HEAD>
<TITLE>Animation Examples</TITLE>
</HEAD>
<BODY>
<FRAMESET COLS="20%,80%">
<FRAMESET ROWS="20%,80%">
<FRAME SRC=empty.html NAME=JSAnimate>
<FRAME SRC=empty.html NAME=Empty>
</FRAMESET>
<FRAME SRC=jsanimate.html NAME=Source>
</FRAMESET>
</BODY>
</HTML>
```

As you can see, we have named the frame where we plan to display our animation "JSAnimate". The frame below it is named "Empty", and the main frame is named "Source". We preload the two lefthand frames with empty.html, an HTML file that does nothing more than set a background color. Our "Source" window is loaded with "jsanimate.html", the document containing the JavaScript code for the animation. Let's take a look at jsanimate.html now. Here it is:

```
<HEAD>
<TITLE>Animation Control</TITLE>
<SCRIPT LANGUAGE="JavaScript">
function writeframe(countdown){
    var i = parseInt(countdown);
    if (i++ < 10) {
        parent.JSANIMATE.location.href="globe" + i + ".gif";
        var timerstring = "writeframe(" + i + ")";
        timer=setTimeout(timerstring,1000);
    }
}
{
writeframe("0");
}
```

```
</SCRIPT>
</HEAD>
<BODY BGCOLOR=#FFFFFF>
<H1>Animation Control</H1>
```
        -- Document text removed for brevity --

Our script makes use of the ability for a document in one frame to update information in a sibling frame. Thus, all we need to do to refresh the frame that is to contain our animation is to update the "location.href" property for that frame. The frame where we wish to place the animation is named JSANI-MATE. We place our images in this frame by updating its URL through the *href* property:

```
parent.JSANIMATE.location.href="globe" + i + ".gif";
```

Here *parent* is a predefined name that refers to the "parent" of the current frame.

Customizing the Script

The first step in customizing the animation script is to set up a frame document. Reserve a frame for your animation and make sure that you name it JSANIMATE. If you are not sure how to do this, please refer to the section on frames in the chapter on Tables and Frames. Next you will need to have a set of images in either GIF or JPEG format that make up your animation. They should be placed in files with a name in the format: myimage1.gif, myimage2.gif, myimage3.gif and so on.

Place the script in a document that will be loaded into one of the other frames in the window. Replace "10" in this line:

```
if (i++ < 10) {
```

with the total number of images in your animation. In this line, replace "globe" with the name of your file:

```
parent.JSANIMATE.location.href="globe" + i + ".gif";
```

If you use JPEG images rather than GIF images, replace "gif" with "jpg" or "jpeg", depending on what you use in your image filenames. Load your frame document, and you should see your animation.

JavaScript Forms Checker

Our final JavaScript script does some preprocessing on Ozone Books' order form. The original form was processed by a CGI program. This meant that the form had to be transmitted to Ozone Books' server, the CGI program had to process it, and if any problems were found, a warning message was returned to the reader. As a result, a single transaction might require several network connections. Since network connections take time, this slowed things down for the customer. By shifting the burden of the processing to the local system, we reduce the time the customer must wait for the form to be processed. Our script adds the following functionality:

- **Order-total calculator.** We add a new button that allows readers to calculate and review their order total *before* submitting the form. Readers no longer need to calculate subtotals for themselves—all they have to do is enter the number of items and the cost of the items. The script takes care of the rest.

- **Required information check**. Rather than submitting a form that may be incomplete, we use the notempty function developed for our database script to check whether readers have filled in certain fields (in this case we check for phone and e-mail). If the field is empty, the form is not submitted and a warning message is displayed.

Order-Total Calculator

We first look at the portion of the script that totals the order. Our goal is to create an extra button that will allow users to check their order total without having to submit the form. For example, a user may enter:

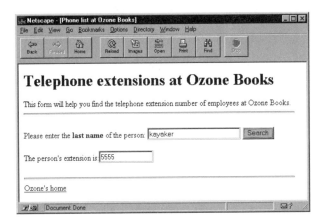

and then click on the "Total my order" button to get:

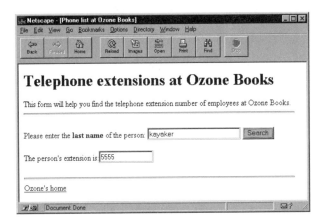

We achieve this with three new functions: PrintNumber, subtotal, and totalorder. We also use the notempty function from our database script.

Our first function, PrintNumber, addresses the problem of dealing with floating-point numbers. Floating-point numbers are not always treated precisely. For example, on some platforms, 4.6 becomes 4.5999999.... Obviously we cannot display figures like this! To avoid this problem, we turn our floating-point number into integers and deal with the fractions in separate steps.

We accomplish this by using the Math object with the *round* method. This method takes a number or numeric expression and rounds it to the nearest integer. Here is PrintNumber:

```
// Round a floating-point number to the correct value and
// convert it to a string
function PrintNumber(InNum){
        var dollars = Math.round(InNum * 100);
        var pennies = (dollars % 10);
        dollars = Math.round((dollars - pennies)/10);
        var dimes = dollars % 10;
        dollars = Math.round((dollars - dimes)/10);
        return(dollars + "." + dimes + pennies);
}
```

Our next function, subtotal, takes two input strings. It first checks to see if there is anything in the strings using the notempty function we developed for our database application. If both strings contain input, it converts them to numerical values with the parseFloat method, multiplies the result, and uses the *return* statement to return the total. If either string did not contain input, it returns 0.

```
//Get a subtotal for an item. Input consists of two strings
// containing price and quantity. The function returns the
// sum of the two.
function subtotal(quantity,price){
    if (notempty(quantity) && notempty(price)) {
        var subtotal = parseFloat(quantity) *
            parseFloat(price);
    }
    else {
        var subtotal = 0;
    }
    return subtotal;
}
```

Before looking at the next function, let us first review the portion of the form that contains the list of books being ordered. We have abbreviated the form to allow space for only three items. Here it is:

```
<FORM METHOD=post NAME="OrderForm"
ACTION="mailto:orders@ozone.com">

-- Form address information removed for brevity --

<TABLE>
<TR><TH>Product
Number<TH>Title<TH>Qty<TH>Price<TH>Total
<TR><TD><INPUT NAME="PN1" TYPE=text MAXLENGTH=5 SIZE=5>
<TD><INPUT NAME="TITLE1"
TYPE=text MAXLENGTH=40 SIZE=40> <TD><INPUT NAME="QTY1"
TYPE=text MAXLENGTH=5
SIZE=5><TD><INPUT NAME="PRICE1" TYPE=text MAXLENGTH=6
SIZE=6><TD><INPUT NAME="TOTAL1"
TYPE=text MAXLENGTH=9 SIZE=9>

<TR><TD><INPUT NAME="PN2" TYPE=text MAXLENGTH=5 SIZE=5>
<TD><INPUT NAME="TITLE2"
TYPE=text MAXLENGTH=40 SIZE=40> <TD><INPUT NAME="QTY2"
TYPE=text MAXLENGTH=5
SIZE=5><TD><INPUT NAME="PRICE2" TYPE=text MAXLENGTH=6
SIZE=6><TD><INPUT NAME="TOTAL2"
TYPE=text MAXLENGTH=9 SIZE=9>

<TR><TD><INPUT NAME="PN3" TYPE=text MAXLENGTH=5 SIZE=5>
<TD><INPUT NAME="TITLE3"
TYPE=text MAXLENGTH=40 SIZE=40> <TD><INPUT NAME="QTY3"
TYPE=text MAXLENGTH=5
SIZE=5><TD><INPUT NAME="PRICE3" TYPE=text MAXLENGTH=6
SIZE=6><TD><INPUT NAME="TOTAL3"
TYPE=text MAXLENGTH=9 SIZE=9>

<TR><TD> <TD><TD COLSPAN=2><STRONG>Order
Total:</STRONG><TD><INPUT NAME="GRANDTOT" TYPE=text
MAXLENGTH=9 SIZE=9>
</TABLE>
```

Each order item has five input fields:

- PN*x*: the part number
- TITLE*x*: the book's title

- QTY*x*: the number of copies requested
- PRICE*x*: the book's price
- TOTAL*x*: the total cost for this item

Note that *x* represents the item number (e.g.: PRICE1, PN2, and so on). Our function, totalorder, looks at the QTY*x* and PRICE*x* input fields from our form to calculate a subtotal for each item. It accesses these fields by using the appropriate document subobject. When we created our form, we used the NAME attribute to name it "OrderForm":

```
<FORM METHOD=post NAME="OrderForm" ...>
```

We use this name to access the form through the document object's *form* subobject. Since we want to access a specific field in the form, we also need to use the appropriate form subobject. Thus, to access the value in the PRICE1 field, we enter:

```
document.OrderForm.PRICE1.value
```

The totalorder function also sums the subtotals to provide the total cost for the order. It sends the output to the form by setting the *value* subobject for the fields that have been set up for this purpose: TOTAL1, TOTAL2, TOTAL3, and GRANDTOTAL. Since our concern is with the order's cost, we do not check the part number or title. Now here is the function itself:

```
//Calculates the total cost of the order, and writes it out
// to the appropriate place in the form.
function totalorder(){
    var total1 = subtotal(document.OrderForm.QTY1.value,
        document.OrderForm.PRICE1.value);
    document.OrderForm.TOTAL1.value = PrintNumber(total1);
    var total2 = subtotal(document.OrderForm.QTY2.value,
        document.OrderForm.PRICE2.value);
    document.OrderForm.TOTAL2.value=PrintNumber(total2);
    var total3 = subtotal(document.OrderForm.QTY3.value,
        document.OrderForm.PRICE3.value);
    document.OrderForm.TOTAL3.value=PrintNumber(total3);
    document.OrderForm.GRANDTOT.value=PrintNumber(total1+
        total2+total3);
}
```

Of course we do not want these functions to automatically calculate the order as soon as the reader enters information in the form's fields. Instead we set up a button field that will allow the reader to click on it to trigger this part of our script. Here is the HTML used to create the button:

```
<INPUT TYPE="button" VALUE="Total my order"
ONCLICK="totalorder()">
```

Note that the button type is not a part of standard HTML. It was added by Netscape so that custom buttons (rather than only the standard SUBMIT and RESET) could be tied to other actions.

Required Field Checker

Our form requests some contact information. Part of the information requested includes an e-mail address and phone number:

```
<B>ZIP:</B> <INPUT NAME="zip" TYPE=text MAXLENGTH=30 SIZE=10>
<TR><TD><B>E-mail:</B>       <TD><INPUT NAME="email"
TYPE=text MAXLENGTH=50 SIZE=50>
<TR><TD><B>Daytime Phone:</B> <TD><INPUT NAME="phonenum"
TYPE=text MAXLENGTH=30 SIZE=20>
```

We do not want readers to be allowed to submit the form unless the e-mail and phone number fields have been completed. Instead, we would like a warning message to be printed:

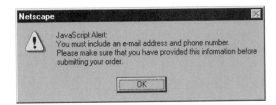

We accomplish this by replacing the submit input field with a button field that calls our input checking function, requireinput:

```
<P><INPUT TYPE=button VALUE="Place My Order"
onClick="requireinput(document.OrderForm)">
```

When the user clicks this button, the function requireinput is called. requireinput uses our notempty function to check whether the e-mail and phonenum fields are empty. If they are, it uses the alert method to create an alert box with a warning message and does not submit the form. If the fields have been completed, requireinput uses the submit method to submit the form:

```
//Used when the form is submitted to see whether the e-mail
// and phone number fields have information. If they don't,
// it prints out a warning and does not submit the form.
function requireinput(CheckForm){
    if (!notempty(CheckForm.email.value) ||
        !notempty(CheckForm.phonenum.value)) {
        var alertmsg = "You must include an e-mail address
and phone number.\nPlease make sure that you have provided
this information before\nsubmitting your order.";
        alert(alertmsg);
    }
    else {
        CheckForm.submit()
    }
}
```

Adapting the Form

If you wish to use our script to check portions of your own order form in, you should start with the template from the CD. You will find it in order-verify.html. Copy the script (everything from <SCRIPT> to </SCRIPT>) at the beginning of the document to your order form.

Now modify the totalorder and requireinput functions to use the names of your form and input fields, rather than the names of our input fields. For example, if you have a form named "myform" with a quantity column named "quantity1" and a price column named "cost2", you would change the line:

```
var total1 = subtotal(document.OrderForm.QTY1.value,
    document.OrderForm.PRICE1.value);
```

to:

```
var total1 = subtotal(document.myform.quantity1.value,
    document.myform.cost2.value);
```

If you have more than three item lines in your form, you should copy the two lines of code used to process an item:

```
var total1 = subtotal(document.OrderForm.QTY1.value,
    document.OrderForm.PRICE1.value);
document.OrderForm.TOTAL1.value = PrintNumber(total1);
```

Place as many copies of these lines before the grand total line as you have items in your form. Then update the lines to reflect the correct field names for your items. Finally, update the grand total line to include all of your items. For example, if you added three items, you would change:

```
document.OrderForm.GRANDTOT.value=PrintNumber(total1 +
total2 + total3);
```

to:

```
document.OrderForm.GRANDTOT.value=PrintNumber(total1 +
total2 + total3 + total4 + total5);
```

To customize the requireinput function, replace *email* and *phonenum*:

```
if (!notempty(CheckForm.email.value) ||
    !notempty(CheckForm.phonenum.value)) {
```

with the names of the input fields you wish to check. You can add extra fields by adding the or operator (||) followed by the notempty function (remember to negate it!) acting on the field.

The Good, the Bad, and the Ugly

Here are some tips to keep in mind while creating documents that incorporate JavaScript scripts:

- Remember that JavaScript output will not be printed when the document is printed by a browser. Don't make the mistake of generating a confirmation notice and asking users to print it!
- Include HEIGHT and WIDTH attributes with any images that you include in a document that uses JavaScript. There have been reports that Netscape Navigator has problems with JavaScript and images if these attributes are omitted.

- If you don't want to take the time to maintain an alternate set of documents for JavaScript-challenged browsers, make sure that you review your documents with other browsers before releasing them! As you can see from our Internet Explorer examples, even when you take the time to try to hide your script with HTML comment lines, you may still run into other accessibility problems.

The biggest challenge when using JavaScript is to create documents that work cleanly with non-JavaScript-aware browsers. For example, here is our order form document in Internet Explorer Version 2 on the Macintosh:

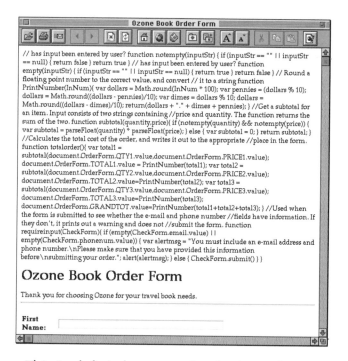

This is definitely not a nice looking document. We can get rid of the JavaScript display by adding an open HTML comment line:

```
<!-- Start script hiding
```

at the beginning of our script (either immediately before or after the <SCRIPT> tag) and another closing comment line:

```
// Now we end our script -->
```

immediately before the closing script tag, </SCRIPT>. After making these changes, we find that Internet Explorer Version 2 displays our document like this:

Ozone Book Order Form

Thank you for choosing Ozone for your travel book needs.

First Name:

Last Name:

Address:

City: State: ZIP:

E-mail:

Daytime Phone:

Product Number	Title	Qty	Price	Total
		Order Total:		

Total my order

Method of Payment: ○ Check or Money Order   ○ Credit Card

Important: We do not accept credit card numbers over the Internet at this time. To complete your order please call us within 48 hours to provide us with your credit card number.

Thank you for your order!

Place My Order   [No Order Right Now]

Now we have a new problem. Do you see a working submit button anywhere? Of course not—because we created our own submit button with the JavaScript input type "button," which this version of Internet Explorer does not see as a submit field. Notice that our total button ends up as a text input field. This happened because Internet Explorer saw it as field with an unknown type and defaulted to a text input field.

To make matters worse, when we check our script in other browsers (such as Lynx), some of the script still shows up. Is there a solution to this mess? Is there something we can do other than place a big warning message at the beginning of our JavaScript documents, telling readers using browsers that do not support JavaScript to go away?

Fortunately there is a partial solution—use JavaScript in combination with frames. This solution is based on the fact that so far the browsers that support JavaScript also support frames. With this in mind, to automatically direct your readers to the appropriate page for their browser, simply access the JavaScript document through a frame document. If your JavaScript document does not use multiple frames, just create a document that looks something like this:

```
<FRAMESET>
<FRAME SRC=javascript.html>
</FRAMESET>
<NOFRAME>
<P>Alternate text for frame and JavaScript-challenged browsers
```

Your JavaScript document will be displayed only if the browser understands frames—and if it knows about frames, it should also have JavaScript support.[2] If it doesn't understand frames, the document that you include in the <NOFRAMES> tag will be displayed instead.

---

2. This was true at the time this book was written. However, we can't guarantee that there will never be a browser that understands frames but not JavaScript, or vice versa.

IN THIS CHAPTER YOU WILL LEARN ESSENTIAL GUIDELINES FOR

- DESIGNING AND LAYING OUT WEB PAGES
- USING GRAPHICS
- SUPPORTING NAVIGATION IN WEB DOCUMENTS
- EFFICIENTLY USING SYSTEM RESOURCES

DESIGN GUIDELINES, STYLES AND TIPS

What's In This Chapter

This chapter pulls together the design guidelines mentioned as we described HTML tags in previous chapters, and introduces overall guidelines for laying out Web documents. In particular, we focus on the following aspects of Web document design:

- Designing and laying out Web pages
- Using graphics
- Supporting navigation in Web documents
- Efficiently using system resources

Introduction

Generally, books, magazine articles and papers are authored with particular audiences or readers in mind. Similarly, Web documents can be authored for a target audience. For example, Web documents containing company policy might be authored for members of that organization.

However, documents that are made part of the Internet World Wide Web are instantly available for browsing by its millions of global members. This means that the documents we author can be browsed by a hugely diverse population. In this case, it is almost impossible to know who our audience might be.

Moreover, users are not simply reading our Web documents—they are interacting with them. Our readers can select hyperlinks, navigate backward and forward between documents and Web sites, and generally choose their own pathway within information spaces in ways that we cannot fully anticipate.

These conditions present interesting and unique challenges for authors wishing to design interesting, appealing and effective Web documents. Although multimedia publishing is a recent desktop reality, little is known about the most effective ways to design digital documents that combine text, images, graphics, movies, and sound in order to best present and convey the intended information.

Fortunately, fields such as human-computer interaction, graphic design, information design and instructional design combined with traditional typography contribute many useful techniques for improving the design and layout of effective Web documents.

Based on our experience in browsing and authoring documents for the Web, we have formulated a set of important authoring principles. Many of these principles have already been highlighted at appropriate spots in the book. In this chapter we review and discuss these design principles, which authors should bear in mind when authoring Web documents.

In particular, we focus on the design and layout of Web pages, the use of graphics and support of navigation in Web documents, and the efficient use of system resources.

Of course, many of these issues are related. For example, a set of documents that are well designed usually enable users to effectively navigate within pages. Similarly, designers wishing for a strong graphical impact will take system and network resources into account. In short, the guidelines we present in the following section should be considered together.

Setting Your Project Up

While many people still create small Web sites for their own enjoyment, there are an ever-growing number of large corporate sites that may be maintained by numerous designers. Regardless of which type of site you have, doing some layout before starting your site can save many hours of work in the long run.

There are two important issues to consider when first creating a site:

- Document structure
- Directory structure

By document structure, we refer to the way in which documents on the site will relate to one another. If numerous people will be working on the site, it is a good idea to visualize how the documents in the site will relate to one another. Some sites start with a top-down approach:

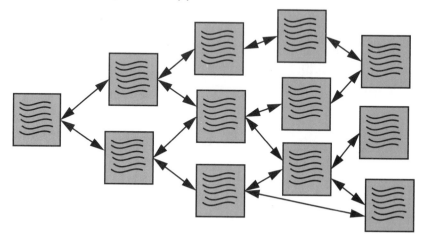

This type of site is designed to have a primary entry point (although the nature of the Web guarantees that there is no way to force people to start transversal of a site at a single point).

Other sites may have a more distributed approach:

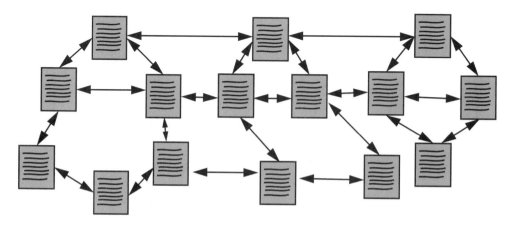

The relationship between the documents on your site should obviously be governed by the type of material being presented. If you are developing an on-line user manual, a top-down approach would work well. On the other hand, the top-down approach would not be well suited for a corporation with many autonomous departments.

Regardless of the type of organizational structure, establishing guidelines for areas that need to be linked before you begin creating your site will greatly reduce the likelihood that links to a main document or set of documents will need to be added or removed from large numbers of documents at a later date. This is especially important if your site will be maintained by more than one designer, and if designers are scattered between different geographic locations.

Now let's consider directory structure. By this we refer to the way that your documents are stored on your system. If you are developing a large site, it is likely that you will have many documents in your Web (this is true even if you expect to develop a small site—documents have a way of multiplying when you aren't watching). If you do not develop a plan for storing related documents, you will quickly find that you have huge numbers of documents in a single directory—making it difficult to find outdated documents or the document that you need to update. By establishing guidelines for document storage before you begin your project you can save yourself hours of maintenance work later on.

For example, you may wish to establish a convention for the storage of images. Images associated with a specific set of documents could be stored in a directory named "Images", with a special Image subdirectory to be created in any directory that holds documents. Thus, all references to images can safely be made to:

images/myimage.gif

Even if the document is moved to another point in the directory structure, as long as the corresponding images are also moved, there will be no need to modify the document to point to a new location. Images that may need to be shared between all documents in a site (such as logos) stored in a common, top-level "Image" directory. In a similar fashion, you may wish to set up guidelines for the organization of the documents themselves. For example, if you are creating an on-line manual, you may wish to group documents relating to a specific topic into separate subdirectories.

Page Design and Layout

When authoring a set of related documents, it is important to keep a consistent design style and organization across documents. When authors use a repeated organization of text and graphics across documents, readers will come to know what to expect and where to locate pertinent information. Such patterns will help make your documents more understandable and legible.

Within one document, do not mix a large number of colors and fonts. While you may find this cute, it makes a bad visual impression.

Header Elements

In particular, you should have the following header elements at the top of each document. These elements should be positioned with the same screen location in each document.

The title of the document

Do not confuse this with the title tag, which you should also include in the document. The title of the document should be included in a header tag at the beginning of the document.

Banner, logo, or seal identifying the organization or institution (if applicable)

This banner can also be a hyperlink that points back to the organization's top-level page, or it could be an image map that provides links to various locations within the organization's pages. If you choose to use an image map, make sure that you offer an alternative table of contents so that readers who cannot use graphics are still able to navigate through your pages.

For example, the following header is used on the top level of Kelly Kayaker's business pages:

```
<A HREF="/cgi/imagemap/obrwa>
<IMG SRC=wahine/obralogo.gif ISMAP ALT="[Ozone Books and
Raging Wahine Logos]"></IMG></A>
<H1 ALIGN=CENTER>Welcome to</H1>
<H1 ALIGN=CENTER>Ozone Books and Raging Wahine Adventures</H1>
```

Although it is not included here, a table of contents that provides equivalent navigational opportunities is included beneath the first paragraph in the document. Here is how this header looks in Netscape Navigator:

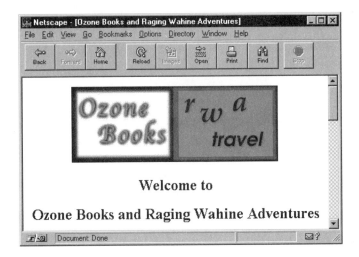

Footer Elements

You should have the following elements at the bottom of documents (sometimes called footers). To give your pages a consistent look, these elements should be similarly positioned in all documents.

The author's name and contact information

This information is typically placed within an <ADDRESS> tag. It is a good idea to include an e-mail address with a mailto link. You may also wish to include a hyperlink from the author's name to the author's personal home page.

Link to a top-level or home page

This is important! Remember that anyone can make a link to any page. If you don't include a link back to your top-level page, and someone gets to your page via a link outside your pages, it may not be easy for them to find your top-level page. If you want to encourage people to look at all of your pages, make it easy for them to get to your starting point!

Links to related documents (if applicable)

Like a link to your top-level page, links to related documents help your readers to navigate through your pages. These links don't have to go to other parts of your web, although typically links in footers do.

Last modification date of document

While this isn't absolutely necessary, it is often helpful for readers to know how recently information has been updated.

Copyright status of document (if applicable)

If you have disclaimers or other restrictions on your pages, you can avoid having to include your list on every page by making a page with this information and then linking a copyright notice to that page.

Let's look at the footer for Ozone Books' catalog. It includes an address, an e-mail contact, and links to relevant top-level pages. Since the catalog itself is dated, we do not include a last modification date, and since they want the catalog to be distributed as widely as possible, there is not copyright restriction notice on this page.

```
<ADDRESS>
Raging Wahine Adventures and Ozone Books<BR>
P.O. Box 600<BR>
Wellington, New Zealand<BR>
<A HREF="mailto:queries@ozwa.com">queries@ozwa.com.nz</A><BR>
</ADDRESS>
<HR>
<A HREF="../ozwatop.html"><IMG SRC="../images/ozwahome.gif"
ALT="[Ozone/Wahine Home Page]"></A>
<A HREF="../wahine/raging.html"><IMG
SRC="../images/wahihome.gif"
ALT="[Raging Wahine Home Page]"></A>
<A HREF="index.html"><IMG SRC="../images/ozhome.gif"
ALT="[Ozone Books Home Page]"></A>
```

Here is how our footer looks in Netscape Navigator:

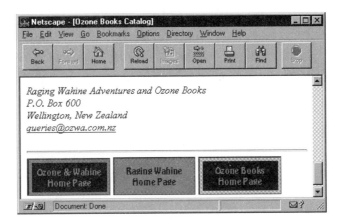

Using Graphics and Other Multimedia Items

The Web has made networked desktop publishing a reality for many people. Naturally, as authors, we are tempted to take maximum advantage of this new ability to integrate multimedia elements such as graphics, animations, audio and video into our documents.

However, there are many reasons to use such items with caution. Many users have limited network bandwidth and hence choose to browse the Web with images "turned off." Others access Web documents using text-only browsers, such as Lynx. These users are completely lost upon encountering a graphics-intensive page.

DON'T MAKE AN IMAGE MAP THE ONLY WAY FOR READERS TO NAVIGATE THROUGH YOUR DOCUMENTS.

Using image maps as a navigational tool for your Web pages is a tempting way to make flashy-looking pages. However, don't make image maps the only way for readers to navigate through your documents. These graphics often take a long time to load for users connecting to the Web with a less-than-high-speed network connection. Many of these users will not have the patience for documents designed in this manner. Others will be incapable of viewing them.

This is especially important in your top-level document. While this kind of top-level navigation approach is visually appealing and supports graphical navigation, you will lose users browsing without images.

For example, our header example from page 321 includes a clickable image. We provide a text-based navigation option equivalent to this image later in the document. However, as you can see when we display the beginning of the document in Lynx, our readers would be unable to navigate to our other related documents if we did not do this.

```
                    OZONE BOOKS and RAGING WAHINE TRAVEL (p1 of 3)

    [Ozone Books and Wahine Adventures Logos]

                    OZONE BOOKS & RAGING WAHINE TRAVEL


    Welcome to Ozone Books and Raging Wahine Adventures. Ozone Books and
    Raging Wahine have teamed together to provide for all your adventure
    travel needs. Ozone books is a publisher of travel books, specializing
    in adventure travel. For those of you that prefer firsthand
    experience, Raging Wahine Adventures provides travel expeditions.
    ----------------------------------------------------------------

Ozone Books



    Ozone Books has been publishing and selling travel and adventure books
    since 1987. We are based in Alberta, Canada. We hope that you enjoy
-- press space for more, use arrow keys to move, '?' for help, 'q' to quit
  Arrow keys: Up and Down to move. Right to follow a link; Left to go back.
  H)elp O)ptions P)rint G)o M)ain screen Q)uit /=search [delete]=history list
```

One way to be sure that you do not lose readers who do not wish to view images is to offer two sets of pages—one with graphic-based navigational links, and another set with text-based links. Then, on your top-level page offer readers the choice of which set of pages to use.

If you do choose to keep only one set of pages that use images or image maps for navigation, be sure to offer an alternative text-based navigation route. You can use the ALT tag to show your readers what they are missing, and offer text-based links for users with text-only browsers.

Image Style Issues

From the point of view of style, you should use graphics only to improve and enhance the presentation and content of your document. You shouldn't cram your page full of graphics, icons, and buttons simply for their sex appeal. Make sure these offer real added value to your document and your document Web space. For example, an inlined graphic of your organization's logo used as a banner at the top of every page is an effective use of graphics, since it provides a visual identity for documents. This banner can also be used as a hyperlink back to the organization's home page.

When designing graphics for inclusion into Web documents, use a graphical format that most computer platforms can display. Presently, the two most common formats are GIF and JPEG. A new format, Portable Network Graphics (PNG), has been developed in response to the legal uncertainties surrounding GIF, and the limitations in the JPEG standard. Although support for the PNG format is very limited at this time, there is strong interest among developers to add PNG capabilities to their products. However, for now, GIF is the most widely supported format, with JPEG following closely behind.

KEEP THE SIZE OF INLINED IMAGES AS SMALL AS POSSIBLE.

Again, out of deference to network transfer time, try to keep the size of your inlined images as small as possible. If you have a large image, use a small icon representation to convey to users the content of a graphical image; then make the icon a hyperlink to the actual item. Using the icon representation, users can better decide if they wish to retrieve the entire image. You should also give users an estimate of the size of the full image. For example, next to the icon you might say "(Full image is 100 kb)." This will allow users to estimate network transfer time, and help them decide if they want the full image.

Here is a sample page for a children's art gallery that uses this technique:

```
<H1><IMG SRC=kidpictures/logo.gif ALIGN=BOTTOM ALT="KidArt
Logo"> Kids Art Gallery</H1>
<P>Welcome to our art gallery! These pictures were created by
children in local preschools. If your school would like to
```

```
participate in this gallery please <A
HREF="mailto:gallerymaster@kidstuff.org">contact us</A>.

<HR>
<P>Here are a couple of the most recent additions to our
gallery:</P>
<TABLE BORDER=3 CELLPADDING=10>
<TR><TD><A HREF="kidpictures/kidpict1.gif"><IMG
SRC="kidpictures/kidpict1-thumb.gif" ALT="[Picture
1]"></A>33Kb image
<TD><A HREF="kidpictures/kidpict2.gif"><IMG
SRC="kidpictures/kidpict2-thumb.gif" ALT="[Picture 1]">
</A>44Kb image
</TABLE>
```

Here it is in Netscape:

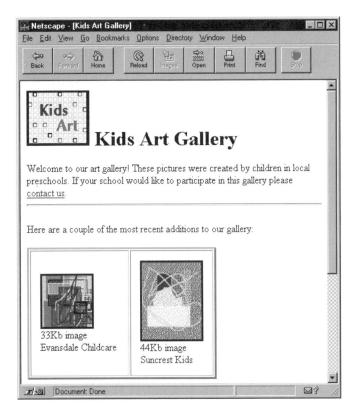

Notice that we included only two pictures besides the logo in our top-level page.

AVOID USING MANY SMALL IMAGES IN A SINGLE DOCUMENT.

Although small images can be transferred quickly, a new network connection must be initiated for each image. Since it takes additional time to open each connection, it ends up taking more transfer time than a single image that is equivalent in size to the total amount of space used by the small images. Additionally, some browsers have problems loading large number of images in a single document.

There are a couple of techniques that you should consider to minimize these problems. If you use multiple images for navigation, try to reuse the same images on all of your pages. Browsers usually keep copies of images in a local memory cache and will be able to reuse them without needing to download them repeatedly. Alternatively, you could combine your images into a single image map. This way, only a single image will need to be transferred.

If possible, provide your images in an interlaced format. Although interlacing does not speed up transfer time, it allows your readers to more quickly determine what the complete image will look like. This way they do not have to wait for the entire image to be transferred before deciding whether they want to see it.

Finally, many authors make the mistake of designing images that are too wide. The sides of these images then get chopped off when loaded in a browser set to the standard size. Avoid this problem by designing your graphics such that they fit within the standard browser size, which is usually on a 13-inch screen with 640 by 480 pixels.

Supporting Navigation

Navigation within and between sets of Web documents is an issue of paramount importance. Document design must support effective navigation among related documents, while avoiding the "lost in hyperspace" syndrome. In this syndrome, links are so convoluted and complex that users forget their location, cannot retrace their steps, and cannot locate items of interest. We now discuss supporting effective navigation for your users.

INCLUDE A TABLE OF CONTENTS.

Having to browse through a large document using a scroll bar is tiresome and disorienting, and makes navigation slow and cumbersome. It is better to keep your documents short and put a table of contents at the top of each high-level, introductory document. Items in the table of contents should be hyperlinks to the actual items. The table of contents provides users with a overview of the document or set of documents and gives an estimate of the coverage. The hyperlinks allow users to quickly locate items of interest and form their individual information pathways.

There are a number of styles for tables of contents. For a fairly short table of contents it is popular to enclose the list in square brackets, with vertical bars separating the topics. For example:

```
<P>[<A HREF="kayak2.htm#gear">kayaking gear</A> |
<A HREF="kayak2.htm#seakayak">sea kayaking</A> |
<A HREF="kayak2.htm#paddle">paddle information</A> |
<A HREF="kayak2.htm#resources"> kayaking resources</A>]</P>
```

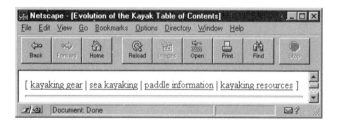

Another simple style uses an unordered list:

```
<UL>
<LI><A HREF="kayak2.htm#gear">kayaking gear</A>
<LI> <A HREF="kayak2.htm#seakayak">sea kayaking</A>
<LI> <A HREF="kayak2.htm#paddle">paddle information</A>
<LI> <A HREF="kayak2.htm#resources"> kayaking resources</A>
</UL>
```

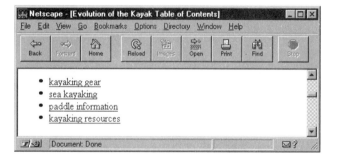

A fancier version of a table of contents uses clickable images as bullets. If you choose this style and your images do not explicitly tell readers what they are linked to, make sure that you include a text description along with the picture. You should also include an ALT attribute with a description of the link to further accommodate readers with line-mode browsers.

```
<P><A HREF="kayak.htm#gear"><IMG SRC="gif/kayak.gif"
ALT="[Kayak Icon]"> kayaking gear</A>
<P><A HREF="kayak.htm#seakayak"><IMG SRC="gif/sea.gif"
ALT="[Sea Icon]"> sea kayaking</A>
<P><A HREF="kayak.htm#paddle"><IMG SRC="gif/paddle.gif"
ALT="[Paddle Icon]"> paddle information</A>
<P><A HREF="kayak.htm#resources"><IMG SRC="gif/kayak2.gif"
ALT="[Kayak Icon]"> kayaking resources</A></P>
```

It looks like this in Netscape Navigator:

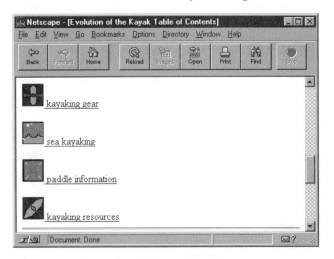

Here it is in the Lynx browser:

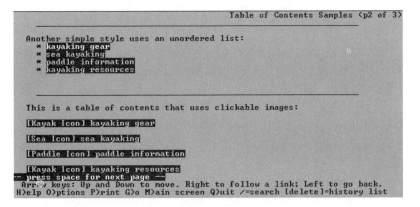

Notice that we placed our text in the ALT attribute in square brackets. Many line-mode browsers do not do anything special to indicate that text comes from an ALT attribute. By putting our text in square brackets, we separate it visually from the rest of the document's text and help to clarify that it is an alternative to an image.

Although the version with images is visually appealing, it wastes screen space. We do a final cleanup by lining our images up in two columns using a table:

```
<PRE><TABLE BORDER=3><TR>
<TR><TD><A HREF="#gear"><IMG SRC="images/kayak.gif"
ALIGN=MIDDLE> kayaking gear</A>
<TD><A HREF="#seakayak"><IMG SRC="images/sea.gif"
ALIGN=MIDDLE> sea kayaking</A>
<TR><TD><A HREF="#paddle"><IMG SRC="images/paddle.gif"
ALIGN=MIDDLE> paddle information</A>
<TD><A HREF="#resources"><IMG SRC="images/kayak2.gif"
ALIGN=MIDDLE> kayaking resources</A>
</TABLE></PRE>
```

Notice that our table is contained in a PRE tag. This is to accommodate our readers with line-mode browsers and browsers that do not support tables. The PRE tag prevents these browsers from running all the text in our table together. At the same time it does not affect the presentation of the table in our table-aware browser.

DON'T GO HYPERLINK-WILD.

While hyperlinks allow individual users to locate items of personal interest within large document spaces, they should be used judiciously. Presenting the user with too many options can be overwhelming and clutters up the document's look. Find a happy medium, based on the content of your document.

DON'T FALL INTO THE "CLICK HERE" TRAP.

When implementing a hyperlink don't say, "If you want to see more, click here." This is redundant. It can also confuse readers, since most browsers try to highlight links in some fashion. If you fall into this trap, your reader will be confronted with a page of "heres." Instead, embed the hyperlink within the referring text.

PROVIDE NAVIGATION BUTTONS.

In a large set of related documents, provide buttons that allow users to move to the "next" document in the series, the "previous" document in the series, and the top-level table of contents. For example, a computer manual stored as a set of Web documents can use the "Next" button to take the user to the subsequent section. Similarly, the "Previous" button will take the user to the preceding section. Finally, a "Top" or "Home" button returns the user to the table of contents. These buttons can be represented as actual graphical buttons with hyperlinks to the appropriate page, or the buttons can simply be text hyperlinks. Supporting such navigation will allow users to effectively and quickly locate information of interest.

PROVIDE A WAY "HOME".

This is actually an extension of the idea of providing navigation buttons, but it is important enough to warrant a separate mention. You should always provide a way to jump back to your top-level document. Remember that links may be made to any document on the Web from any other document—so you may have readers who get to your documents from some starting point over which you have no control. You can help these readers to find all of your documents by providing them with a link to your top-level document.

We have included a number of arrow icons on the CD that can be used as navigation buttons. You can find a catalog of these icons in the document *icon-index.html*. Here is an example of some navigational icons at the end of a document:

```
<TABLE BORDER=5>
<TR><TD ALIGN=CENTER WIDTH=50%><A HREF=index.html><IMG
SRC=gif/larrow4.gif ALIGN=middle ALT="[Home]" BORDER=0><BR>
Home</A>
<TD ALIGN=CENTER WIDTH=50%><A HREF=next.html><IMG
SRC=gif/rarrow4.gif ALIGN=middle ALT="[Next Page]"
BORDER=0><BR>Next</A><BR>
</TABLE>
```

Here is how this looks in Netscape Navigator: .

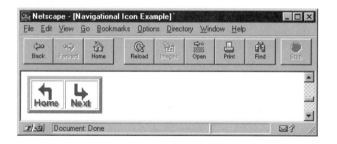

CHECK YOUR DOCUMENT IN DIFFERENT BROWSERS.

Our navigation example makes use of a table and a number of Netscape extensions to create arrows in beveled buttons. But what happens when our document is viewed in a browser that does not support all of the Netscape extensions or in a browser that does not support tables? What happens in a line-mode browser—does our use of images still make sense?

We use a version of the Macintosh EINet browser that does not support tables to see what happens to the display in the first situation. This is what we find:

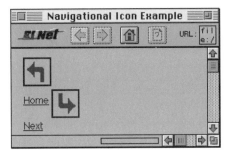

We've lost the beveled-button effect. Even worse, "Home" appears on the same line as the arrow that actually goes with "Next." Fortunately there is an easy fix for this problem. We modify our source to include a BR tag at the end of each cell. Table-aware browsers should ignore the BR tag at the end of the cell, so this change does not affect the way that it looks in those browsers. Now our document is more understandable:

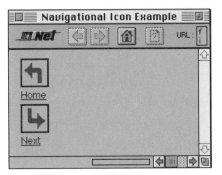

Now let's take a test drive in a line-mode browser. Here it is in Lynx:

The navigation is still clear, but it looks a little awkward. Since there are actually two links—one image-based and one text-based—to each destination, we see duplicate text in our line-mode browser. The simplest solution to this problem is to move the text into our images so that we no longer need double links. Here is the HTML source used with our updated images:

```
</TABLE>
<TABLE BORDER=5 CELLPADDING=0>
<TR><TD><A HREF=index.htm><IMG SRC=gif/HomeArrow.gif
ALIGN=middle ALT="[Home]" BORDER=0></A>
<TD> <A HREF=next.htm><IMG SRC=gif/NextArrow.gif ALIGN=middle
ALT="[Next Page]" BORDER=0></A>
</TABLE>
```

As you can see, even the source is simpler. As you can see in our example, the resulting display in Netscape Navigator is nicer as well:

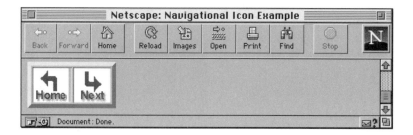

Let's check it with ElNet's browser to see how it fares without tables:

Since the buttons are on the same line, it takes up less space. It looks better too. Now the line-mode test:

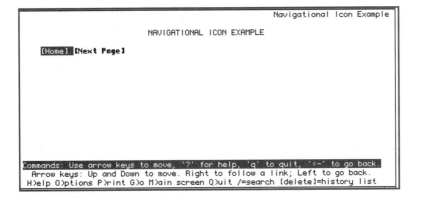

Without the text link, only our ALT attribute is displayed. As you can see, this is an improvement as well.

By viewing our document in three types of browsers, we were able to make changes that improved its appearance in all of the browsers. We also eliminated confusion that might have arisen when the original document was displayed in some of the browsers. While it is not always practical to view every document in multiple browsers, you should always try to review at least the framework you plan to use.

Centering Text

Centering text is something that almost every author will want to do. It is also something that can be done many ways—with each method supported by only a subset of browsers. As you may recall from Chapter 2, there are three methods for centering sections of text:

- CENTER
- DIV with the ALIGN=CENTER attribute
- Specific tags (such as P, H1, H2, and so on) with the ALIGN=CENTER attribute

Although all of these tags and attributes are included in the HTML 3.2 standard, the CENTER tag is a Netscape creation and was not included in previous versions of the HTML standard. The DIV tag is a relative newcomer, although its roots are in the HTML standards process. This leaves the ALIGN=CENTER attribute in combination with specific tags as the only method for centering text in earlier versions of HTML.

Why should you as an author of HTML documents care about this? Simple—because browser writers do. If you are authoring documents that will be viewed in Netscape, you can stick to the CENTER tag and be fairly confident that sections of your document that have been designated for centering will appear centered. However, if you don't have control over the browser that will be used to view your document, and you want to be sure that your centered sections show up in a centered fashion, you will need to use a different strategy.

For example, browsers that were written with earlier versions of the HTML standard in mind did not support the CENTER tag. NCSA Mosaic 2.0.1 on the Macintosh is one such browser—but since it was created before DIV was introduced, the only way to center text in this browser is to use ALIGN=CENTER with the tag for a specific block of text.

The simplest way to be sure that the elements you wish to center actually appear as you desire is to include all the center-related tags that are applicable to the item(s) you wish to center. For example, if we have a second-level heading and a table that we wish to center, we might include them as follows:

```
<CENTER>
<DIV=CENTER>
<H2 ALIGN=CENTER>Kayaking in New Zealand</H2>
<TABLE ALIGN=CENTER>
<TR><TH>River<TH>Difficulty Level
<TR><TD>Karamea River<TD>2
<TR><TD>Rangitikei River<TD>3.5
</TABLE>
</DIV>
</CENTER>
```

While this may seem like overkill, it covers every possible combination of centering tags. If a browser supports some form of centering, we can be assured that these elements in our document will be centered.

Use of System Resources

Well-designed Web pages take into account the impact that different types of elements have on the systems on which the page is viewed. Beautiful pages will be of little use to the majority of readers if they are difficult or time consuming to load into a browser. Nontext elements should be of particular concern when designing your pages. We have already gone over some of the ramifications of the use of images in the "Using Graphics" section. Now we will go over some of the other system-related issues you need to consider.

Minimize Document Size

Recall that in a networked environment, delays can occur when transferring large documents. Moreover, users throughout the Internet have different amounts of bandwidth in their network connection. The larger the number of bytes in a document, the longer it takes for a browser to load it. Users without high-bandwidth connections will usually not have the patience to wait long periods of time for documents to be loaded.

Although images, video, and audio usually contribute the largest number of bytes to documents, it is possible to create large documents primarily composed of text. If you find yourself with such a document, you should review its structure and see if it can be divided into smaller documents that are linked to one another.

Therefore:

- Minimize the number of multimedia elements within documents in order to minimize byte size.
- If you find that you have a very long document composed primarily of text, examine the document's contents to see if it may be broken into smaller documents connected with links.

Test Your Documents

It can be very frustrating to encounter a poorly or incorrectly formatted document on the Web. Users may form negative opinions about a Web site based on a single substandard document. Therefore:

ALWAYS TEST THE DISPLAY OF YOUR DOCUMENTS BEFORE PUBLISHING THEM.

If possible, test documents using multiple graphical and text-only browsers. Recall that different flavors of browsers may result in subtle variations in document display. If you currently have only one browser, you can use browsers.html on the CD to download Mac and Windows browsers.

Ideally, you should also check your documents on multiple platforms. There are significant differences between the way that Windows systems and Macintoshes display color. You may find that the beautifully balanced image on your Windows system looks completely washed out on a Macintosh. While it may not be possible to make an image that looks perfectly balanced on all platforms, it should be possible to find an acceptable median point.

DON'T RELY ON THE APPEARANCE OF A PARTICULAR STYLE.

Remember that many browsers allow users to modify the way that logical and physical styles are displayed. Therefore, you cannot be sure how a style will look, even if you know which browser your reader uses. Use styles with consistency.

ALWAYS CHECK THE ACCURACY OF THE URLs IN YOUR DOCUMENTS

If your documents contain links, Make sure that you check your links both before and after your documents have been moved to a server. If you used relative paths in your URLs, some links may not work after your documents are moved to a server. There are a number of automated tools that you can use to check your URLs. We were unable to locate any Mac-based checkers, but many are available for UNIX systems.

Checking and Verifying Your Web Documents

As we demonstrated with our multiple TITLE example in Chapter 2, creating documents that violate the rules can result in unexpected and sometimes unpleasant results. Before making your Web pages public, you should check them to ensure that they are using accurate and correct HTML. You could, of course, check everything by hand, but this is painstaking and time consuming. It is also easy to miss errors this way.

Fortunately, many tools are available for checking your HTML documents for errors and verifying link accuracy. These validation tools come in two general formats. First, they exist as software that can be downloaded and run on your own computer. The second option is simpler if you have Internet access. Validation services exist on Internet Web sites to which you can send the URL of the page you want checked.

Typically, you use your Web browser to access the Web checking site. You are then usually presented with a form, which asks you to enter the URL of the document or documents you wish to have checked. Some services allow you to specify which version of HTML you are using, while others use the DOCTYPE listed in your document. If your document does not have a DOCTYPE, and you want to add one, you can find a list of valid DOCTYPEs at:

```
http://ugweb.cs.ualberta.ca/~gerald/validate/lib/catalog
```

You submit the form, and the checker presents you with a new document listing the HTML errors found in your document. You must, of course, have Internet access for this service to work.

There are many such checking and verifying programs available on the Internet. Of the services that we have tried, Dr. HTML is our favorite. Not only does it do HTML verification, but it can also provide an analysis of the amount of time it will take to download a page and associated images. You can find Dr. HTML at:

```
http://imagiware.com/RxHTML/
```

Although we like Dr. HTML, we recommend trying several services, since they vary quite a bit. For each of these services, you can use the listed URL and your Web browser in order to access the site.

Weblint sources:

`http://www.khoral.com/staff/neilb/weblint.html`

Weblint form-based checking service:

`http://www.unipress.com/weblint/`

Webtechs:

`http://www.webtechs.com/html-val-svc/`

Kinder, Gentler Validator:

`http://ugweb.cs.ualberta.ca/~gerald/validate/`

You will find a listing of many validation services at:

`http://www.ccs.org/validate/validate.html`

For example, we used the Unipress form service to check a small HTML document. The form looks like this:

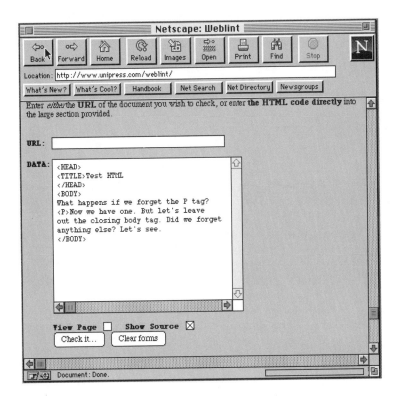

Even in a short document it is possible to make numerous errors. Finding all of the errors by hand can be difficult. Can you spot the errors in the HTML document that we entered in the form?

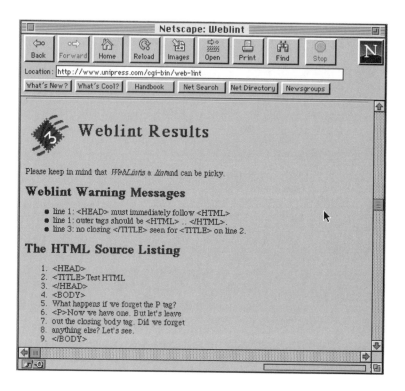

As you can see, Weblint had no problems finding them. Try it yourself and see how much easier it is than manual checking.

In Closing

It is easy to write a document that can be displayed by a Web browser. Even a plain ASCII file can be linked into the Web. The difficult part of Web publishing is to make an *inviting* set of documents—ones that your readers will enjoy and be able to use easily. In this chapter we reviewed the guidelines that will help you to create a set of documents that do this. In the next chapter we'll show you how to apply these principles to actual document design.

- Avoid a tangled or broken web: provide clear navigational links on **every** page.
- Validate your documents.
- Either view your document over a slow link or find the total number of bytes your document and all the associated in-line images use. If it's over 50 kb, cut down!
- Check your document in multiple browsers, and make sure that one of them is a line-mode browser.
- Check your document with image loading turned off (be sure to empty your disk cache before you do this!).

IN THIS CHAPTER YOU WILL LEARN HOW TO CREATE
DIFFERENT TYPES OF HOME PAGES INCLUDING

- PERSONAL HOME PAGES
- BUSINESS HOME PAGES

  *All of the home pages in this chapter can be found
  on the CD.*

DESIGNING HOME PAGES

What's In This Chapter

This chapter explains how to author a number of types of
home pages, including a personal, autobiographical page, an
on-line travel guide, and a set of pages for a business. You can
find all of the pages in this chapter on the CD.

Personal Home Pages

One of the most popular uses for HTML is the creation of
personal home pages. We will present several sample pages to
give you some ideas for your own page.

Kelly Kayaker's Home Page

In this example we will create a personal home page for Kelly Kayaker. Kelly is a writer and editor of travel guides for a publishing company, Ozone Books, Inc., which maintains a Web server on the host ozone.com. Kelly has two children, Ray and Neil. As hobbies, Kelly likes to bicycle, white-water kayak, and play Ultimate Frisbee. Kelly is indeed a busy woman!

We begin by creating the file that will contain our initial document. Since it is an HTML document, we give it the .html extension. We call our document kelly-homepage.html. Following good html practice, we include the following:

```
<HTML>
<HEAD>
<TITLE>Kelly Kayaker Home Page</TITLE>
</HEAD>
<BODY>
</BODY>
</HTML>
```

We include our closing tags so that we don't forget them, even though we are not yet done with the document.

We put Kelly's name in a large heading and include a thumbnail picture of Kelly, which is linked to a full-size picture. We also include a section on Kelly's work. To minimize the size of the document, we use a black-and-white picture of Kelly. Where possible, we add the appropriate hyperlinks. For example, since Kelly works for a publishing company we include a link to the company's catalog. Now our document contains the following:

```
<H1>Kelly Kayaker
<A HREF="gif/kelly.gif"><IMG ALIGN=middle
SRC="gif/kellthum.gif" ALT="My photo"></A>
</H1>
I am a writer and editor of travel books at Ozone Books,
Inc., a small publishing company. I am currently writing a
book on kayaking. My book includes an  <A
HREF=kelkayak.html>HTML document about kayaking</A>.
<HR>
```

```
<H2>Ozone Books</H2> <A
HREF="http://ozone.com/ozone.html">Ozone Books, Inc</A> is a
small publishing company. We specialize in <EM>travel
books</EM>. <P> Our <A
HREF="http://ozone.com/catalogue.html">catalogue of books</A>
is available on the Web. Books can also be <A
HREF="http://ozone.com/order-form.html"> directly ordered
</A> on the Web
<HR>
```

Note that the links to Kelly's publishing company are to a different system, so we have used complete URLs for these files. Here is the first part of Kelly's home page:

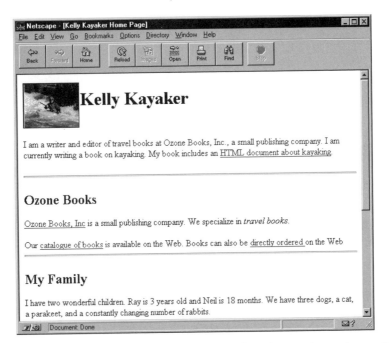

Now we add more personal information about Kelly—we describe her children, pets, and hobbies. We have used partial URLs for the links in this section, since they are Kelly's files and are kept on the same system as her personal home page. Because we wish to keep the file small in order to minimize network transfer time, we have not directly included the GIF files of her children. Instead, users may load the images by clicking on the hyperlinks.

```
<H2>My Family</H2>
I have two wonderful children. <A HREF="ray.gif">Ray</A>
is 3 years old and <A HREF="neil.gif">Neil</A> is 18
months. We have three dogs, a cat, a parakeet, and a
constantly changing number of rabbits.
<HR>
<H2>My Hobbies</H2>
I have several hobbies that keep me very busy. I wish
there were more hours in the day!
<DL>
<DT><B>Bicycling</B>
<DD>I own a tandem bicycle, and my husband and I ride
frequently in the hills near our home.
<DT><B>White-water kayaking</B>
<DD>I have been <A HREF="kayak.htm">kayaking </A> for 5
years in the rivers and creeks in the mountains near our
home.
<DT><B>Ultimate Frisbee</B>
<DD>I play frisbee on a woman's ultimate frisbee team.
</DL>
<HR>
```

We end Kelly's page with an address. We make Kelly's e-mail address a "mailto" link, so that it will be easy for people to contact her over the Net.

```
<ADDRESS>Kelly Kayaker, <A
HREF="mailto:kelly@ozone.com">kelly@ozone.com</A><BR>
Ozone Books, Inc.</ADDRESS>
```

The rest of the file appears as follows:

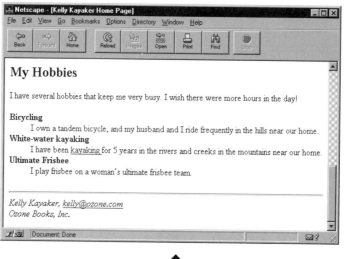

Kelly's Kayaking Document

On page 3 we described a kayaking document that Kelly was writing. The document consisted of a number of kayaking-related pictures, which were linked to documents about each picture. The descriptions of the pictures were written and maintained by Kelly's kayaking friends. The document ended with a guest book, so that readers could leave comments about it. Let's take a look at that document now. Here is the first part:

```
<HTML>
<HEAD>
<TITLE>Kayaking with Kelly Kayaker and Friends</TITLE>
</HEAD>
<BODY BGCOLOR=#FFFFFF>
<H1 ALIGN=CENTER>Kayaking with</H1>
<H1 ALIGN=CENTER>Kelly Kayaker and Friends</H1><HR>
<P><I>Page Under Construction</I></P>
<P>This is my kayaking hot spot list. I've gotten together
with some of my kayaking buddies to put together descriptions
of some of our favorite kayaking spots. I'm looking for help
with my descriptions of rivers in the US and New Zealand. If
you have an awesome run that you would like to add to this
list, please sign the guest book at the end of the document
or send me <A HREF="mailto:kayaker@ozone.com">e-mail</A>.
I'll be in touch.<P>
<P>[ <A HREF=#newzealand>New Zealand</A> | <A HREF=#usa>United
States</A> | <A HREF=#guest>Guest Book</A> ]
<HR>
```

Here it is:

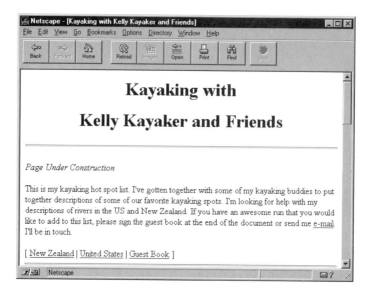

The first thing you should notice about this page is the *Page Under Construction* notice. Kelly is not really done with this page, but she wanted to make it available so that people could begin to use it. By encountering at the beginning of the document a notice that it is a work in progress, people know that it is still evolving, and this provides motivation to revisit the page later.

Right now the document is in one file. However, as more listings are added, the file will grow and may become too large to easily download and navigate. Kelly has planned for growth by dividing the document into sections that may easily be split into separate files later. She includes a table of contents at the beginning of the document to allow easy navigation between these sections. In the current document the links point to locations within the same file. However, it will be easy for her to split sections into separate files as she adds more listings.

The next part of the document is a section on rivers in New Zealand.

```
<H2><A NAME=newzealand></A>New Zealand</H2>
<P>Kayaking and other river sports are very popular
recreational activities in New Zealand. Popular rivers for
these sports are:</P>
<H3><A HREF="http://river.net/funstuff/shot.html"><I>The
Shotover River, South Island</I></A></H3>
<P><A HREF="http://river.net/funstuff/picture.gif"><IMG
SRC=images/mimithum.gif ALIGN=LEFT>Image of the Shotover
River, 65Kb</A></P>
<P>A hair-raising tale of a run down the Shotover by Joe
Paddle, Last Updated: Nov. 13, 1995<BR CLEAR=LEFT>
<H3><A HREF="http://kayak.net/descrip/buller.html"><I>The
Buller River, South Island</I></A></H3>
<P><A HREF="http://river.net/funstuff/picture.gif"><IMG
SRC=images/lavathum.gif ALIGN=LEFT>Image of the Buller River,
78Kb</A></P><P>A moving description of a solo journey down
the Buller by Sally Shooter, Last Updated: July 8, 1996</P>
```

Here it is:

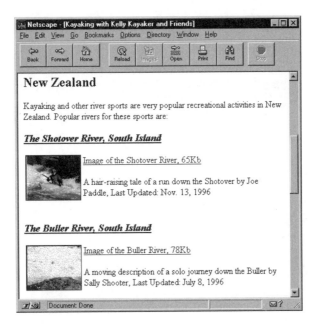

Notice that each link is accompanied by a brief description and the date it was last updated. This makes it easy for people who may revisit the page to determine if anything has changed since their last visit. The thumbnail pictures, which are linked to full-size images, are labeled with the size of the full image to help readers decide if they want to download the picture.

The next section illustrates some useful design ideas for evolving pages.

```
<H3><A HREF="http://kayak.net/descrip/karamea.html"><I>The
Karamea River, South Island</I></A><IMG
SRC=images/newred.gif></H3>
<P><A HREF="http://river.net/funstuff/picture.gif"><IMG
SRC=images/terrthum.gif ALIGN=LEFT>Image of the Karamea
River, 56Kb</A></P>
<P>The exciting saga of a blind kayaker's excursion down the
Karamea River by Darla Daring. Last Updated: April 10,
1995</P>
<BR CLEAR=LEFT>
<H3><I>Still Under Construction...</I></H3>
<UL>
<LI>The Rangitikei River, North Island
<LI>The Mohaka River, North Island
</UL>
```

Here it is:

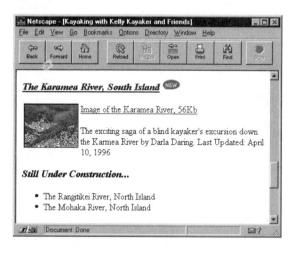

Kelly has only recently added the description for the Karamea River, so she includes an image of the word "new" in a red cloud. This makes it easy for people to notice the addition. Kelly has also left place holders for two other rivers that still need images and stories.

Kelly's Guest Book

Now let's look at the guest book. Kelly has requested that interested readers let her know if they have descriptions that they would like to add to her document. She also wants general comments about her page. She provides two methods for people to give her feedback. They can send her e-mail or fill out the guest book form at the end of her document. The form is fairly simple, since she needs only a few fields to get the information that she wants.

```
<H2><A NAME=guest></A>Kayaking Guest Book</H2>
<P>Like this page? Hate this page? Want to tell me about your
kayaking experiences? I'd like to hear from you -- please
sign in!</P>
<FORM METHOD=post ACTION="http://ozone.com/cgi/guest">
<P><B>First Name:</B> <INPUT NAME="fname" TYPE=text
MAXLENGTH=30 SIZE=30></P>
<P><B>Last Name:</B> <INPUT NAME="lname" TYPE=text
MAXLENGTH=30 SIZE=30></P>
<P><B>E-mail Address:</B> <INPUT NAME="eaddr" TYPE=text
MAXLENGTH=50></P>
<P><B>Tell me about your favorite kayaking run.</B><BR>
<TEXTAREA NAME="comments" ROWS=4 COLS=60>
</TEXTAREA>
</P>
<P>Thanks for visiting - come again soon.</P>
<P><INPUT TYPE=SUBMIT VALUE=" Finished - Submit ">
<INPUT TYPE=RESET Value=" Restart - Clear "></P>
```

Kelly ends the page with her contact information, a last update date, and a copyright notice:

```
<HR>
<ADDRESS>Kelly Kayaker, <A
HREF="mailto:kelly@ozone.com">kelly@ozone.com</A><BR>
Ozone Books, Inc.<BR>
Last Update: April 15, 1996</ADDRESS>
<P>&#169 1996 Kelly Kayaker</P>
```

Mimi's Home Page

Now we'll look at a real home page—Mimi's. Mimi is a lecturer at a university in New Zealand. She has made it easy for readers to load her home page by leaving all images out of her top-level page. Instead, there are links to pages with images. In her description of her work history, she has included links to the pages for the places she has worked and studied.

```
<!DOCTYPE HTML PUBLIC "-//W3O//DTD W3 HTML 2.0//EN">
<HTML>
<HEAD>
<TITLE>Mimi Recker</TITLE>
</HEAD>
<BODY>
<H1><A HREF="mimipics.html">Mimi Recker</A></H1>
I am a lecturer affiliated with the University Teaching
Development Centre (UTDC) at  <A
HREF="http://www.vuw.ac.nz">Victoria University</A> in
Wellington, New Zealand.<P>
I received a Ph.D. from the <A
HREF="http://www.berkeley.edu">University of California,
Berkeley</A>, in 1992, and a B.A. from the <A
HREF="http://www.upenn.edu">University of Pennsylvania</A>,
both in the U.S.A.<BR>
More recently, I was employed as a research scientist in the
<A HREF="http://www.cc.gatech.edu">College of Computing</A>,
at  <A HREF="http://www.gatech.edu">Georgia Tech</A>.
<P>
```

Let's see how this looks.

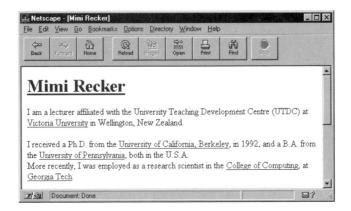

Rather than including her lengthy list of publications in her home page, Mimi keeps a separate document with a list of her publications and makes a link to this page. This keeps the top-level page short so that it loads quickly. It also makes it easy to maintain the list, which she may want to incorporate in other documents. Mimi also provides a way for readers to contact her by including a "mailto" link to her e-mail address.

```
<H2>Some recent papers and publications</H2>
Click to see recent <A HREF="mimipubs.html">papers and
publications</A>. Send <A
HREF="mailto:mimi.recker@vuw.ac.nz">email</A>
if you have trouble downloading a particular paper.
<HR>
<ADDRESS>UTDC<BR>
Victoria University of Wellington<BR>
P.O. Box 600<BR>
Wellington New Zealand<BR>
mimi.recker@vuw.ac.nz<BR>
+64 4-472.1000 x8868 </ADDRESS>
</BODY>
</HTML>
```

Here is the rest of Mimi's page:

Business Home Pages

In this section we present a couple of examples of how a business might set up its home pages. When you set up home pages for a business, you should first decide what portions of your business are to be presented. Are you advertising the business as a whole? Do you want to give control of various pieces to different departments? Will you allow people to order your products through forms in some of your pages? Do you want customer feedback?

In our first example we will look at a small business. Our first example will be for Kelly Kayaker's publisher, Ozone Books, and its affiliate, Raging Wahine Adventures. Ozone Books is a publisher of travel books, and Raging Wahine Adventures is a travel company specializing in adventure expeditions.

We create a top-level page that includes a logo for each division of the company. We have placed both of the logos into the same image and created a map file for the image. Readers may click on the logo for a division to go to the home page for that division. We also include a short overview of both companies.

```
<HTML>
<HEAD>
<TITLE>Ozone Books and Raging Wahine Travel</TITLE>
</HEAD>
<BODY>
<A HREF="http://ozone.com/cgi/imagemap/obrwa>
<IMG SRC=wahine/obralogo.gif ISMAP ALT="[Ozone Books and
Raging Wahine Logos]"></IMG></A>
<H1 ALIGN=CENTER>Welcome to</H1>
<H1 ALIGN=CENTER>Ozone Books and Raging Wahine Adventures</H1>
<P>Ozone Books and Raging Wahine have teamed together to
provide for all your adventure travel needs. Ozone books is a
publisher of travel books, specializing in adventure travel.
For those of you who prefer
firsthand experience, Raging Wahine Adventures provides
travel expeditions.</P>
```

We displayed this page in the design chapter on page 321. Next, we add short summaries for each division. If you have several divisions in your company, you may wish to add a table of contents to make it easier for readers to find the section they want. However, since this company has only two divisions, we do not use a table of contents. The description for each division includes links to the division's home pages.

```
<HR>
<H2><A HREF=ozone/index.html>Ozone Books</A></H2>
<P>Ozone Books has been publishing and selling travel and
adventure books since 1987. We are based in Alberta, Canada.
We hope that you enjoy our <A
HREF=ozone/catalog.html>catalog</A>. Our books are available
at many bookstores, or you may <A HREF=ozone/order.html>order
them directly</A> from
us.</P>
<HR>
<H2><A HREF=wahine/raging.html>Raging Wahine
Adventures</A></H2>
<P>Raging Wahine Adventures is an adventure travel company,
based in Wellington, New Zealand. We have been offering
adventure travel trips since 1988. We provide all levels of
trips -- from the backcountry novice to the most hardened
thrill-seeker.</P>
```

We store the documents for the two divisions in separate folders. All the pages related to Ozone Books are kept in the Ozone folder, while Raging Wahine Adventures' pages may be found in the Wahine folder. This separation of pages makes it easy to find the pages for the relevant division and provides a consistent structure so that links may be made in a consonant fashion.

Notice that for the Ozone division we have included links to Ozone's order form and catalog. This allows readers who may wish to place an order or look up a specific book to jump directly to the document of interest.

Finally, we end the page with contact information, as well as an e-mail address. The e-mail address is a mailto link, to make it as easy as possible for customers to contact the company:

```
<HR>
For more information, you may send us <A
HREF="mailto:queries@ozwa.com">
electronic mail</A>, or write to us at the address below.<P>
We look forward to hearing from you.
<P>
<ADDRESS>
Raging Wahine Adventures and Ozone Books<BR>
P.O. Box 600<BR>
Wellington, New Zealand<BR>
<AHREF="mailto:queries@ozwa.com">queries@ozwa.com.nz</A><BR>
</ADDRESS>
</BODY>
</HTML>
```

Here is how this section looks:

Back   Forward   Home   Reload   Images   Open   Print   Find   Stop

Ozone Books

Ozone Books has been publishing and selling travel and adventure books since 1987. We are
based in Alberta, Canada. We hope that you enjoy our catalog. Our books are available at many
bookstores, or you may order them directly from us.

Raging Wahine Adventures

Raging Wahine Adventures is an adventure travel company, based in Wellington, New Zealand.
We have been offering adventure travel trips since 1988. We provide all levels of trips -- from the
backcountry novice to the most hardened thrill-seeker.

For more information, you may send us electronic mail, or write to us at the address below.

We look forward to hearing from you.

Raging Wahine Adventures and Ozone Books
P.O. Box 600
Wellington, New Zealand
queries@ozwa.com.nz

Document: Done

Now let's look at Ozone's pages. We divide Ozone's pages
into two sections—one that describes books, and one that
allows people to submit orders. Ozone's top-level page is a
description of Ozone along with links to the other sections.

We start our top-level page with Ozone's logo. Notice that
we have included the logo in a consistent location for all of the
pages used in this company. Next, we include a short description of the company.

```
<HTML>
<HEAD>
<TITLE>OZONE BOOKS</TITLE>
</HEAD>
<IMG SRC=images/ozlogo.gif><H1>Welcome to Ozone Books</H1>
<P>Ozone Books publishes travel books. with an emphasis on
adventure travel. You can find a complete listing of our
books in our <A HREF=catalog.html>catalog</A>. Many of our
books are available at bookstores. You can also order books
directly from us by filling out this <A HREF=order.html</A>
order form. You can also place orders over the phone.
```

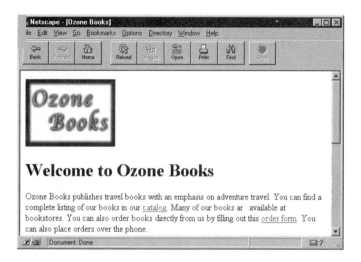

Ozone's Order Form

Ozone Books sells books over the Internet. We will now develop an on-line form for book orders. In keeping with our desire to have a similar look for all of the business's home pages, we include a logo at the top of the form. However, since this is a form, we do not want to use up too much space with a logo, so we use a thumbnail version.

We start the form with some information about Ozone. We include contact numbers for telephone and fax support. It is always a good idea to provide alternate contact information since network problems may prevent people from reaching you via the Internet.

```
<HTML>
<HEAD>
<TITLE>Ozone Book Order Form</TITLE>
</HEAD>
<BODY BGCOLOR=#FFFFFF>
<H1><IMG SRC=../images/ozsmall.gif> Ozone Book Order Form</H1>
Thank you for choosing Ozone for your travel book needs. In
addition to Internet orders, we also accept orders over the
phone and via FAX. Our staff is available Monday through
Friday from 9 a.m. to 5 p.m. Eastern Standard Time to take
your orders and answer your questions. FAX orders may be sent
at any time. Phone Orders: (304) 555-1368. FAX: (304) 555-
3712.
<HR>
```

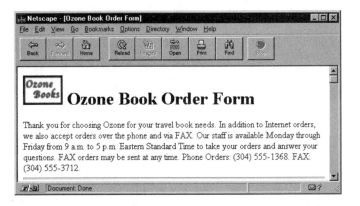

The data input portions of the form make heavy use of the TABLE tag to align input fields. As you may recall from our discussion about navigational buttons in a table, it is important to include the BR tag at the end of each row when you use TABLE. This accommodates readers using line-mode browsers and other browsers that do not understand the TABLE tag.

Next we provide areas for the customer's name and address:

```
<FORM METHOD="POST" ACTION="http://ozone.com/cgi/orderform">
<TABLE>
<TR><TD><B>First Name:</B> <TD><INPUT NAME="fname" TYPE=text
MAXLENGTH=30 SIZE=30><BR>
<TR><TD><B>Last Name:</B> <TD><INPUT NAME="lname" TYPE=text
MAXLENGTH=30 SIZE=30><BR>
<TR><TD><B>Address:</B> <TD><INPUT NAME="add1" TYPE=text
MAXLENGTH=45 SIZE=45><BR>
```

```
<TR><TD><B>Address:</B><TD><INPUT NAME="add1" TYPE=text
MAXLENGTH=45 SIZE=45><BR>
<TR><TD><B>City:</B> <TD><INPUT NAME="city" TYPE=text
MAXLENGTH=30 SIZE=20>
<B>State:</B> <INPUT NAME="state" TYPE=text MAXLENGTH=2
SIZE=2>
<B>ZIP:</B> <INPUT NAME="zip" TYPE=text MAXLENGTH=30 SIZE=10>
<BR>
<TR><TD><B>E-mail:</B> <TD><INPUT NAME="E-Mail" TYPE=text
MAXLENGTH=50 SIZE=50><BR>
<TR><TD><B>Daytime Phone:</B> <TD><INPUT NAME="phonenum"
TYPE=text MAXLENGTH=30 SIZE=20><BR>
</TABLE>
```

Netscape - [Ozone Book Order Form]

File Edit View Go Bookmarks Options Directory Window Help

Back Forward Home Reload Images Open Print Find Stop

First Name:

Last Name:

Address:

Address:

City: State: ZIP:

E-mail:

Daytime Phone:

Document: Done

Next, we create the section for placing orders. Since we allow people to order gift certificates, we preload one of the lines with our gift certificate code. Note that customers can overwrite our predefined values in this line.

```
<TABLE>
<TR><TH>Product<BR>
Number<TH>Title<TH>Qty<TH>Price<TH>Total<BR>
<TR><TD><INPUT NAME="PN1" TYPE=text MAXLENGTH=5 SIZE=5>
<TD><INPUT NAME="TITLE1" TYPE=text MAXLENGTH=40 SIZE=40>
<TD><INPUT NAME="QTY1" TYPE=text MAXLENGTH=5
SIZE=5><TD><INPUT NAME="PRICE1" TYPE=text MAXLENGTH=6
SIZE=6><TD><INPUT NAME="TOTAL1" TYPE=text MAXLENGTH=9
SIZE=9><BR>
```

<similar lines removed for brevity>

```
<TR><TD><INPUT NAME="PN6" TYPE=text MAXLENGTH=5 SIZE=5>
<TD><INPUT NAME="TITLE6" TYPE=text MAXLENGTH=40 SIZE=40>
<TD><INPUT NAME="QTY6" TYPE=text MAXLENGTH=5
SIZE=5><TD><INPUT NAME="PRICE6" TYPE=text MAXLENGTH=6
SIZE=6><TD><INPUT NAME="TOTAL6" TYPE=text MAXLENGTH=9
SIZE=9><BR>
<TR><TD><INPUT NAME="GIFT" TYPE=text MAXLENGTH=5 SIZE=5
VALUE="GIFT"> <TD><INPUT NAME="TITLEG" VALUE="Gift
Certificate" TYPE=text MAXLENGTH=40 SIZE=40> <TD><INPUT
NAME="QTYG" VALUE=0 TYPE=text MAXLENGTH=5 SIZE=5><TD><INPUT
NAME="PRICEG" VALUE=0 TYPE=text MAXLENGTH=6 SIZE=6><TD><INPUT
NAME="TOTALG" VALUE=0 TYPE=text MAXLENGTH=9 SIZE=9><BR>
</TABLE>
```

Notice that although the fields from line to line look almost identical, each one has a unique NAME attribute. When setting up forms with multiple lines that are fairly similar, be sure to check that each field has a unique NAME—otherwise you will have problems when you try to sort out the data that is returned by the form!

Our next section allows the customer to enter address information for a gift certificate. Since this section is essentially the same as the section for entering customer information, we will not display it here.

Now we include a payment section. We use radio boxes to allow the customer to pick one of four payment options.

```
<STRONG>Method of Payment:</STRONG>
<INPUT NAME="payment" VALUE="check" TYPE=radio>Check or Money
Order
<INPUT NAME="payment" VALUE="VISA" TYPE=radio>VISA
<INPUT NAME="payment" VALUE="Discover" TYPE=radio>Discover
<INPUT NAME="payment" VALUE="MC" TYPE=radio>MasterCard<BR>
```

If you plan to create a form that requests credit card information, you should try to make sure that your pages are placed on a secure server. Secure server technology provides a way for information that is exchanged between the browser and server to be transmitted in an encrypted format. This means that the browser scrambles the information before sending it to the server, so that a casual observer would not be able to understand it. When the browser receives the information, it unscrambles it.

Servers that do not use secure technology make it easy for someone watching network traffic to see the numbers. Since Ozone Books does not use a secure server, they do not allow people to send their credit card information in the form. Instead, they request that customers call to confirm the order and provide a credit card number.

```
<STRONG>Important:</STRONG> We do not accept credit card
numbers over the Internet at this time. To complete your
order please call us within 48 hours to provide us with your
credit card number. At your request, we will retain your
credit card information in our files so that future orders
may be completed without additional calls. Credit card orders
which have not been completed with 48 hours will be
cancelled. Checks must be received within one week of the
order. Books will not be shipped until the check is
received.</P>
```

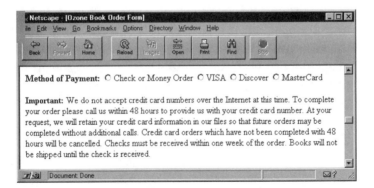

We end the input part of the form with a comment box so that our customers can give us feedback. We also provide submit and reset buttons.

```
<P>Please enter any additional comments here:<BR>
<TEXTAREA NAME="comments" ROWS=2 COLS=60>
</TEXTAREA>
</P>
</PRE>
<P>Thank you for your order!</P>
<P><INPUT TYPE=SUBMIT VALUE="Finished - Submit">
<INPUT TYPE=RESET Value="Restart - Clear All Fields"></P>
</FORM>
```

We finish off the form with some detailed information about Ozone's policies. At the very end we put our standard contact information along with some navigational buttons to allow customers to go back to the Ozone/Raging Wahine Home Page or to the Ozone Home Page.

```
<ADDRESS>
Raging Wahine Adventures and Ozone Books<BR>
P.O. Box 600<BR>
Wellington, New Zealand<BR>
<A HREF="mailto:queries@ozwa.com">queries@ozwa.com.nz</A> <BR>
</ADDRESS>
<HR>
<A HREF="../ozwatop.htm"><IMG SRC="../gif/ozwahome.gif"
ALT="[Ozone/Wahine Home Page]"></A>
<A HREF="../wahine/raging.htm"><IMG SRC="../gif/wahihome.gif"
ALT="[Raging Wahine Home Page]"></A>
<A HREF="index.htm"><IMG SRC="../gif/ozhome.gif" ALT="[Ozone
Books Home Page]"></A>
</BODY>
</HTML>
```

You can see how this looks on page 323 in the design chapter.

We included ALT values for each of our navigational buttons so that readers with line-mode browsers or who have image loading turned off will still be able to use the links. For example, here it is with image loading turned off:

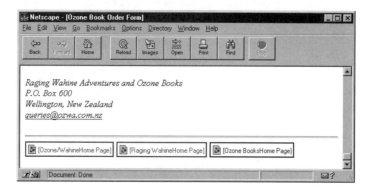

As you can see, the navigational links are usable even without the corresponding images.

Finding More Examples

We've presented a number of examples to illustrate the principles of good Web document design. However, you will find millions of other examples (both good and bad) on the Web itself. You can learn more about document design by looking at the HTML sources for any of these pages. Most Web browsers provide a way to view the source for the HTML document being displayed. Take advantage of this ability! Look at sources for both good and bad pages. This way, you will learn what to avoid as well as what to do.

PUBLICIZING YOUR WEB PAGES

What's In This Chapter

Once you have finished authoring documents for your Web site, you naturally want to encourage people to visit them. This chapter provides some ideas to help you to get people to visit your pages.

HTML is constantly changing. We've done our best to explain how things work at the time this book was written. However, there are a number of places on the Internet that you can go for more help. Toward this end we've listed a number of HTML-related mailing lists and newsgroups at the end of this chapter. Finally, we provide the URL for this book's Web page.

Generating Traffic

Once you are done setting up your piece of the Web you will undoubtedly want people to visit. The best method for encouraging people to visit your Web pages depends, of course, on their contents. Before publicizing new pages, consider who the best and most appropriate audience might be. Don't announce your pages in an unsolicited way to groups and people who haven't requested the information because you are likely to quickly antagonize them. With this caveat in mind, we mention here some of the most common means for publicizing new Web pages and sites.

Personal Home Pages

For personal pages, people are increasingly including the URLs of their home pages in their "signatures" attached to electronic mail. In addition, many people are listing their URLs on their business cards.

You can add your page to GNN's Netizens directory at:

```
http://gnn.com/gnn/netizens/addform.html
```

Announcing to Newsgroups

A common approach is to advertise your new Web pages in a relevant USENET newsgroup or mailing list. If you choose to do this, you must make sure that the group or list you target is appropriate and that your announcement is directly related to it. Otherwise, your announcement might be treated as "spam," and you risk receiving angry complaints.

In addition, there is a moderated newsgroup for announcing generally interesting and useful Web sites, called comp.info-systems.announce. Before submitting to this group, please read the charter posting and several of the group's postings to get an idea of what is considered appropriate.

Announcing to the Web

Naturally, you can use the Web to publicize your pages or Web server. For ongoing traffic, you will need to have your pages listed in the popular Web catalogs (also known as search engines) such as Yahoo!, Alta Vista, or Lycos. These sites collect URLs (and also search the Web itself) in order to generate catalogs of Web documents. These catalogs can then be searched by Web users in order to find documents of interest.

Most of these catalogs fall into two categories—manually maintained indices and automatically generated harvesters. The manual indices are typically annotated lists of URLs that have been sorted by category. They are similar to the table of contents in a book. Yahoo! is the most popular catalog of this type. To get your site or a specific page listed in this type of catalog, you usually need to submit your URL along with a description and contact information.

The other type of catalog uses an automated "Web harvester" program. These catalogs take a URL, and then use a program to search and catalog the document, as well as any links found in the document. This type of catalog is like a book's index. Alta Vista is one such search engine. To list your site in this type of catalog, you typically submit the URL for your "top-level" page. The robot will then go to your site and catalog all of your pages.

There are many such catalogs, and we provide only the URLs of a few of them here. You can use the listed URLs in order to access the site of each of these catalogs. This will enable you to both search their databases and submit the URLs of your Web pages for inclusion in the catalogs.

Indexing Tips

Each web index uses a different method to categorize pages. Understanding how an index categorizes a page can help you to set your pages up so that they show up whenever someone searches for a topic covered by your pages. In particular, indexing schemes typically consider meta tags, comments, repetitions of terms, early mention of terms, and titles.

For example, here are factors for a few of the most popular search indices.

Alta Vista

In the absence of any other information, all words in your document (except for comments) are indexed, with the first few words of the document used as a short abstract.

If META tags are included with name="description" and name="keywords", the description will be used as an abstract instead of lines from the document, and the keywords will be indexed in addition to the full-text index.

Lycos

Builds the catalog entry from the title and text of a Web page. Search results show the title, abstract (about the first 200 characters) and an outline (it looks for header tags [H1, H2, etc.])

Web Crawler

Full-text indexing. Takes the total number of times each of the words in a query appears in the document and divides it by the total number of words in the document.

Since search engines do change their criteria or harvesting methods occasionally, you should consult the information at the search engine in which you want your site to be listed to be sure that you understand how your pages will be indexed.

Popular Web Indices

You can submit your URL to the "What's New Page" at NCSA. This page will provide you with information on how to send in your listing:

```
http://www.ncsa.uiuc.edu/SDG/Software/Mosaic/Docs/whats-new.html
```

Table 12–1 contains a list of some of the most popular Web indices. You can submit your pages for inclusion in these indices by going to the URL for the index, and choosing the link for adding a link.

TABLE 12–1 Popular Web Indices

Index	URL
Alta Vista	http://www.altavista.digital.com/
Excite	http://www.excite.com/
Infoseek	http://www.infoseek.com/
Lycos	http://www.lycos.com/
Yahoo!	http://www.yahoo.com
ALIWEB index	http://web.nexor.co.uk/aliweb/doc/aliweb.html

Indices of Web Search Engines

There are so many Web indices now, that a number of sites devoted to indexing the indices have been created. Some of these sites listed in Table 12–2 are specifically aimed toward simultaneously adding links to multiple indices while others provide a good starting point for finding a specific index.

TABLE 12–2 Indices of Web Search Engines

Index	URL
Submit It!	A form that allows you to submit an announcement to many indices at one time: http://www.cen.uiuc.edu/~banister/submit-it/
WebStep Top 100	http://www.mmgco.com/top100.html
Multi-submit!	Pointers to numerous search engines: http://www.cetlink.net/~yinon/multi-sub/index.html
C|NET	Alphabetical listing of many search engines: http://www.search.com/alpha.html

Announcing a Server

If you are adding a server rather than just a single page or set of pages, you can also register in the WWW list of servers maintained by the World Wide Web Consortium. The URL for this resource is:

```
http://www.w3.org/hypertext/DataSources/WWW/Geographical_gener
ation/new-servers.html
```

Hiding Your Site

If you do not want your Web page to be indexed by the automatic Web indexing robots used by many search engines, you will need to add the URL for your pages to the robots.txt file for your site. The entries in this file have two fields:

User-agent

The name of the robot that is to be excluded from the site. "*" may be used to specify all robots.

Disallow

A partial URL of the document(s) that should not be indexed.

For example:

```
User-agent: *
Disallow: /kayaker/working/ # Kelly's in-progress stuff
```

For more information on the robots.txt file, see the "Standard for Robot Exclusion" at

```
http://info.webcrawler.com/mak/projects/robots/norobots.htm
```

Checking Your Site Status

If you've gone to all the trouble of submitting your site at multiple search engines or have created an exclusion file to prevent your file from being indexed, it is nice to know whether your efforts have worked. One of the easiest ways to determine whether your site is listed in a specific search engine is simply to enter your own URL in the search engine's search form. If you're listed, you should show up. This has the side benefit of also showing any links to your site from other locations that are indexed in that search engine as well.

Making an Even Bigger Splash

So far, we've described only standard Internet locations for announcing Web pages. However, the Web is attracting a wider audience every day. If you're developing pages that you wish the general public to visit—for example, if you're developing an on-line store—you'll need to advertise your site in other ways. Depending on the audience you want to reach, and your advertising budget, here are some places you should consider including your URL:

- Business cards
- Print advertisements
- Radio and television advertisements
- Billboards

Many popular Web sites take advertisements in the form of a banner with a link to the advertised site that pops up before displaying the rest of their pages. Placing an advertisement on one of these sites (such as Yahoo) is a good way to increase the traffic to your site.

Getting Mentioned in the News

Getting a mention of your site's page in traditional print media can help increase traffic. Many newspapers and magazines include technology columns, and some even have columns specifically about the Web. You can increase the likelihood that your site will be reviewed or referenced by contacting the appropriate reporters. For example, targeting reporters at special-interest magazines that cover the same topics that your site does may help.

You can sometimes find the e-mail address of reporters that cover specific areas by checking the byline. You can then send a short description of your site. In addition to the description be sure to include:

- the URL
- the site's name
- target audience
- your contact information

Places to Go for More Help

We've presented some ideas on ways to get people to visit your site. If you're interested in getting more help in this area, or simply want to find other people with similar interests, there are a number of Internet e-mail lists that address this topic.

Resources for All Levels

HTML Writer's Guild

URL: http://www.hwg.org/

The Charter of the HTML Writers Guild: To build awareness within and beyond the Internet community of Web page authoring and related services as a skilled pursuit; to assist members in developing and enhancing their capabilities; to communicate to prospective users of Web services what they should expect from a Guild member and demand from others offering these services; and to contribute to the development of the Web and Web technical standards and guidelines.

Intermediate Level Resources

The resources listed in this section require familiarity with HTML. If you have gone through this book, you should be able to participate in the forums listed in this section. First we list a number of e-mail lists.

List Name: web-support@mailbase.ac.uk

> **Subscription Address:** mailbase@mailbase.ac.uk
>
> **Subscription Instructions:** Send a message to the subscription address with:
>
> ```
> JOIN web-supportFirstName LastName
> ```
>
> in the body of the message.
>
> **Description:** This list is based in the United Kingdom and has a European orientation.

Advanced Resources

List Name: ADV-HTML

> **Subscription address:** LISTSERV@UA1VM.UA.EDU
>
> **Subscription Instructions:** Send a message to the subscription address with:
>
> ```
> SUBSCRIBE ADV-HTMLFirstName LastName
> ```
>
> in the body of the message.
>
> **Description:** A moderated discussion list for the discussion of both advanced hypertext markup language and other advanced Web topics. Archives are available at:
>
> ```
> http://risc.ua.edu/adv-html
> ```

List Name: WWW-MANAGERS

> **Subscription Address**: majordomo@lists.stanford.edu
>
> **Subscription Instructions**: Send a message to the subscription address with:
>
> ```
> sub www-managers
> ```
>
> in the body of the message.
>
> **Description**: This list is for managers of WWW servers and sites to get answers to specific questions about the setup and maintenance of HTTP servers and clients. It is not for discussions—answers are to be mailed back to the person who asked the question, who then has responsibility for summarizing the relevant answers and posting back to the mailing list.

The Latest Book News

You can find the Web page for this book at:

`http://catalog.com/vivian/win95.html`

We'll put up errata sheets there as well as a list of sites that used this book to get started. If you've found this book instrumental in getting your site up and would like to be listed, drop us a line (you'll find a link on the book's page) with the URL for your site. While we can't promise to list everyone, we'll try to put up links to our favorite sites.

ISO Latin 1 Entities in HTML

HTML Tag	Character	Description
&AElig;	Æ	capital AE diphthong (ligature)
&Aacute;	Á	capital A, acute accent
&Acirc;	Â	capital A, circumflex accent
&Agrave;	À	capital A, grave accent
&Aring;	Å	capital A, ring
&Atilde;	Ã	capital A, tilde
&Auml;	Ä	capital A, dieresis or umlaut mark
&Ccedil;	Ç	capital C, cedilla
&ETH;	Ð	capital Eth, Icelandic
&Eacute;	É	capital E, acute accent

HTML Tag	Character	Description
&Ecirc;	Ê	capital E, circumflex accent
&Egrave;	È	capital E, grave accent
&Euml;	Ë	capital E, dieresis or umlaut mark
&Iacute;	Í	capital I, acute accent
&Icirc;	Î	capital I, circumflex accent
&Igrave;	Ì	capital I, grave accent
&Iuml;	Ï	capital I, dieresis or umlaut mark
&Ntilde;	Ñ	capital N, tilde
&Oacute;	Ó	capital O, acute accent
&Ocirc;	Ô	capital O, circumflex accent
&Ograve;	Ò	capital O, grave accent
&Oslash;	Ø	capital O, slash
&Otilde;	Õ	capital O, tilde
&Ouml;	Ö	capital O, dieresis or umlaut mark
&THORN;	Þ	capital THORN, Icelandic
&Uacute;	Ú	capital U, acute accent
&Ucirc;	Û	capital U, circumflex accent
&Ugrave;	Ù	capital U, grave accent
&Uuml;	Ü	capital U, dieresis or umlaut mark
&Yacute;	Ý	capital Y, acute accent
&aacute;	á	small a, acute accent
&acirc;	â	small a, circumflex accent
&aelig;	æ	small ae diphthong (ligature)
&agrave;	à	small a, grave accent
&aring;	å	small a, ring
&atilde;	ã	small a, tilde
&auml;	ä	small a, dieresis or umlaut mark
&ccedil;	ç	small c, cedilla
&eacute;	é	small e, acute accent

HTML Tag	Character	Description
&ecirc;	ê	small e, circumflex accent
&egrave;	è	small e, grave accent
&eth;	ð	small eth, Icelandic
&euml;	ë	small e, dieresis or umlaut mark
&iacute;	í	small i, acute accent
&icirc;	î	small i, circumflex accent
&igrave;	ì	small i, grave accent
&iuml;	ï	small i, dieresis or umlaut mark
&ntilde;	ñ	small n, tilde
&oacute;	ó	small o, acute accent
&ocirc;	ô	small o, circumflex accent
&ograve;	ò	small o, grave accent
&oslash;	ø	small o, slash
&otilde;	õ	small o, tilde
&ouml;	ö	small o, dieresis or umlaut mark
&szlig;	ß	small sharp s, German (sz ligature)
&thorn;	þ	small thorn, Icelandic
&uacute;	ú	small u, acute accent
&ucirc;	û	small u, circumflex accent
&ugrave;	ù	small u, grave accent
&uuml;	ü	small u, dieresis or umlaut mark
&yacute;	ý	small y, acute accent
&yuml;	ÿ	small y, dieresis or umlaut mark

ASCII Table

00	nul	16	syn	2c	,	42	B	58	X	6e	n
01	soh	17	etb	2d	-	43	C	59	Y	6f	o
02	stx	18	can	2e	.	44	D	5a	Z	70	p
03	etx	19	em	2f	/	45	E	5b	[	71	q
04	eot	1a	sub	30	0	46	F	5c	\	72	r
05	enq	1b	esc	31	1	47	G	5d	]	73	s
06	ack	1c	fs	32	2	48	H	5e	^	74	t
07	bel	1d	gs	33	3	49	I	5f	_	75	u
08	bs	1e	rs	34	4	4a	J	60	`	76	v
09	ht	1f	us	35	5	4b	K	61	a	77	w
0a	nl	20	sp	36	6	4c	L	62	b	78	x
0b	vt	21	!	37	7	4d	M	63	c	79	y
0c	np	22	"	38	8	4e	N	64	d	7a	z
0d	cr	23	#	39	9	4f	O	65	e	7b	{
0e	so	24	$	3a	:	50	P	66	f	7c		
0f	si	25	%	3b	;	51	Q	67	g	7d	}
10	dle	26	&	3c	<	52	R	68	h	7e	~
11	dc1	27	`	3d	=	53	S	69	i	7f	del
12	dc2	28	(	3e	>	54	T	6a	j		
13	dc3	29	)	3f	?	55	U	6b	k		
14	dc4	2a	*	40	@	56	V	6c	l		
15	nak	2b	+	41	A	57	W	6d	m		

USEFUL URLS

There are many HTML resources for authors available on the Web. Here are some useful links.

General HTML and WWW Information

The World Wide Web Consortium

http://www.w3.org/

RFC 1866: Hypertext Markup Language Specification Version 2.0

ftp://ds.internic.net/rfc/rfc1866.txt.

WWW Frequently Asked Questions

http://www.boutell.com/faq/index.htm

Introductions to HTML

http://www.ncsa.uiuc.edu/demoweb/html-primer.html

List of DOCTYPES

http://ugweb.cs.ualberta.ca/~gerald/validate/lib/catalog

HTML Style Guides

http://www.w3.org/hypertext/WWW/Provider/Style/Overview.html

http://info.med.yale.edu/caim/StyleManual_Top.HTML

HTML Writer's Guild

http://www.hwg.org/

HTML Working Group Mailing List Archive

http://www.ics.uci.edu/pub/ietf/html/

HTML Bibliographies

http://www.utirc.utoronto.ca/HTMLdocs/NewHTML/bibliography.html

http://info.med.yale.edu/caim/M_Resources.HTML

Browser Information

BrowserCaps, a catalog of HTML support by different browsers

http://www.pragmaticainc.com/bc/

BrowserWatch

http://browserwatch.iworld.com/

HTML Elements

Image Map Information

http://hoohoo.ncsa.uiuc.edu/docs/setup/admin/Imagemap.html

Forms Information

http://www.ncsa.uiuc.edu/SDG/Software/Mosaic/Docs/fill-out-forms/overview.html

Table Information

http://www.hpl.hp.co.uk/people/dsr/html/tables.html

CGI Information

Documentation

http://hoohoo.ncsa.uiuc.edu/docs/

http://hoohoo.ncsa.uiuc.edu/cgi/overview.html

Scripts for NCSA httpd: C Routines

ftp://ftp.ncsa.uiuc.edu/Web/httpd/Unix/ncsa_httpd/cgi/ncsa-default.tar.Z

Scripts for NCSA httpd: Perl routines

ftp://ftp.ncsa.uiuc.edu/Web/httpd/Unix/ncsa_httpd/cgi/cgi-lib.pl.Z

CGI Standard

http://hoohoo.ncsa.uiuc.edu/cgi/overview.html

Matt's Script Archive

http://worldwidemart.com/scripts/

HTML Validation

Dr. HTML

http://imagiware.com/RxHTML/

Weblint form-based checking service

http://www.unipress.com/weblint/

Weblint sources

http://www.khoral.com/staff/neilb/weblint.html

Webtechs

http://www.webtechs.com/html-val-svc/

Kinder, Gentler Validator

http://ugweb.cs.ualberta.ca/~gerald/validate/

Listing of many validation services

http://www.ccs.org/validate/validate.html

Multimedia

GIF Animation: Royal E. Frazier's GIF89a Document

http://members.aol.com/royalef/

Bandwidth Conservation Society

http://www.infohiway.com/faster/index.html

Independent JPEG Group's JPEG FAQ

http://www.cis.ohio-state.edu/hypertext/faq/usenet/jpeg-faq/top.html

Apple's Quicktime Site

http://quicktime.apple.com

Netscape's Background Image Repository

http://home.netscape.com/assist/net_sites/bg/backgrounds.html

JavaScript and Java

Netscape's JavaScript Resource List

http://home.netscape.com/comprod/products/navigator/version_2.0/script-/script_info/index.html

JavaScript FAQ

http://www.freqgrafx.com/411/l

JavaScript examples

http://www.c2.org/~andreww/javascript/

Sun's Java Developer's Kit

http://java.sun.com/

WWW Service Providers

This appendix contains a list of Web service providers. New service providers seem to pop up every day, so if you do not find a service provider that suits your needs listed here, there are a number of places you can check for additional listings on the Internet.

Criteria for Choosing a Provider

There are an overwhelming number of Web service providers around. Choosing the right one is important, since your provider will be an integral part of your business. Switching providers can also be painful, so getting it right the first time can make your life much simpler. To help you find a match, we've provided a list of questions to consider when choosing a provider. Not all of the questions may apply to your situation, since the requirements for a site to host a personal home page are very different than the requirements for a business.

- What type of bandwidth does the provider have? If your customers can't reach you, you will lose business. A provider with connections to multiple sources and a high-speed connection is a must.

- Does the provider allow access to the CGI directory? If not, does the provider have generic CGI programs that can be tailored to meet your needs?

- Support. Does the provider have 24-hour support? What are its procedures for dealing with outages?

- Price. There are many methods for charging for services. In general, you can expect to receive a fixed amount of disk space for your monthly service charge. Some providers allow an unlimited amount of transmission as part of the basic service, while others may place a surcharge on transmissions in excess of a base amount. If you anticipate building a high-volume site, you will probably find it more economical to choose a service provider with no limit on transmission. On the other hand, providers that do not charge for transmission may also have difficulty maintaining enough bandwidth to service all of their customers.

- Availability of a secure server. If you plan on conducting financial transactions as part of your site, you should make sure that your provider has a server that uses secure service technology.

When choosing a Web provider, keep in mind that the Web is a global entity. Your audience may be located anywhere in the world; so as long as *you* have a way to get onto the Internet, your Web provider does not need to be close to you (as opposed to a general Internet service provider, for which you would probably want to have a local access point).

Each provider is listed in the following format:

Provider name
Surface mail address (if available)
Phone number
Fax number
Internet e-mail address
URL

If you are a provider and would like to be added to this list in future editions of this book, please send your update to Vivian@catalog.com.

World Wide Web Service Providers

a2i communications
1211 Park Avenue #202
San Jose, CA 95126–2924
408–293–8078
Fax: 408–263–0461
support@rahul.net
http://www.rahul.net/

Able Technical Services
ABLECOM.NET
P.O. Box 26530
San Jose, CA 95159
408–441–6000
howard@ablecom.net
http://www.ablecom.net/

Access Nevada, Inc.
702–294–0480
Fax: 702–293–3278
info@accessnv.com
http://www.accessnv.com/

Achilles Internet Limited
613–723–6624
Fax: 613–723–8583
office@achilles.net
http://www.achilles.net/

Advanced Network Solutions
http@adnetsol.com
http://www.adnetsol.com/

Berbee Information Networks Corp.
455 Science Drive
Madison, WI 53711–1058
608–233–5222
Fax: 608–233–9795
info@binc.net
http://www.binc.net/

Best Internet Communications, Inc.

421 Castro Street
Mountain View, CA 94041
415–964–2378
Fax: 415–691–4195
info@best.com
http://www.best.com/

BlueMarble

Bloomington, IN
support@bluemarble.net
http://www.bluemarble.net/

BBN Planet Corporation

150 Cambridge Park Drive
Cambridge, MA 02140
800–472–4565
Fax: 617–873–5620
net-info@bbnplanet.com
http://www.bbnplanet.com/

Board of Directors Internet Service

303-571-5271 voice
303-571-5273 FAX
lc@bod.net
http://www.bod.net/

Canada Connect Corporation

201 1039 17 Avenue SW
Calgary, Alberta T2T 0B2
Canada
403–777–2025
Fax: 403–777–2026
info@canuck.com
http://www.canuck.com/

Charm.Net

2228 E. Lombard St.
Baltimore, MD 21231
410–558–3900
Fax: 410–558–3901
admin@Charm.Net
http://www.charm.net/

CERFnet

California Education and Research
   Federation Network
P.O. Box 85608
San Diego, CA 92186–9784
800–876–2373
619–455–3900
Fax: 619–455–3990
sales@cerf.net
http://www.cerf.net/

CHANNEL 1 Communications

1030 Massachusetts Avenue
Cambridge, MA 02138
617–864–0100
Fax: 617–354–3100
support@channel1.com
http://www.channel1.com/

CICNet

Committee on Institutional Cooperation
   Network
ITI Building
2901 Hubbard Drive
Ann Arbor, MI 48105
313–998–6703
800–947–4754
info@cic.net
http://www.cic.net/

CityNet

P.O. Box 3235
Charleston, WV 25332
304–342–5700
http://www.citynet.net/

Clarknet

Clark Internet Services, Inc.
10600 Route 108
Ellicott City, MD 21042
800–735–2258
410–254–3900
Fax: 410–730–9765
info@clark.net
http://www.clark.net/

Colorado SuperNet (CSN)

SuperNet Inc.
One Denver Place
999 18th Street
Denver, CO 80202
303–296–8202
Fax: 303–296–8224
help@csn.net
http://www.csn.net/csn/

Computer Service Langenbach GmbH

Germany
http://www.csl-gmbh.net/csl/

Connect.com.au pty ltd

129 Hawthorn Road
Caulfield
Victoria 3161 Australia
61–3–528–2239
1–800–818–262 (Australia-wide)
Fax: 61–3–528–5887
connect@connect.connect.com.au
http://www.connect.com.au/

Crossroads Communications

P.O. Box 30250
Mesa, AZ 85275
602–813–9040
800–892–7040
Fax: 602–545–7470
http://xroads.xroads.com/home.html/

CTS Network Services (CTSNET)

Division of Datel Systems Inc.
4444 Convoy Street, Suite 300
San Diego, CA 92111–3761
619–637–3637
Fax: 619–637–3630
info@crash.cts.com (server)
support@crash.cts.com (human)
http://www.cts.com/

CyberGate, Inc.

305–428–4283
Fax: 305–428–7977
info@gate.net
http://www.gate.net/services.html/

Data Basix

Ray Harwood
P.O. Box 18324
Tucson, AZ 85731
602–721–1988
Fax: 602–721–7240
info@data.basix.com (server)
sales@data.basix.com (human)
http://data.basix.com/

Dayton Internet Services

Dayton Internet Services
3131 South Dixie Drive
Suite 103
Dayton, OH 45439
513–643–0188
Fax: 513–643–0190
http://www.firstnet.net/About.html/

Demon

Demon Internet Systems (DIS)
44–081–349–0063
internet@demon.co.uk
http://www.demon.co.uk/

Direct Network Access

2039 Shattuck Avenue, Suite 206
Berkeley, CA 94704
510–649–6110
Fax: 510–649–7130
info@dnai.com (Automated response)
support@dnai.com (User technical
    support)
http://www.dnai.com/

Dreamscape Online

315–446–2626
Fax: 315–446–2626
http://www.dreamscape.com/

EmeraldNet

1718 East Speedway
Suite #315
Tucson, AZ 85719
520–670–1994
Fax: 520–670–1922
INFO@Emerald.NET
http://www.emerald.net/

EUnet Communications Services BV

Singel 540
1017 AZ Amsterdam
The Netherlands
31–20–623–3803
Fax: 31–20–622–4657
info@EU.net
http://www.eu.net/

Frontier Internet

303–385–4177
jbd@frontier.net
http://www.frontier.net/

Frontier Internet Services

London, UK
01–71–242–3383
Fax: 01–71–242–3384
support@ftech.co.uk
http://www.ftech.co.uk/frontier/frontier.htm/

GetNet International, Inc.

7325 North 16th Street, Suite #140
Phoenix, AZ 85020
602–943–3119
info@getnet.com
http://www.getnet.com/

Global Enterprise Service, Inc.

3 Independence Way
Princeton, NJ 08540
800–358–4437
609–258–2400
Fax: 609–897–7310
market@jvnc.net
http://www.jvnc.net/

Helix Internet

#902–900 West Hastings
Vancouver, B.C., V6C–1E6
Canada
604–689–8544
Fax: 604–685–2554
accounts@helix.net
http://www.helix.net/sub/about.html/

HoloNet

Information Access Technologies, Inc.
46 Shattuck Square, Suite 11
Berkeley, CA 94704–1152
510–704–0160
Fax: 510–704–8019
info@holonet.net
http://www.holonet.net/holonet/

HookUp

HookUp Communication Corporation
519–747–4110
Fax: 519–746–3521
info@hookup.net
http://www.hookup.net/

IDS World Network

InteleCom Data Systems
5835 Post Rd., Suite 214
East Greenwich, RI 02818
800–IDS–1680
Fax: 401–886–4050
info@ids.net
http://www.ids.net/idstext.html/

IndyNet

5348 N. Tacoma Ave.
Indianapolis, IN 46220
317–251–5208
http://gopher.indy.net/index.html/

InfoCom Networks

P.O. Box 590343
Houston, TX 77259–0343
helpdesk@infocom.net
http://www.infocom.net/

Inter'Acces

Montreal, Quebec
Canada
514–367–0002
sales@Interax.net
http://www.interax.net/

InterAccess

3345 Commercial Avenue
Northbrook, IL 60062
800–967–1580
708–498–2542
Fax: 708–671–0113
http://www.interaccess.com/

Internet Direct, Inc.

800–879–3624
602–274–0100 (Phoenix)
602–324–0100 (Tucson)
Fax: 602–274–8518
sales@direct.net
http://www.indirect.com/

Internet Express

800–592–1240
info@usa.net
http://www.usa.net/

The Internet MainStreet

334 State Street, Suite 106
Los Altos, CA 94022
415–941–1068
info@mainstreet.net
http://www.mainstreet.net/

KAIWAN

Knowledge Added Information Wide Area
   Network Corporation
18001 Sky Park Circle, Suite J
Irvine, CA 92714
714–638–2139
Fax: 714–638–0455
info@kaiwan.com
http://www.kaiwan.com/

Klink Net Communications

Gloversville, NY
518–725–3000
800–KLINK–123
admin@klink.net
http://www.klink.net/

Lanka Internet Services, Ltd (LISL)

5th Floor, IBM Building
48 Nawam Mawatha
Colombo 2, Sri Lanka
94–1–342974
Fax: 94–1–343056
info@lanka.net
http://www.lanka.net/lisl.html/

LinkAGE Online

webmaster@hk.linkage.net
http://www.hk.linkage.net/

LinkNet

318–442–LINK
Fax: 318–449–9750
support@linknet.net
http://www.linknet.net/

The Little Garden

3004 16th St., #204
San Francisco, CA 94103
415–487–1902
Fax: 415–552–6088
sales@tlg.net
http://tlg.org/

Maestro

Maestro Technologies, Inc.
29 John Street, Suite 1601
New York, NY 10038
212–240–9600
Fax: 212–566–0315
info@maestro.com (server)
staff@maestro.com (human)
http://www.maestro.com/

Magic Online Services

1483 Pembina Hwy. #150
Winnipeg, Manitoba R2T 2C6
Canada
204–949–7777
Fax: 204–949–7790
sbrooker@magic.mb.ca
http://www.magic.mb.ca/

MCSNet

1300 West Belmont, Suite 405
Chicago, IL 60657
312–248–8649
Fax: 312–248–8649
support@mcs.com
http://www.mcs.net/

Michigan BizServe

Online Technologies Corporation
staff@BizServe.com
http://bizserve.com/

Milwaukee Internet X

Mix Communications
P.O. Box 17166
Milwaukee, WI 53217
414–962–8172
wwwinfo@mixcom.com
http://www.mixcom.com/

MindVOX

Phantom Access Technologies, Inc.
175 Fifth Avenue, Suite 2614
New York, NY 10010
800–MindVox
212–989–2418
Fax: 212–989–8648
info@phantom.com
http://www.phantom.com/

MSEN, Inc.

320 Miller Avenue
Ann Arbor, MI 48103
313–998–4562
Fax: 313–998–4563
info@msen.com
http://www.msen.com/

MUC.DE e.V.

Muenchner Technologiezentrum
Frankfurter Ring 193 a
80807 Muenchen
Germany
089–324683–0
vorstand@muc.de
http://www/muc.de/

Mundo Internet

Centro de Investigación y de Estudios
    Avanzados del IPN
Unidad Mérida
Sección de Telemática
km 6 Antigua Carretera a Progreso
Apdo. Postal 73 Cordemex Mérida, Yuc. CP
    97310
99–812960, ext. 265
Fax: 99–812923
http://w3mint.cieamer.conacyt.mx/

NeoSoft, Inc.

1770 St. James Place
Suite 500
Houston, TX 77056
800–GET–NEOSOFT
713–968–5800
sales@neosoft.com
http://www.neosoft.com/

Netcom Online Communication Services

P.O. Box 20774
San Jose, CA 95160
408–554–8649
info@netcom.com
http://www.netcom.com/

NETConnect

Cedar City, UT
801–865–7032
http://www.tcd.net/

NetHeaven

518–885–1295
800–910–6671
stpeters@NetHeaven.com
http://www.netheaven.com/

Netrail, Inc.

2007 N. 15 St., Suite 5
Arlington, VA 22201
703–524–4800
Fax: 703–524–5510
sales@netrail.net
http://www.netrail.net/

Network Wizards

PO Box 343
Menlo Park, CA 94026
415–326–2060
Fax: 415–326–4672
info@nw.com
http://catalog.com/

North Shore Access

Eco Software, Inc.
145 Munroe Street, Suite 405
Lynn, MA 01901
617–593–3110
info@northshore.ecosoft.com
http://northshore.ecosoft.com/

NovaLink

Inner Circle Technologies, Inc.
79 Boston Turnpike, Suite 409
Shrewsbury, MA 01545
800–274–2814
508–754–9910
info@novalink.com
http://www.novalink.com/

Nuance Network Services

904 Bob Wallace Avenue, Suite 119
Huntsville, AL 35801
205–533–4296
info@nuance.com
http://www.nuance.com/

OnRamp

1950 Stemmons Freeway
Suite 5061 – INFOMART
Dallas, TX 75207
214–746–4710
Fax: 214–713–5400
Faxback: 214–746–4852
info@onramp.net
http://www.onramp.net/

Open Door Networks, Inc.

110 S. Laurel St.
Ashland, OR 97520
503–488–4127
help@opendoor.com
http://www.opendoor.com/

OuterNet Connections

8235 Shoal Creek, #105
Austin, TX 78758
512–345–3573
info@outer.net
http://www.outer.net/

Panix Public Access Unix

110 Riverside Drive
New York, NY 10024
212–741–4400
infobot@panix.com
http://www.panix.com/

Pavilion Internet

Brighton, Sussex
44–0–1273–607072
Fax: 44–0–1273–607073
info@pavilion.co.uk
http://www.pavilion.co.uk/

Performance Systems International, Inc. (PSI)

510 Huntmar Park Drive
Herndon, VA 22070
800–827–7482
Fax: 800–329–7741
info@psi.com
http://www.psi.net/

Pacific Information eXchange, Inc. NETwork (PIXINET)

1142 Auahi Street, Suite 2788
Honolulu, HI 96814
info@pixi.com
http://www.pixi.com/

Pegasus Networks

PO Box 284
Broadway Q 4006
Australia
61–7–257–1111
Fax: 61–7–257–1087
pegasus@peg.apc.org
http://www.peg.apc.org/

PIPEX

Unipalm Ltd.
44–223–424616
Fax: 44–223–426868
pipex@unipalm.co.uk
http://www.pipex.net/

Planet Access Networks

55 Rt. 206 – Suite E
Stanhope, NJ 07874
201–691–4704
info@planet.net
http://www.planet.net/

Portal Communications, Inc.

20863 Stevens Creek Boulevard
Suite 200
Cupertino, CA 95014
408–973–9111
http://www.portal.com/

Power Net

Los Angeles, CA
310–643–4908
sales@power.net
http://www.power.net/

QuakeNet Internet Services

830 Wilmington Road
San Mateo, CA 94402
415–655–6607
Fax: 415–377–0635
info@quake.net
http://www.quake.net/

RainDrop Laboratories

5627 SW 45th
Portland, OR 97221–3505
info@agora.rain.com
http://www.rdrop.com/agora/

Real/Time Communications

6721 N. Lamar, Suite 103
Austin, TX 78752
512–451–0046
Fax: 512–459–3858
sales@realtime.net
http://www.realtime.net/

RedIRIS

Secretaria RedIRIS
Fundesco
Alcala 61
28014 Madrid
Spain
34–1–435–1214
Fax: 34–1–578–1773
secretaria@rediris.es
http://www.rediris.es/

Renaissance Internet Services

Phase IV Systems, Inc.
Huntsville, AL
custsrv@ro.com
http://www.ro.com/

Seanet

OSD, Inc.
Columbia Seafirst Center
701 Fifth Avenue, Suite 6801
Seattle, WA 98104
206–343–7828
Fax: 206–628–0722
seanet@seanet.com
http://www.seanet.com/

Sierra-Net

Lake Tahoe/Northern Nevada
702–832–6911
Fax: 702–831–3970
info@sierra.net
http://www.sierra.net/

South Coast Computing Services, Inc.

713–661–3301
Fax: 713–917–5005
info@sccsi.com
http://www.sccsi.com/

SSNet

302–378–1386
800–331–1386
info@ssnet.com
http://ssnet.com/

Structured Network Systems, Inc.

503–656–3530
800–881–0962
Fax: 503–656–3235
sales@structured.net
http://www.structured.net/

Suburbia PAN

P.O. Box 2031
Barker 3122
Australia
helpdesk@suburbia.apana.org.au
http://suburbia.apana.org.au/

Supernet

800–746–0777
info@supernet.net
http://www.supernet.net/

SWITCH

SWITCH Head Office
Limmatquai 138
CH–8001 Zurich
Switzerland
41–1–268–1515
Fax: 41–1–268–1568
info@switch.ch
http://www.switch.ch/

Systems Solutions Inc.

2108 East Thomas Road, Suite 200
Phoenix, AZ 85016–7758
602–955–5566
Fax: 602–955–0085
webmaster@syspac.com
http://www.syspac.com/

Tachyon Communications Corporation

100 Rialto Place, Suite 747
Melbourne, FL 32901
407–728–8081
Fax: 407–725–6315
sales@tach.net
http://www.tach.net/

TANet

Computer Center, Ministry of Education
12th Floor, Number 106
Sec. 2, Hoping East Road
Taipei, Taiwan
Attn: Chen Wen-Sung
886–2–7377010
Fax: 886–2–7377043
nisc@twnmoe10.edu.tw
http://www.edu.tw/

Teleport

Beaverton, OR
503–223–4245
info@teleport.com
http://www.teleport.com/

TerraNet, Inc.

729 Boylston Street, Floor 5
Boston, MA 02116
617–450–9000
sales@terra.net
http://www.terra.net/

Texas Metronet

1701 W. Euless Blvd.
Metro Center, Suites 130, 131b
Euless, TX 76040–6819
214–705–2900
Fax: 817–267–2400
info@metronet.com
http://www.metronet.com/

UltraNet Communications, Inc.

910 Boston Post Road, Suite 220
Marlboro, MA 01752
508–229–8400
info@ultranet.com
http://www.ultranet.com/

UniComp Technologies International Corporation

15851 Dallas Parkway, Suite 946
Dallas, TX 75248
214–663–3155
Fax: 214–663–3170
info@unicomp.net
http://www.unicomp.net/

UUNET Canada Inc.

1 Yonge Street
Suite 1801
Toronto, Ontario, M5E 1W7
Canada
416–368–6621
Fax: 416–369–0515
info@uunet.ca
http://www.uunet.ca/

UUNET Technologies, Inc.

3060 Williams Drive
Fairfax, VA 22031–4648
800–488–6383
703–206–5600
Fax: 703–206–5601
info@uu.net
http://www.alter.net/

Vector Internet Services

12 South 6th Street
Minneapolis, MN 55402
612–288–0880
Fax: 612–288–0889
info@visi.com
http://www.visi.com/

Vnet Internet Access, Inc.

PO Box 31474
Charlotte, NC 28231
800–377–3282
info@vnet.net
http://www.vnet.net/

WestNet Internet Services

Westchester County, NY
914–967–7816
chris@WestNet.com
http://www.westnet.com/

Water Wheel Systems

Marlton, NJ
609–596–0032
info@waterw.com
http://www.waterw.com/

Whole Earth 'Lectronic Link (WELL)

27 Gate Five Road
Sausalito, CA 94965
415–332–4335
info@well.sf.ca.us
http://www.well.sf.ca.us/

WIDE

c/o Prof. Jun Murai
KEIO University
5322 Endo, Fujisawa, 252
Japan
81–466–47–5111 ext. 3330
jun@wide.ad.jp
http://www.wide.ad.jp/

Wimsey Information Services Inc.

8523 Commerce Court
Burnaby, BC V5N 4A3
Canada
604–257–1111
Fax: 604–257–1110
info@wimsey.com
http://www.wimsey.com/wimsey/

@wizard.com

Las Vegas, NV
702–871–4461
Fax: 702–871–4249
gajake@wizard.com
http://www.wizard.com/

WombatNet

236 Hamilton Avenue
Palo Alto, CA 94301
415–462–8800
Fax: 415–462–8804
info@batnet.com
http://www.batnet.com/

The World

Software Tool & Die
1330 Beacon Street
Brookline, MA 02146
617–739–0202
office@world.std.com
http://world.std.com/

World Web Limited

906 King Street
Alexandria, VA 22314
support@worldweb.net
http://www.worldweb.net/

WorldWide Access

P.O. Box 285
Vernon Hills, IL 60061–0285
708–367–1870
Fax: 708–367–1872
http://www.wwa.com/

The Xensei Corporation

Boston South Shore area
617–376–6342
info@xensei.com
http://www.xensei.com/

XNet Information Systems

3080 E. Ogden Ave. , #202
Lisle, IL 60532
708–983–6064
Fax: 708–983–6879
info@xnet.com
http://www.xnet.com/

Zilker Internet Park

1106 Clayton Lane, Suite 500W
Austin, TX 78723
512–206–3850
Fax: 512–206–3852
support@zilker.net
http://www.zilker.net/

zNET

777 South Pacific Coast Highway
Suite 204
Solana Beach, CA 92075
619–755–7772
Fax: 619–755–8149
info@znet.com
http://www.znet.com/

GLOSSARY

ACK

Acknowledgment. A message sent to indicate that data has been received.

anchor

One of the ends of a hypertext link.

anonymous FTP

A mechanism that allows public files to be copied from systems on the Internet without having a login account on the system. It uses the login name "anonymous" with a password of "guest" or the e-mail address of the person using anonymous login. Browsers use anonymous FTP when an FTP URL is chosen.

ASCII

American Standard Code for Information Interchange. It is a 7-bit code that can represent up to 128 characters. Appendix B contains a list of ASCII characters.

attribute

An optional indicator that can be added to markup tags in order to specify a variation in the way the tag is displayed.

browser

An application used to display HTML documents. Browsers may be used to display local HTML documents or to retrieve documents across the Internet. Some popular browsers are Netscape Navigator and NCSA Mosaic.

cache

Hold information in memory. Many browsers temporarily keep copies of documents in a cache directory on the local hard disk so that they do not have to be reloaded over the network each time they are referenced.

cello

Along with NCSA Mosaic, one of the first graphical browsers available for Windows. It was created at the Cornell Legal Information Institute (LII).

CERN

European Center for Particle Physics, located in Geneva, Switzerland. Birthplace of the Web.

CGI

Common Gateway Interface. An interface for running external programs or scripts under an information server, such as a Web server. A common use of a CGI script is handling data from HTML forms.

clickable image

See Image map.

client

A general term for a computer or application that can access and retrieve information from a server computer. A Web client is usually called a Web browser.

container

See Markup Tag.

CSLIP

Compressed SLIP. See the entry for SLIP.

dial-up

A connection made between machines using phone lines and modems.

DTD

Data Type Definition for the HyperText Markup Language; provides a formal description of HTML with respect to SGML.

element

A portion of an HTML document delineated by markup tags.

entity

An HTML symbol representing a special character. A list of ISO character entities may be found in Appendix B.

e-mail address

The address that is used to send electronic mail to a specified destination. For example, Vivian's e-mail address is "vivian@catalog.com".

FAQ

Frequently Asked Questions. List of frequently asked questions and their answers.

finger

An application that shows information about all of the users logged on to a system. It can also display information about a particular user. It typically shows full name, last login time, idle time, terminal line, and terminal location (where applicable). It may also display plan and project files left by the user.

form

Fill-out forms are HTML tags that were added to HTML 2.0, which enable documents to display interactive elements used on forms, such as radio buttons, checkboxes, and text-entry boxes.

FTP

File Transfer Protocol. The protocol that defines the way in which files are exchanged around the Internet. FTP also refers to the name of the application that uses the FTP protocol.

FYI

For Your Information. FYI also represents a series of informational documents about the Internet published by the Internet Engineering Task Force (IETF).

gateway

A program or device that passes information between networks or applications.

GIF

Graphic Interchange Format. An image storage format developed by Compuserve. It is the most widely supported image format on the Web.

Gopher

A menu-driven information service developed at the University of Minnesota that makes information across the Internet available through a single application. Gopher clients can get information from any accessible Gopher server, providing the user with a single "Gopher space" of information.

head

The beginning of an HTML document. The head portion of an HTML document should contain the document's title.

host

A computer; usually one that is connected to a network.

home page

A browser's home page refers to the first document that is loaded when the browser is started up. A user's personal home page refers to a Web page that describes and introduces that individual. A company or organization home page is its top-level or starting Web page.

hostname

The name given to a computer.

HTML

HyperText Markup Language. The language in which Web documents are written; what this book is about.

HTTP

HyperText Transfer Protocol. The protocol used to transfer HTML documents on the Web.

hotlist

The term used in Mosaic to describe the list of URLs that it remembers; also known as a bookmark list.

hypermedia

Hypermedia is hypertext which may include nontext elements such as images, video and sound. The Web is a hypermedia system.

hypertext

A hypertext document contains links to other parts of the document or to other documents. Users can select hypertext links in order to view documents in a nonlinear and individual way. The term was coined by Ted Nelson in 1965.

IETF

Internet Engineering Task Force. The technical group that works on protocol standards used on the Internet.

image map

An image map is a graphical image containing "hot spots." When a hot spot is clicked on by a user, the browser loads the corresponding document.

Interlaced GIF

The scanlines in an interlaced GIF have been rearranged so that when it is viewed in a browser with appropriate support, it first appears with poor resolution and then, over time, improves in resolution until the entire image is loaded. This is a useful technique for giving users a quick impression of the image, without having to wait for it to be entirely loaded.

inline image

Inline images in HTML documents are images that appear as part of the document rather than shown by an external viewer.

internet

While an internet is a network, the term "internet" is usually used to refer to a collection of networks interconnected with routers.

Internet

(Note the capital "I.") The Internet is the largest internet in the world.

internet address

An IP address that uniquely identifies a node on an internet. An Internet address (capital "I") uniquely identifies a node on the Internet.

Internet Relay Chat (IRC)

A worldwide "party line" protocol that allows one to converse with other people on the Internet in real time via typed comments.

IP address

The 32-bit address defined by the Internet Protocol in STD 5, RFC 791. It is usually represented in dotted decimal notation; for example, 10.0.0.51.

ISO

International Organization for Standardization. An international standards body that defines many technical standards.

JPEG

Joint Photographic Experts Group. A standard format for image storage created by this group. It is a popular image storage format on the Web.

knowbot

Knowbots (or softbots) are programs that wander the Web collecting document titles and URLs. These are then indexed and can be searched by users.

line-mode browser

A nongraphical Web browser. These browsers may be used on dumb terminals. Although they cannot display graphics, most of the other features in a graphics-based browser may still be accessed with such browsers. Lynx is one of the most popular browsers of this type.

link

A link (or hyperlink) is the pointer in a hypertext document that points to another location or another document.

Lynx

A line-mode browser developed at the University of Kansas. Versions are available for many platforms, including DOS.

mail gateway

A computer that connects two or more electronic mail systems (including dissimilar mail systems) and transfers messages between them.

mail server

A software program that distributes files or information in response to requests sent via e-mail. Internet examples include Almanac and netlib. Mail servers have also been used in Bitnet to provide FTP-like services.

mailing list

A list of e-mail addresses used to send e-mail messages to groups of people. Generally, a special-interest group mailing list is used to discuss a specific topic.

markup language

A language that is used to specify document formats by embedding tags within the document. These tags are then interpreted by browsers in order to properly display the document.

MIME

Multipurpose Internet Mail Extension. An extension to Internet e-mail which provides the ability to transfer nontextual data, such as graphics, audio and fax. It is defined in RFC 1341.

Mosaic

One of the most popular Web browsers. The first widely used graphical browser. See also NCSA.

MPEG

Motion Picture Experts Group. One of the most widely used formats for storing video on the Internet.

NCSA

National Center for Supercomputing Applications based at the University of Illinois. This is where NCSA Mosaic was developed.

netiquette

A pun on "etiquette" referring to proper behavior on a network.

Netnews

A bulletin board system.

NNTP

Network News Transfer Protocol. The protocol used to transfer network news. It is defined in RFC 977.

OS

Operating System. The program that controls a computer's hardware. Operating systems typically control the use of the CPU (through a scheduler), memory, and peripheral devices (through device drivers). User applications send requests to the operating system to access the computer.

Perl

Practical Extraction and Report Language. It is an interpreted language created by Larry Wall. Originally based on UNIX systems, it is now available on other platforms, including DOS. A number of useful HTML filters have been written in Perl.

PPP

Point-to-Point Protocol—defined in RFC 1171. It provides a method for transmitting packets over serial point-to-point links.

POP

Post Office Protocol. A protocol designed to allow single-user hosts to read mail from a server. There are three versions: POP, POP2 and POP3. Later versions are not compatible with earlier versions.

post

To send a message to a newsgroup or e-mail list. Also, a method for accessing a CGI application.

protocol

A standard communication format allowing networked computers to exchange information. Protocols are developed for each kind of information exchange; for example, electronic mail uses the SMTP protocol, and the Web uses, among others, the HTTP protocol.

proxy server

A proxy server acts by keeping local copies of documents requested by users. When a local user requests a document, the proxy server is first consulted to see if a copy is held there. If it is, the user receives the document much more quickly than were it remotely retrieved.

Quicktime

A digital video and audio standard developed by Apple Computer.

RFC

Request For Comments. A document series, begun in 1969, which describes the Internet suite of protocols and related experiments. Not all (in fact, very few) RFCs describe Internet standards, but all Internet standards are written up as RFCs.

RFC 822

The Internet standard format for electronic-mail message headers. Mail experts often refer to "822 messages." The name comes from "RFC 822," which contains the specification (STD 11, RFC 822). 822 format was previously known as 733 format.

RFC 1392

Internet Glossary. If you run across an Internet-related term that isn't defined here, check the Internet Glossary. It is available at ftp://ds.internic.net/rfc/rfc1392.txt

RFC 1866

Hypertext Markup Language Specification Version 2.0. It is available at ftp://ds.internic.net/rfc/rfc1866.txt.

robot

See knowbot.

server

A program that handles certain types of requests on a continuous basis. For example, a mailing list server handles requests for list subscriptions and may also handle archive file requests from list members.

SGML

Standard Generalized Markup Language. SGML is a broad language used to define specific markup languages. HTML is a particular application of SGML.

signature

The three- or four-line message at the bottom of a piece of e-mail or a Usenet article which identifies the sender. Many mail programs allow you to set up a signature and automatically attach it to all the messages that you send. Long signatures (over five lines) are generally frowned upon.

SLIP

Serial Line IP. A protocol used to run IP over serial lines, such as telephone circuits or RS-232 cables, interconnecting two systems. SLIP is defined in RFC 1055.

SMTP

Simple Mail Transfer Protocol. A protocol defined in STD 10, RFC 821, used to transfer electronic mail between computers. It is a server-to-server protocol, so other protocols are used to access the messages.

spider

See knowbot.

tag

See markup language.

TCP/IP Protocol Suite

Transmission Control Protocol over Internet Protocol. This is a common shorthand which refers to the suite of transport and application protocols which runs over IP.

Telnet

Telnet is the Internet standard protocol for remote terminal connection service. It is defined in STD 8, RFC 854, and extended with options by many other RFCs.

UNIX

One of the most popular operating systems in use on the Internet today.

URL

Uniform Resource Locator. The address for a document on the Web. The format for a URL is

```
protocol://pathname
```

URN

Uniform Resource Name.

Usenet

A collection of thousands of topically named newsgroups, the computers which run the protocols, and the people who read and submit Usenet news. Not all Internet hosts subscribe to Usenet, and not all Usenet hosts are on the Internet.

viewer

A special-purpose application program for displaying data in specific formats. For example, a GIF viewer is used to display GIF images.

WAIS

Wide Area Information Servers. A distributed information service which offers simple natural-language input, indexed searching for fast retrieval, and a "relevance feedback" mechanism which allows the results of initial searches to influence future searches.

whois

An Internet program which allows users to query databases of people and other Internet entities, such as domains, networks, and hosts. The original whois databases are kept at the Internet Network Information Center (NIC) or Data Defense Network (NIC), depending on what you need, but many companies and educational institutions also make whois databases available now. The information for people shows a person's company name, address, phone number and e-mail address.

WWW

World Wide Web (W3). A hypertext-based, distributed information system created by researchers at CERN in Switzerland. Users may create, edit or browse hypertext documents.

Zine

On-line magazine.

INDEX